THE SECOND BATTLE
— OF —
CABIN CREEK

THE SECOND BATTLE
— OF —
CABIN CREEK

BRILLIANT VICTORY

STEVEN L. WARREN

Foreword by William L. Shea
Series Editor Douglas Bostick

Charleston   London

THE
History
PRESS

Published by The History Press
Charleston, SC 29403
www.historypress.net

Cover image: In the early morning hours of September 19, 1864, a ragtag Confederate force made up of Texans and Indian troops led by Brigadier Generals Richard M. Gano and Stand Watie attacks the station at Cabin Creek, Indian Territory, in an effort to capture a three-hundred-wagon Union supply train. Well-placed rounds from Howell's Texas Battery panics the driverless mule teams. *Illustration by Royce Fitzgerald.*

Some of the illustrations featured in this book are by Royce Fitzgerald, from the television documentary *Last Raid at Cabin Creek*. Copyright 1992, Warren Entertainment. All rights reserved.

First published 2012

Previously published in hardback by Gregath Publishing Company, Oklahoma, 2002.
Copyright 2002, Steven L. Warren. All rights reserved.

Manufactured in the United States

ISBN 978.1.60949.832.0

Library of Congress CIP data applied for.

For my parents, Leon and Mary. This is the result of stopping the car at every fort and historical site to let your kids out to explore and dream.

For our daughters, Emma and Alli. Always remember to protect our nation's battlefields and historic sites. They're a part of you—a part of what it is to be an American.

For my wife, Amy. Thank you for letting me go off to fight the war.

Contents

CONTENTS

Foreword

Most inhabitants of the Indian Territory in 1861 had no ideological or emotional attachment to either the United States or the Confederacy. They were understandably wary of being dragged into a conflict not of their own making and simply wanted to be left alone. Nevertheless, the war came, and the Indian Territory experienced incursions, raids and widespread brigandage. Tribal factionalism added another layer of violence. The conflict devastated and depopulated large areas. Disease and hunger stalked the land. Thousands died or fled into exile. Impoverishment, recriminations and revenge killings plagued the tribes for decades after the war. No part of the country suffered more.

The Civil War in the Indian Territory has never received the attention it deserves, even though events there were part and parcel of the larger struggle in Arkansas, Missouri and Kansas. The scale of the fighting in the Indian Territory was smaller than in other theaters but no less intense, and the losses and hardships were no less painful. Yet the number of campaign and battle narratives, the mainstay of Civil War literature for the past century and a half, is disappointingly small. And so it is with pleasure and a measure of relief that we welcome the appearance of Steve Warren's stirring account of the Second Battle of Cabin Creek, a significant addition to the literature of the Civil War in the West.

—William L. Shea

Preface

Future years will never know the seething hell and the black infernal background of countless minor scenes and interiors (not the official surface courteousness of the Generals, not the few great battles) of the Secession War.
—Walt Whitman

When poet and ex–Civil War nurse Walt Whitman wrote this prediction, I sincerely doubt that he ever had the Civil War battles of Indian Territory in mind. When you study the war as it was in Indian Territory, however, you can see that his statement readily fits. The military authorities on both sides regarded the territory as a backwater of the war. Unfortunately, some historians still consider it that way. There are many fascinating aspects of the Civil War and its effects on the Five Civilized Tribes. As in the East, the "White Man's War" meant that brother fought against brother and father fought against son. But it also caused division within the individual tribes themselves, the effects of which are still felt among the tribes even today. The war in Indian Territory was described by historian Edwin C. Bearss as "war to the knife and the knife was usually to the hilt."

It was indeed a war within a war as the blood feuds of old rose again to fever pitch. When it was over, the Cherokee, Creek, Chickasaw, Choctaw and Seminole nations had lost more than just the lives of their people and their property. Within a span of less than forty years, the five tribes would also lose their lands and their sovereignty. The federal government conveniently forgot about the service of the three regiments of Indian Home Guards made up of members from these five nations. Or perhaps they thought all of these Native Americans lived in Kansas?

I attended a presentation on a Civil War general several years ago, and I heard the speaker say something I have carried with me to this day. "I got this information out of a book. Since the facts were written down in a book, they must be correct. Right?" she asked.

Being polite, no one in attendance moved to challenge her theory. I will challenge her statement here. I say, "Just the facts, ma'am." As a member of the fourth estate who has worked in newsrooms for different TV stations and networks around the country, writing stories that have appeared in all of the various media available today, I would remind the reader that we who study history must constantly strive for the correct historical facts.

In the preparation of this manuscript, I uncovered facts about the Second Battle of Cabin Creek that had not been seen before. Some were discovered using a relatively new research tool: the Internet. It proved to be very useful in helping find the descendants of some of the participants in the battle. Some of those descendants—like Claire Witham and Mrs. Gene Rain, granddaughters of General Gano—even found me. If Rick Harding and I were producing the *Last Raid at Cabin Creek* television documentary today, I believe it could easily stretch to a four-hour television special or miniseries.

I have researched this engagement for more than twenty years, giving presentations to audiences across the country, never dreaming that someone from my own family had fought in the battle. But then, almost by accident, I found him—Private John W. Clanton, a distant cousin who fought at Cabin Creek with the Thirtieth Texas Cavalry. So cue the *Twilight Zone* music.

Jess Epple and Marvin J. Hancock were the first historians to try to look back in time to that fateful night in September 1864 when Confederate brigadier generals Richard M. Gano and Stand Watie, and their commands, captured a Union supply train of three hundred wagons far behind enemy lines. I'm sure both Mr. Epple and Mr. Hancock would join me in telling you to challenge each of our works. Their articles and books inspired me to find out more about the battle and its participants. Perhaps this book will inspire someone to start his or her own journey of discovery. It is my hope that future historians will uncover more information about the Civil War in Indian Territory.

To the future bold adventurer, I leave this one small wish: may you have as much fun as I did.

Acknowledgements

B ooks don't just happen. It takes a lot of help to gather the material and write a book. I would like to thank the following people for their help and for making my first book a truly rewarding experience: Jack and Norma Jean Mullen, Rod Martin, Stephen B. McCartney, Herman and Olivia Stinnett, Joe Poplin, Brian Watts, Rick Harding, Dick Harding, William R. McCright, Royce Fitzgerald, Claire Witham, Mrs. Gene Rain, Curtis Payne, Robert DeMoss, Paul and June Venamon, Kelly Kirkpatrick, Margaret Johnson, Fredrea Cook, Carrie Cook, Dan Jones, Raymond Sweatland, Rick Frost, Steve Cox, Joan Bull, Howard Coleman Jr., Truitt Bradly, Shirle Williams, Daniel W. Gano, Stephen M. Gano, John Gano, Wanda Holder, Dr. Alfred Nofi, Chuck Larson, Anne C. Jones, Lori N. Curtis, Whit Edwards, Sara Stone, Sarah Irwin, Robert A. McInnes, Virgil W. Dean, Donaly E. Brice, Michael V. Hazel, Dr. Donald W. Olson, Peggy Fox, Steve Mullinax, Pat Sutherland Mittelsteadt, Hannah and Jason Puckett, William L. Shea and Don Vickers.

I would also like to thank the following institutions: Oklahoma Historical Society; Kansas Historical Society; Fort Scott National Historic Site; State Historical Society of Missouri; Leavenworth County Historical Society; Johnson County Historical Museum; Cherokee National Museum; Friends of Cabin Creek Battlefield Inc.; Indian Territory Treasure Hunters Club; Thomas Gilcrease Museum; University of Tulsa's McFarlin Library; Olathe Public Library; Texas State Library; Dallas Historical Society; U.S. Army Military History Institute at Carlisle Barracks, Pennsylvania; National

Archives, Washington, D.C.; Smithsonian Institution, Washington, D.C.; the staff of the Westside Regional Library; Tulsa City-County Library, Tulsa, Oklahoma (for what probably seemed like thousands of interlibrary loans I requested); Western History Collections, University of Oklahoma Libraries; Abilene Christian University Library; Wichita State University Library; and The History Press.

CHAPTER 1

The Historic Cabin Creek Ford

H istory happened where the old Texas Road still crosses a northeastern Oklahoma stream known as Cabin Creek. The land surrounding the Cabin Creek ford is one of the most historic areas in the Sooner State. If one could give the rocks, hills and trees the ability to speak, just think of the tales they would tell. You would hear stories of daring explorers, brave soldiers and bloodthirsty outlaws who passed this way a long time ago. Stories about the blood and fire of Civil War battles, including the tale of an Indian Territory pioneer family named Martin, a prosperous ranch and a way of life now gone forever.

The site of the Cabin Creek crossing or ford is located about eight miles east of Adair, Oklahoma, and three and a half miles north of the small community of Pensacola. Near this crossing, the Civil War battles of Cabin Creek were fought. Historians give the names of the First and Second Battles of Cabin Creek to the engagements fought by Union and Confederate forces on July 1–2, 1863, and on September 19, 1864, respectively.

There were actually as many as seven battles of Cabin Creek when counting all of the documented battles and skirmishes fought near the historic ford. Historians usually agree that there were at least eighty-nine Civil War battles and skirmishes fought in Indian Territory. However, while doing research for a book, author Whit Edwards uncovered written documentation of at least twenty-one more battles fought within the territory during the bloody years of our nation's history between 1861 and 1865. Through his research, Edwards has accounted for six battles at Cabin Creek:

Two of the Union cannons placed on the ridge overlooking the Cabin Creek ford keep up a brisk fire on Confederate positions at the First Battle of Cabin Creek, July 1–2, 1863. The Southern force made up of Texans and Indians could only answer with small arms fire, and their attempt to capture a wagon train turned into a rout. *Courtesy Warren Entertainment.*

- May 6–19, 1862—skirmishes near the Creek Agency and Cabin Creek at Martin's House
- July 1–2, 1863—engagement at Cabin Creek
- July 20, 1863—skirmish at Cabin Creek
- May 2, 1864—skirmish at Cabin Creek (not mentioned in the *Official Records*)
- September 19, 1864—Battle at Cabin Creek
- October 23, 1864—action at Cabin Creek (not mentioned in the *Official Records*)[1]

One battle of Cabin Creek not noted by Edwards is a skirmish that took place on November 22, 1864, between a group of Southern guerrillas numbering twenty-six men reportedly led by Fletcher Taylor and a detachment of thirty-two Union cavalrymen led by First Lieutenant Emmett Goss of Company M, Fifteenth Kansas Cavalry. This account first appeared in a story in the *St. Louis Dispatch* in 1873. The story was purported to be the fruit from interviews with Frank James and Jesse James, as well as friends and acquaintances of Cole and John Younger.

According to the story, Taylor, the James brothers and the rest of the guerrillas were riding down the Texas Road, where they had a chance meeting near the Cabin Creek ford with several Jayhawkers riding up the road in the direction of Fort Scott. A fight ensued. "Nothing so weak as the Kansas detachment could possibly live before the deadly prowess and pistol practice of the Missourians."[2] Jesse James reportedly shot and killed Goss, as well as U.P. Gardner, who identified himself as the chaplain of the Thirteenth Kansas Cavalry. Of the thirty-two Union men, only three survived the battle. The Southern irregulars counted four dead.

Some believe that Goss was murdered by Colonel Charles R. Jennison while in charge of foraging parties in the vicinity of Cane Hill, Arkansas. It is interesting to note that a story has also been passed down through the Martin family about Jesse James and his apparent killing of two men near the Cabin Creek ford.[3] This account could be the retelling of the killing of Goss and Gardner during the November 22, 1864 battle at Cabin Creek.

The battle is also documented in J.P. Burch's book *A True Story of Charles W. Quantrell and His Guerrilla Band.*[4] Burch wrote the book from the account of Captain Harrison Trow, who rode with Quantrill during the war. Trow reportedly served the entire war with the ruthless guerrilla leader. However, it seems strange that Trow couldn't recall his leader's name correctly as William Clark Quantrill. Even though he apparently wasn't very good with names, Trow seems to have been able to remember faces. He was asked by Missouri governor Crittenden to identify the body of Jesse James after Bob Ford assassinated the outlaw in 1882. Trow agreed to do this, providing that he could go armed to protect himself. He identified the corpse as James for the governor at St. Joseph, Missouri.[5]

Located at the end of a rural northern Mayes County, Oklahoma road, the ten-acre Cabin Creek Battlefield is owned by the State of Oklahoma. The site was originally owned by the Vinita Chapter of the United Daughters of the Confederacy. The Vinita UDC chapter had purchased the site because its membership believed the land to be the burial place of Confederate soldiers killed in the Second Battle of Cabin Creek.

The battlefield was added to the National Register of Historic Places on July 27, 1971.[6] In 2011, eighty-eight more acres were added to the battlefield with the help of the Civil War Trust, a nonprofit organization dedicated to battlefield preservation. The battlefield is currently maintained by the

1ST KANSAS COLORED VOLUNTEER INFANTRY 79TH U.S.C.T.

The 1st Kansas Colored Volunteer Infantry was the first black unit to engage in battle during the Civil War. On July 2, 1863, while escorting a wagon train bound for Fort Gibson, the 1st Kansas Colored was attacked here by Stand Watie's Confederates where the Texas Road crossed Cabin Creek. After a Union artillery barrage the 1st Kansas Colored, supported by the 3rd Indian Home Guard, forded waist deep Cabin Creek under heavy small arms fire. Emerging with bayonets fixed, the 1st Kansas Colored secured the ford, forcing the Confederates to retreat.

A monument to the First Kansas Colored Infantry (later the Seventy-ninth U.S. Colored Troops) stands on the eastern side of the Cabin Creek Battlefield Park north of Pensacola, Oklahoma. The First Kansas holds the distinction of being the first black regiment to see combat during the Civil War, fighting first at Island Mound, Missouri, October 27–29, 1862. At the First Battle of Cabin Creek, July 1–2, 1863, the regiment made history by fighting alongside white soldiers for the first time. No other Kansas regiment lost as many men during the war. *Courtesy Jack and Norma Jean Mullen.*

Friends of Cabin Creek Battlefield Inc., a local volunteer organization headquartered in nearby Vinita.

Within a stone's throw of the battlefield's circular drive is the very spot were the First Kansas Colored Infantry, a regiment made up of black volunteers, fought beside white soldiers for the first time in the war and in the history of the U.S. Army. It happened on July 1–2, 1863, during the First Battle of Cabin Creek—a full two weeks before the Fifty-fourth Massachusetts Infantry (whose exploits are famous due to the 1989 motion picture *Glory*) led the attack on Fort Wagner near Charleston, South Carolina. A monument to the valor and bravery of First Kansas Colored regiment was dedicated at the eastern end of the battlefield park by the Friends group on July 7, 2007.

A large granite monument to the Confederate victory at the Second Battle of Cabin Creek is prominent as one drives the gravel road, down into a large ravine and up the small rise to the park. The monument was dedicated by the Vinita Chapter of the United Daughters of the Confederacy on June 2, 1961.[7] A group of smaller monuments placed around the short circle drive of the park show approximate Union and Confederate lines during the rare night battle. However, they do not mark the actual battle positions of the various units engaged. Visitors to the battlefield always have questions about the battle, including how the action took place in "such a small area."[8] In reality, the entire battlefield encompassing the sites of both actions is spread out over an area of two to three miles.

It is interesting to note that of all the battles in Indian Territory mentioned in the *Official Records of the War of the Rebellion*, more pages are devoted to the Second Battle of Cabin Creek than any other battle in the territory.

Except for the occasional sound of an airplane passing overhead, the modern world has bypassed this corner of Oklahoma. The surrounding countryside looks much the same as it did in the mid-1860s when the American Civil War was raging.[9] The only real difference in the landscape is the creek's appearance. Similar waterways in the region hold backwater for man-made lakes. Cabin Creek is no exception, as it holds backwater from the nearby Markham Ferry Reservoir and empties into the Grand (or Neosho) River three miles to the southeast. The toll of the backwater has made the creek wider due to the constant erosion of its banks, and in some places, it is deeper than it was during the time of the Civil War. Rod Martin, the son of D.E. "Bill" Martin, whose family once owned the land surrounding the historic ford, recalled when he was a small boy that "you could walk across the creek and not even get your feet wet."[10] The creek

A large granite monument to the Confederate victory at the Second Battle of Cabin Creek stands within the battlefield park. It was placed by the Vinita Chapter of the United Daughters of the Confederacy, which dedicated it in June 1961. The UDC chapter acquired ten acres that it thought contained graves from Confederates buried after the 1864 battle. Today, the land makes up the small battlefield park. *Author's collection.*

continues to be a haven for wildlife. Fishing for bass and crappie is a popular pastime for local residents.

The historic events that happened at the Cabin Creek ford on the Texas Road were in part due to a natural highway. Ten thousand years ago, the Osage Indians followed a buffalo trail that forded the creek. As time passed, word spread about the "Osage Trace," and the white man eventually used the trail leading to Texas, naming it the "Immigrant Road."[11] Originally, the road ran from St. Louis, Missouri, into Kansas and then followed a course south through Indian Territory into Texas. In time, the "Texas Road," as it commonly became known, was the main highway for thousands of settlers headed west. As early as 1829, the government surveyed the road. Lieutenant Washington Hood, a topographer with the expedition, kept a journal in which he described the countryside that he observed.[12] During the Civil War, a portion of the road was used as a supply line between Fort Scott, Kansas, and Fort Gibson, Indian Territory, thus acquiring the name of the "Military Road" or the "Texas-Military Road."

Many famous and infamous men crossed the Cabin Creek ford as they rode down the Texas Road to their appointments with destiny. The first recorded explorer who visited the area was Washington Irving, noted author and scholar. Irving wrote in his book *A Tour of the Prairies* about his visit to Cabin Creek or Planch Cabin Creek on October 5–6, 1832. Irving's book helped to popularize the Texas Road to people all over the early United States. Using a copy of Irving's original journal, notes and other research materials, amateur historians Paul and June Venamon of Pryor, Oklahoma, pinpointed Irving's first campsite, across Cabin Creek to the north of the present Cabin Creek Battlefield. The Venamons believe that Irving's party entered what is now Oklahoma on the old Texas Road and camped the night of October 5 east of Cabin Creek. The next morning, on the sixth, they did not cross Cabin Creek at this point but instead traveled south of the Hopefield Mission. The party had lunch there and then crossed Cabin Creek at the old ford. The ford was about half a mile upstream from the mouth of the creek. After crossing Cabin Creek, they followed the Texas Road on south to Chouteau's trading post.[13]

Other notable figures from U.S. history who crossed the Cabin Creek ford include Sam Houston, who lived with the Cherokees and took a Cherokee wife named Tiana Rogers. (Tiana is buried in the officer's circle at the Fort Gibson National Cemetery.) Before living with the Cherokees, he had held public office as a United States congressman from Tennessee and later served as the state's governor. He was the commander in chief of Texas forces in the Texas War for Independence against Mexico. Groomed for public service, he later became the first president of the Republic of Texas. After Texas was admitted to the Union, Houston served as both U.S. senator and governor of the state of Texas.

Zachary Taylor served as a major general in the United States Army in the Mexican-American War and would later be elected as the twelfth president of the United States. Jefferson Davis also rode down the Texas Road as a second lieutenant in the First United States Dragoons to his assigned post at Fort Gibson, Indian Territory.[14] He would later serve as secretary of war before becoming the first and only president of the Confederate States of America. William C. Quantrill, the Confederate guerrilla leader whose band of ruthless raiders included the James brothers, used the Texas Road frequently during the Civil War. Quantrill's band of cutthroats, as well as other guerrillas, used the Texas-Military Road to travel through Indian Territory frequently during the Civil War.

There was also a bold breed of pioneer men and women who traveled the Texas Road to what they hoped would be a new and better life. Some came freely. Others came by force. Many members of the Five Civilized Tribes would make the journey to the Indian Territory over another road in what was known as the "Trail of Tears."

CHAPTER 2

"Greenbrier Joe" Martin and His Pensacola Ranch

One of the first Cherokee families to travel from Georgia to the Indian Territory was the John Martin family. Martin was born into the Cherokee tribe on October 2, 1781. His father, Joseph Lynch Martin, had served as brigadier general of the Twentieth Virginia Brigade during the Revolutionary War. Martinsville, Virginia, was named in honor of General Martin.[15] John would become the first treasurer of the Cherokee nation in 1819 and would be named the first chief justice of the Supreme Court of the Cherokee nation in 1821.[16] Martin brought his family west in 1828, settling near the area of the Grand River known as the Grand Saline. His two wives, Nellie and Lucy McDaniels, were sisters. Together they parented sixteen children. Judge John Martin died on October 17, 1840. His grave can still be visited in the community of Fort Gibson, Oklahoma.[17]

Joseph Lynch Martin, one of John's sons, was born on August 20, 1820, and named in honor of his grandfather. This Joseph L. Martin later became affectionately known by the nickname of "Greenbrier Joe" because of a house he built at a place that he called Greenbrier.[18] Because of his influential father, he was well known within the Cherokee tribe and other tribal circles. Among the wealthiest landowners in Indian Territory at the time, Joe Martin's Pensacola Ranch was a sprawling 100,000 acres. Martin had chosen the name "Pensacola," which meant "land of many beautiful flowers." Some of the land he owned, while the rest was leased from the Cherokee nation.[19] The present-day community of Pensacola, Oklahoma, was named for the old Martin Ranch.

"Greenbrier Joe" Martin rose to the rank of major, serving in the quartermaster department of Watie's Indian brigade. When the war was over, he spent the rest of his life trying to regain what his family had lost. Some people said that when he died in 1891, "he died of a broken heart." *Author's collection.*

Greenbrier Joe Martin was married several times in his lifetime. His wives included Julia Lumbard, Sallie Chambers, Lucy Rogers, Caroline Garrett and Jennie Harlan. He fathered fifteen children between all of them.[20]

Martin built two large antebellum houses on his ranch. The first one, Greenbrier, he constructed on the southern part of this ranch. The house stood on the site of the present-day Greenbrier Baptist Church near Strang, Oklahoma.[21] The other house was built just south of the Cabin Creek ford on the Texas Road. A portion of the road crossed directly in front of the house.[22] It has been described by family members as a two-story brick antebellum-style house.[23] As with most houses built on the frontier, it was surrounded by a large fence for protection. Both houses were furnished with the very latest fashions and furniture from St. Louis and New Orleans.[24] Like other large plantation owners in Indian Territory, Martin was also a slave owner. At one time, he had more than 103 slaves working on his ranch.[25] One of Martin's slaves, named William, rose to be the overseer or foreman of the ranch.[26] William had four sons and three daughters, all of whom were born into freedom after the Civil War.[27] William took the surname of Martin after the war. One of William's sons, Tobe Martin, lived in Vinita, Oklahoma, where he died in 1972 at the age of 104.[28]

Stories have been passed down in the Martin family about slaves who refused to leave the devastated Cabin Creek house and the outbuildings when Union forces occupied the Pensacola Ranch from 1863 to 1865. Many years after the war, some of Martin's former slaves would often come to visit him, call him "Massa Joe," sit at his feet and cry for the old times.[29]

One other interesting story about the Martin household has also survived. Instead of using slaves as house servants, Greenbrier Joe hired fourteen full-blood Cherokees as servants. He wanted his children to learn Cherokee as a second language to English. He thought the children would have to learn the Cherokee language in order to converse with the servants. The plan backfired, however, when the children taught the Cherokee servants how to speak English.[30]

The Cabin Creek ford was a popular overnight stop for settlers traveling by wagon train. There was abundant water, as well as ample grass for grazing animals. It was a perfect camping spot. Since a branch of the Texas Road ran right by his house, Martin was in a good spot to see history roll by his window. Almost every day, it seemed, the road was full of settlers moving westward, looking for better lives. Martin later recalled counting more than one thousand wagons pass by his house during a six-week period.[31]

Besides the Martin residence, ranch buildings and slave quarters, there was also a small community that sprang up at Cabin Creek. This included a stage station, a blacksmith shop, (both owned by Joe Martin), a few other private residences and a trading post run by a full-blood Cherokee named Tom Knight.[32] Martin also sold supplies and oxen teams to the settlers. Many settlers were coming down the Texas Road, and business was good. Greenbrier Joe and some of his ranch hands occasionally drove wild steers up the Texas Road to Fort Leavenworth, Kansas, to sell to settlers as oxen. In one year, Martin sold more than seven hundred oxen teams at $300 a team.[33]

Like many ranchers of his day, Martin liked racehorses. One particular gray racehorse was his favorite, and it was fast. One day, a man from Missouri came down the Texas Road to arrange a race between his horse

Left: Postwar photo of Richard Martin. A teenager at the time of the Cabin Creek raid, Martin later wrote that he remembered his condition of his uniform was deplorable. "My shirt was without a back, but the defect was covered by a friendly gray jacket with buttons of wood. My pants from the pockets down was only represented by the inner part called 'lining.' My garb was about as respectable as many others in our command." *Courtesy Rod Martin.*

Below: Postwar photo Alexander Martin. He went off with his father and brother to fight the war. *Courtesy Rod Martin.*

and Martin's horse. Each man was to wager $1,000, but the stranger also had one condition: he would choose the day of the race. Martin agreed to the condition, and the man went away. Then one day after a heavy snowfall, the man appeared at the Martin Ranch with his racehorse in tow. The race was held that day, and the contest was not even close. The stranger's horse easily outran Martin's horse. Impressed, Martin asked to see the winning horse's shoes. Apparently, the shoes were made to help the horse have better traction in the snow. Joe bought the horse's shoes from the Missouri man. A few days later, Martin's gray horse ran another race, this time wearing the new snowshoes. The race was held at Rose Prairie, located east of the present-day town of Locust Grove. Martin's horse raced against a horse owned by a man named Leach. This time, Greenbrier Joe wagered $2,000, and his horse won.[34]

At the outbreak of the war in 1861, Martin enlisted in the Confederate army and became a captain commanding Company D in Colonel Stand Watie's Second Cherokee Mounted Volunteers.[35] Martin's oldest son, Alexander, and his other son, Richard, also enlisted in the Confederate army for the duration. As other Confederate Indian volunteers had done, Martin sent the rest of his family south out of harm's way to northern Texas. He told his slaves to watch over the ranch and that, for the time being, they were on their own.[36]

A natural spring used to bubble near the old Texas Road. There is no doubt that the spring was one of the drinking sources for the Martin household, for overnight campers and for a base or "station" built by the Union army. After the Battle of Honey Springs in July 1863, Major General James Blunt ordered the construction of stations along the Texas Road. These stations were garrisoned with a company or two for strength.[37] The Cabin Creek station was the halfway point between Forts Scott and Blunt (Gibson), and thus it seemed logical to fortify it. During November 1863, 170 Cherokees with the Second Union Indian Home Guard were assigned garrison duty at the Cabin Creek station.[38] According to numerous eyewitness and historical accounts, the stockade stood twelve feet high, with heavy timbers set solidly into the ground. It enclosed quarters for officers and enlisted men. The Martin house served as the hospital. The stockade was in the large field located immediately west of the present-day battlefield site. The Civil War changed everything for the little community at Cabin Creek. No traces of the dwellings or the stockade remain.

CHAPTER 3

The War in Indian Territory

By August 1864, the fortunes of war, which had turned against the Confederacy in the East, were being felt strongly in the Trans-Mississippi Department. Since the fall of Vicksburg, Mississippi, in 1863, the Union navy had control of the Mississippi River. The Richmond government's supplies to its Indian allies were few and far between. Worst of all, the civilian population in Indian Territory had suffered greatly. At the start of the war, almost 100,000 people lived in the Indian nations. By the war's end, more than one-third of the population had been killed or had moved out of the territory.[39]

Hanna Hicks Hitchcock, wife of Dr. Dwight Hitchcock, a missionary in Indian Territory, kept a diary about the sufferings of civilian population. According to eyewitness accounts like Hitchcock's, both Union and Confederate troops stole horses, cattle and supplies from the starving populace.[40]

William P. Ross, the son of Cherokee chief John Ross, wrote a letter in December 1864 describing the conditions in Indian Territory:

> *Everything has been changed by the destroying hand of War…but few men remain in their homes…nearly all the farms are growing up in bushes and briars, houses abandoned or burnt…some idea of the great and melancholy change which has come over our once prosperous and beautiful country… livestock of all kinds have become very scarce…We have not a horse, cow or hog left that I know of. Though some few have a yoke of oxen or a mule…*

great increase in the number of wild animals. The wolves howl dismally over the land and the panther's scream is often heard.[41]

With the outbreak of war in 1861, the United States Army abandoned all Federal forts in Indian Territory, including Fort Washita, Fort Cobb and Fort Arbuckle. Deactivated in 1857, Fort Gibson had been turned over to the Cherokee nation.[42] Federal authorities had signed treaties with the tribes promising supplies and military protection. Now they refused to honor their promises. Indian leaders loyal to the government tried in vain to get officials in Washington to hear their pleas. Instead, Washington turned a deaf ear. As expected, Confederate troops swiftly occupied the former Union posts. The Confederate government sent emissaries, including Albert Pike, to the Indian nations in the hopes of gaining allies for the Confederacy.[43]

The Indian nations were known by the name of the "Five Civilized Tribes" (Cherokee, Creek, Chickasaw, Choctaw and Seminole) and were divided in regard to loyalty between the United States and the new Confederate States. Several Indian leaders, including Cherokee chief John Ross, tried to keep their people out of the "white man's war." Like their counterparts in the East, families in Indian Territory were ripped asunder as brother, father and son went off to fight alongside one another and often against one another. The Cherokee nation knew such division. Organizations of full-blood and pure-blood Cherokees aligned themselves with the Union. Those full bloods and other mixed-blooded Cherokees who followed the Southern cause called these Union Indians "Pins." They could easily be identified by the wearing of a pin or crossed pins on their coats.[44] When an invading Union force arrested Chief Ross in 1862, the "Pins" began raiding and looting the homes of Southern sympathizers.

In 1863, Confederate hopes in Indian Territory looked brighter. Brigadier General Sam Bell Maxey became the commander of all Confederate forces in Indian Territory. Originally from Kentucky, Maxey was a graduate of the United States Military Academy at West Point. His roommate during one year was Thomas J. Jackson.[45] At the Battle of First Manassas or Bull Run, Jackson would acquire fame and the legendary nickname of "Stonewall." During the Mexican-American War, Maxey served as a first lieutenant under Captain Robert E. Lee and was decorated for gallantry.[46] Before the outbreak of hostilities in 1861, Maxey was an attorney at law in Texas and had also held the office of district attorney. When the war began, Maxey raised his own company of men, holding various command positions, and was appointed a brigadier general. In March 1862, he commanded a brigade at the Siege of Vicksburg.[47]

Wartime photograph of Major General Samuel B. Maxey, CSA, the able Confederate commander of Indian Territory. It was Maxey who called Stand Watie "that gallant old hero." *Courtesy Harold B. Simpson Confederate Research Center, Hillsboro, Texas.*

Maxey was appointed commander of Indian Territory on December 11, 1863, replacing Brigadier General William Steele.[48] When he arrived in the territory, he found a command filled with problems. He quickly reorganized his command and ruled that no color line would determine rank. His Indian troops numbered about 6,000 on the muster rolls among the various Indian commands. This parlayed into only about 2,000 effective troops.[49] Also assigned to Maxey's department was Brigadier General Richard Montgomery Gano's Fifth Texas Cavalry Brigade, which had a roster of 1,800 troopers. However, due to the lack of equipment, supplies and low morale, full-scale military operations were reduced to guerrilla warfare. Bushwhacking by both sides was a common practice.

Gano was a man of many accomplishments. A native of Lexington, Kentucky, he was born in Bourbon County, Kentucky, on June 17, 1830. His father, John Allen Gano, was a minister of the Disciples of Christ and was associated with Alexander Campbell and Barton W. Stone in what is known today as the Restoration movement. The movement circulated among late nineteenth-century conservative churches with the intent to go back to the Bible and be Christians in name only. Gano's great-grandfather, John Gano, had baptized (immersed) George Washington during the Revolutionary War.[50] The Ganos (pronounced *ga*-noh or *ga*-neaux) were descended from Francis Gano, a leader of the Protestant Huguenots who fled France following an edict from King Louis XIV.[51]

Richard had been baptized into the church at the young age of ten. At twelve, he attended Bacon College (1842–47) in Harrodsburg, Kentucky. At seventeen, he completed his courses at Bethany College (1848–49) in Virginia. He also attended Louisville Medical University (1849–50) at Louisville, graduating under special dispensation in 1850 before he was twenty-one years of age.[52] He practiced medicine in Kentucky for a short time and was a physician at the Louisiana State Penitentiary at Baton Rouge. In 1853, he married Martha (Mattie) J. Welch of Crab Orchard, Kentucky.[53] The couple eventually had twelve children, nine of whom lived to maturity. In 1857, Gano moved his family to Texas and settled at Grapevine Prairie, where he became well known as an Indian fighter and as a state legislator. Part of the old Gano homestead today lies under the runways of the Dallas–Fort Worth International Airport.

Early in the war, Gano had organized and led a cavalry command known as Gano's Texas Cavalry Squadron made up entirely of volunteers from Texas.[54] With two hundred men, he rode to Tennessee to join his good friend, General Albert Sydney Johnston. Unfortunately, Gano and his men arrived one day after the Battle of Shiloh, in which Johnston was killed. The Texas troops then joined the Confederate forces, with Gano personally reporting to General Pierre Gustave Toutant Beauregard, commander of the Confederate Army of the Tennessee. With the help of his old family friend, Major General John C. Breckinridge, Gano's squadron was ordered to join Colonel John Hunt Morgan's Second Kentucky Cavalry regiment at Chattanooga, Tennessee.[55] Gano and his Texans served with distinction as a part of Morgan's Raiders. The Texas volunteers were inducted into the Third Kentucky Cavalry, with Gano serving as the regiment's colonel.

A deeply religious man, Gano neither smoked tobacco nor drank alcoholic beverages or stimulants, including coffee or tea. It was also reported that he never used foul language.[56]

Colonel Gano was never hesitant about maintaining discipline, and on more than one occasion, he tried to convey his morals on the men serving in his

Brigadier General Richard Montgomery Gano, CSA, fought with Morgan's Cavalry in Kentucky before being transferred to Indian Territory in December 1863. After the war, Gano became a Church of Christ/Christian Church evangelist and helped establish many churches in Texas. The former Confederate general also became a millionaire through his business dealings in land, horses and cattle. *Courtesy Claire Witham.*

command. One incident after his command's capture of Harrodsburg, Kentucky, illustrates this conviction. After leaving Harrodsburg, one of his men apparently filled his canteen with whiskey and became drunk. When Gano learned of the matter, he ordered the men lined up along the side of the road and sent an officer to empty every canteen. He told the men they could refill their canteens with fresh water at the next spring they came to. When the officer attempted to empty one particular canteen, the soldier protested that he was pouring out some of the finest old bourbon he'd ever seen. The soldier even tried to get his mouth under the stream draining onto the road. However, Gano had no drunken men in his command that day.[57] As a way to stifle his boredom while in camp, Gano trained his own pets, including a squirrel, a rabbit and a deer.[58]

Gano left active service for a short time due to ill health[59] and was transferred to the Trans-Mississippi Department in late 1863. As acting brigadier general, Gano was assigned to command the Fifth Texas Cavalry Brigade. He was the youngest Confederate general in the sector. The remnants of his original Texas cavalry troop, reduced to less than company size in numbers, went with him to his new command in Indian Territory. The unit was renamed Gano's Guards in his honor and continued to operate as a part of the Fifth Texas.[60]

Since his appointment as brigade commander, Gano had been forced to deal with the overwhelming problem of desertion in the ranks of his Texas troopers. Hunting for deserters was a job detested by those of the rank and file. One soldier commented, "This is a hard business—to take a man away from his home while his wife and children begged and screamed for his release…we tried to look favorably upon the actions of our superior officers, but sometimes it was hard to do."[61]

The brigade was ordered to McKinney, Texas, in late June 1864 to hunt down and arrest Confederate deserters. A court-martial board of thirteen commissioned officers, with General Gano presiding, decided the dispositions of the accused. Sentences included prison terms or the disgrace of being "drummed out of the army." This time, however, an example was made to discourage others from deserting. Some of the men were sentenced to death, including Private Barney McDermott. On June 28, 1864, after hearing all of the evidence against McDermott, the court found him guilty. Gano sentenced McDermott to be shot by a firing squad of twelve men, which was carried out on July 1, 1864.[62]

General Maxey tried to solve many of the overwhelming problems facing his command, including constant desertion from the ranks and the severe shortage of weapons and supplies. His efforts to resolve the situation were unproductive. From his headquarters at Fort Towson in the Choctaw nation on February 25, 1864, Maxey wrote to his wife about the weapons shortages, "The great troubles and the one about which I have the most anxiety than the others is arms. Oh for 5,000 good guns, and I would leave northern Texas in safety. I have the promise, but when will it be fulfilled?"[63]

All of Maxey's troops, white and Indian, were poorly armed. Some of the Indian and Texas troops were equipped with old Enfield, Mississippi and

Texas rifles, together with double-barreled shotguns, small squirrel rifles and mammoth Belgian muskets.[64] Many of the Indian troops also had shotguns, as well as ancient muskets and hunting rifles of many different calibers. Ammunition for these weapons was in short supply.[65] One inspecting officer noted that if the Indians had been properly armed, they would have made an effective offensive fighting force.[66]

To get an even better idea of the small arms used by Confederate forces in Indian Territory, we can look to a letter dated October 26, 1863, that includes details about the small arms used by Brigadier General Douglas Cooper's brigade:

> Cooper's brigade of First and Second Creek regiments, Seminole Battalion, Chickasaw Battalion, Picken's company of Chickasaws, Cherokee regiment, 's (29th) Texas (Cavalry) regiment and Wells' (34th regiment) battalion Texas cavalry was poorly drilled, armed and disciplined…The Texas regiments are well mounted and better armed than the Indians. Many of the later have flintlock rifles and nearly all of them have the common sporting rifle. The majority of the Indians are poorly mounted on Indian ponies.[67]

An inventory of arms from this brigade on August 23, 1863, notes the following type of weapons:

Common rifles, old and worn	460
Shot-guns, old and worn	1,078
Mississippi rifles	76
Sharps rifles [probably carbines]	43
Belgian rifles [i.e., Texas contract rifles]	450
Maynard rifles [carbines]	2
Muskets, old and worn	416
Enfield rifles, good	265
Minié rifles	20
Hall's carbines	4
Minié muskets	25
Colt's rifles	4

The writer of the report noted that a large portion of these guns were old, worn and barely serviceable.[68]

These two reports provide strong evidence that the Confederate Texas and Indian troopers involved in the Cabin Creek raid were armed with a wide and diverse variety of weapons, including percussion shotguns.

Because of the news of Confederate setbacks in the East, Maxey visited the leaders of the Indian nations in order to shore up support for the struggling Confederacy. On May 14, 1864, he published a letter from Jefferson Davis, the president of the Confederate States, intended for all residents of the Indian nations:

> *The soldiers and the people of the Six Nations in Treaty and Animity with us, are regarded by this Government with the same and tender care and solicitude, as are the soldiers and people of all of the Confederate States. Our cause is one and our hearts must be united. We must put forth our whole energy. Cultivate harmony and confidence. Practice fortitude. Bring forth promptly every available man into the field, and resolve to do, and if need be, to die in defense of our birthright. And with the Providence of God to guide and to shield us, victory will perch on our banners and bless us with peace, Independence and prosperity. Accept my best wishes for health and happiness to yourselves and to the people of the Nations, and believe me*
>
> *Very Truly Your Friend,*
> *Jefferson Davis* [69]

CHAPTER 4

Watie's Daring Plan

On February 5, 1864, Colonel Stand Watie proposed a plan to force Union troops from Forts Gibson and Smith. The main part of the plan proposed a strong raid into central Kansas. It was hoped that such a demonstration would cause the withdrawal of Federal troops from the various outposts in Indian Territory to protect Kansas.[70] Watie's plan was submitted by Maxey to Lieutenant General Edmund Kirby Smith, the commander of the Trans-Mississippi Department. Maxey and his field commanders waited seven months for a response to the plan from the Confederate military command.[71]

By 1864, the exploits of Watie were already legendary in both armies. At the start of the war, Watie was commissioned a colonel in the Confederate army, leading his Cherokee Mounted Volunteers. On May 10, 1864, he was promoted to the rank of brigadier general.[72] He was the only Native American to hold a general's commission in either army during the war. More importantly, his name meant fear and apprehension to his Federal enemies stationed along the territory border. His Cherokee name "Degataga" is translated to mean "he stands (on two feet), immovable."[73] He also went by the name of Isaac S. Watie.

Watie was born on December 12, 1806, near Rome, Georgia. He was a member of the Deer clan. His father, David Oowatie, was an important Cherokee leader. His mother, Susana Reese, was the part-Cherokee daughter of Charles Reese, an English trader. His brother was Buck Watie, better known as Elias Boudinot.[74] In his youth, Watie had taken an early

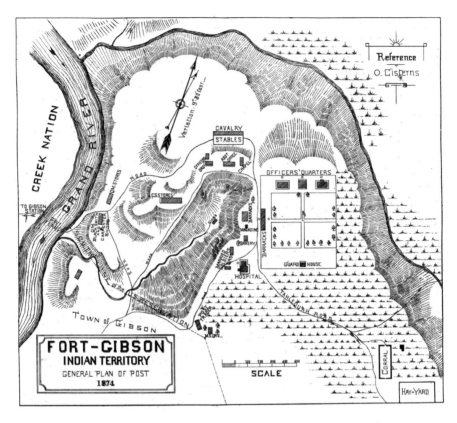

A government map of Fort Gibson, Indian Territory, as it appeared in 1874. *Author's collection.*

interest in Cherokee politics. He signed the Treaty of New Echota, thus marking himself as one of the Treaty Party. Watie was forewarned of the assassinations of Boudinot and Major and John Ridge, but Watie himself managed to escape death. He opposed Cherokee chief John Ross for the rest of his life. After the Cherokee people were forced to walk the Trail of Tears and arrived in Indian Territory, Watie became a member of the Cherokee Council from 1845 to 1861. He was elected the speaker of the council from 1857 to 1859.[75]

Watie and his Indian soldiers had ambushed and captured the Federal steamer *J.R. Williams* on June 15, 1864. Placing his three pieces of artillery on Pheasant Bluff, which overlooked the Arkansas River, Watie and his troops patiently waited for the steamboat to come upriver. The boat was filled with supplies intended for the garrison at Fort Gibson. After unloading a

Postwar photo of Brigadier General Stand Watie, CSA. Watie planned the raid north of the Arkansas River that resulted in the capture of a Union supply train of three hundred wagons at Cabin Creek, Cherokee Nation. He was planning yet another raid when word of General Robert E. Lee's surrender reached Indian Territory. Watie was the last Confederate general in the field to surrender, on June 23, 1865. *Courtesy University of Arkansas at Little Rock Archives, Little Rock, Arkansas.*

portion of sixteen thousand pounds of bacon, 150 barrels of flour and a considerable amount of store goods, Watie ordered the captured boat burned. The blazing vessel was released and floated over a mile before it sank. The loss of the steamer further discouraged river traffic for the Union army. Accordingly, supplies for Indian Territory had to be brought in by wagon train.[76]

General Gano was anxious to assume the offensive. While in camp, he wrote a letter to Maxey on August 29, 1864, concerning his hope for renewed action:

> *The hope secures farther reaching because you are going to send me an order to go north of the Arkansas River and do all the damage to the Yanks I can up there. I have been anxious about it, but there seems so much delaying on our part while the Feds are moving trains and Regiments to and fro and the finest opportunities afforded to whip them in detail. It is true many of my men are dismounted, barefooted and unarmed, but they would be better satisfied actively employed, than idling in camps. And there would be a pretty fair chance to capture arms, horses and clothing. I am satisfied we ought to be up there now. The River is fordable and we are burning away the light of day on the working season. If we were ordered or allowed to go forward, then General Stand Watie would cooperate with us, but General Cooper is very cautious and I am satisfied some good opportunities have and are being presented. What say you?[77]*

The cautious General Cooper Gano referred to in his letter is Major General Douglas H. Cooper, who was now Confederate superintendent of Indian affairs in Indian Territory. On July 17, 1863, Cooper had led the largest Confederate force ever assembled in Indian Territory into the disastrous defeat at the Battle of Honey Springs near present-day Rentiesville, Oklahoma.[78]

Finally, after months of waiting, Watie's plan for a raid was approved by the Confederate high command. However, Kirby Smith ordered that the raid should take place before October 1 to coincide with Confederate major general Sterling Price's planned Missouri Raid.[79] This proved to be perfect timing. In August, intelligence reports were received at Maxey's headquarters at Fort Towson that told of a large Union wagon train being prepared at Fort Scott that would soon move south on the Texas Road. The train would be filled with supplies intended for Indian refugees at Fort Gibson. On August 18, 1864, Colonel William Adair of the Second Cherokee Regiment rode

View of the officers' quarters at Fort Scott, Kansas, during the Civil War. The buildings have been restored and are a part of the Fort Scott National Historic Site. *Author's collection.*

into Maxey's headquarters with an amended plan from General Watie to raid and disrupt Union communications along the Grand River and north of the Arkansas River. The wagon train, if it could be found, would be the primary target.[80]

The Cherokee general did not realize that his plan would take him to the very battlefield where he had met his worst defeat. At the First Battle of Cabin Creek, July 1–2, 1863, Watie had been forced to withdraw after trying to capture another wagon train. Colonel James M. Williams, the Union commander of the wagon train, used his artillery and cavalry, as well as black and Indian infantry, to turn the Confederate withdrawal into a rout.

Just two weeks after Gano wrote his letter to Maxey demanding action, Gano's Texans and Watie's Indian troops were sharing campfires at Camp Pike, located on the Canadian River near present-day Whitefield, Oklahoma.[81] Animosity existed between the two separate brigades, each belonging to different divisions. Gano had expressed to Maxey the lack of confidence and reliance that the white troops placed in their Indian allies. The Texans and Indians had almost fired on one another in an earlier incident that occurred in January 1864. Colonel Charles DeMorse, commanding the Twenty-ninth Texas Cavalry, rode into Fort Washita with his regiment, demanding the commissary be opened up to his command. With his request denied, the Texans commandeered all of the artillery at

Brothers Ira and Robert Haney of the Third Wisconsin Cavalry fought in the First Battle of Cabin Creek. Two weeks later, they saw action at the largest battle of the Civil War in Indian Territory at the Battle of Honey Springs near present-day Rentiesville, Oklahoma. Both brothers survived the war. *Courtesy Hannah and Jason Puckett.*

the post, loaded the guns and turned them on the commissary building and the Indian command. The situation was defused only after the Texans were allowed supplies.[82]

Once the Texas and Indian brigades were combined, Watie and Gano did not ever doubt their effectiveness as a fighting force. On September 12 (at Camp Courser) and September 13 (at Camp Pike), Watie and Gano held planning sessions for the raid. Although both men retain command over their individual units, Watie readily turned command of the expedition over to Gano because his commission predated Watie's by one month. Both Gano and Maxey commended Watie for his

Stand Watie carried this Bowie knife during the Civil War. *Courtesy Cherokee National Museum, Tahlequah, Oklahoma.*

unselfishness, something that up to that time had not been seen by the armies on either side.[83]

Equipment, supplies and ammunition were loaded as the Confederates prepared for the raid into Union-held territory north of the Arkansas River. Gano took 1,200 of his brigade including Colonel Charles DeMorse's Twenty-ninth Texas (Lieutenant Colonel Welch commanding), Thirtieth Texas Cavalry Regiment (Captain Strayhorn commanding) and detachments of Martin's Thirty-first Texas Cavalry (Major Mayrant commanding); Hardeman's Battalion; Head's Company; Welch's Company; and, most importantly, Captain Sylvanus Howell's Texas Artillery Battery with six guns.

Watie had 800 Indian soldiers in his command, including 200 men of the First Cherokee Regiment commanded by Lieutenant Colonel C.N. Vann, 150 men from the Second Cherokee Regiment reporting to Major John Vann, 125 from First Creek Regiment under Lieutenant Colonel Samuel Checote, 200 men of the Second Creek Regiment under Colonel Timothy Barnett and Colonel John Jumper's 120 Seminoles. This gave the Confederate commanders a total combined force of 2,000 men.[84]

On Wednesday, September 14, 1864, the column comprising Watie's Indians and Gano's Texans headed north, splashing across the ford on the Canadian River.[85] The most ragtag force the Confederate army had ever known was on the move. Unknown to Watie, Gano and their men, this was to be the last Confederate raid of the long and bitter war in Indian Territory. This time, things would turn out differently for the Confederates. Their planning would pay off, and this would be a ride into history.

CHAPTER 5

Ridin' a Raid

The Attack on the Hay Camp at Flat Rock

For three days, the Confederate column traveled north. Its commanders knew that such a large force could not go undetected. Watie ordered Major John Vann to throw out scouts from his Second Cherokee Regiment on the right flank as far up the south side of the Arkansas River as possible.[86] Riding with the regiment were Captain Joe Martin and his sons, Alexander and Richard. Watie's oldest son, Saladin, also rode with the column. General Gano also had relatives riding on the raid with him. His son, John T. Gano, served as his aide. Gano's brother-in-law, Captain William G. Welch, was in command of Gano's Guards. Welch's father, Lieutenant Colonel Otis G. Welch, was the acting commander of the Twenty-ninth Texas Cavalry.[87]

Vann's scouts reported no sign of enemy troops. So far, it appeared that the Southern force had been lucky and was undetected. The column camped at Prairie Springs on the night of Wednesday, September 14, then crossed the Arkansas River about six miles from the Creek Agency at about noon on the fifteenth.[88] The river was so swollen with recent rains that it became necessary to pack over all the artillery ammunition by hand and on horseback. It was difficult work. It took more than six hours to cross the river with the wagons, artillery pieces and supplies. Each man had to be cautious as he felt his footing as the area was laced with treacherous quicksand.[89]

Union officers had realized the vulnerability of their supply lines and were alert for a Confederate strike. Scouts had been detailed across the countryside to look for any organized Confederate activity. A lone Union

Indian scout approached the river and observed the large rebel force at the ford. He was observed by the Confederates and fired upon but escaped.[90]

Speed was now imperative for the Confederates. Within a few hours, the Federal commander at Fort Gibson would know that the Southern force was north of the Arkansas. Major Vann's command proceeded to the Creek Agency, located five miles west of the old Confederate Fort Davis and ten miles west of Fort Gibson. This was as close as the Confederates came to the Union post during the raid. Located near the Creek Agency was a tall hill known today as Fern Mountain. From a point on top of the mountain, observers could have warned the main Confederate column if a Federal force appeared.[91]

The Confederates made their camp at a site Watie called "Camp Pleasant" in his report. The Southern force was located about eleven miles north and west of Fort Gibson. In early morning hours of Friday, September 16, the Confederate force crossed the Verdigris River at the Sand Town ford. That afternoon, scouts discovered a Union haying party at Flat Rock, twelve miles northwest of Fort Gibson on the west side of the Grand River.[92] Flat Rock was the principal hay camp for the fort. Several smaller hay camps intervened between the principal hay camp and the edge of the timber four miles north of Fort Gibson along the Texas-Military Road.[93]

Working at a hay camp was one of the most tedious assignments a soldier in the Army of the Frontier could receive. With black soldiers cutting and hauling hay, mounted patrols of white soldiers watched the fords at the river crossings, circling the perimeter of the main camp and constantly watching for Confederate regulars and bushwhackers.

The large column halted as scout Bill McCracken led Watie and Gano as well as other staff officers to the top of a high hill located to the northeast to spy on the Federal troops.[94] Known today by the name of Blue Mound, the hill is located about three miles west of present-day Wagoner, Oklahoma. From the top of the hill through field glasses, Watie and Gano could "view the enemy camps" and watch black soldiers in blue, using horse-drawn mowing machines to cut hay over a three-mile area, the black troops "little dreaming" that rebels were watching them.[95] The chance to fight a large contingent of the "Corps d' Afrique" was not going to be missed by the Southern commanders.

General Gano ordered Gurley's regiment (Thirtieth Texas) to the rear of the hay camp to cut off any chance of the Federal troops taking to the Grand River timber.[96]

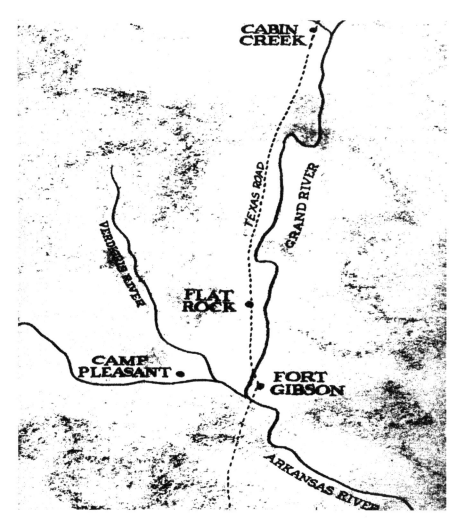

Flat Rock was the principal haying camp for Fort Gibson. This map shows the proximity to the fort and the Confederate camp, which Watie called "Camp Pleasant" in his report. The Cabin Creek stockade was located about thirty-five miles north of the Flat Rock hay camp. *Courtesy Warren Entertainment.*

When the rest of the column came within a mile or two of the Federal camp, Gano deployed the Twenty-ninth and Thirty-first Texas Regiments to the right and Watie's command to the left. Gano's Guards, Martin's Regiment, Howell's Texas Battery and the two detached companies remained with Gano at the center of the Confederate line. The general had a clear view of the field and could see the Confederate columns as they circled the camp to cut off any retreat. Gano reported that he could distinctly see Captain Strayhorn formed in the enemy's rear. "The clouds looked somber and the V-shaped procession grand as we moved forward in the work of death," he later wrote in his report.[97]

Captain Edgar A. Barker and a detachment of soldiers from Fort Gibson had been assigned the duty of guarding the haying operation. Barker's detail consisted of men from Company C, Second Kansas Cavalry, along with detachments from Companies G and L. First Lieutenant David M. Sutherland, a white officer, had reinforced him with a detachment from Company K of the First Kansas Colored Volunteer Infantry. Barker's total force numbered 125 men.[98]

A native of Junction City, Kansas, Barker had quickly risen through the ranks of Company C. On November 30, 1861, he had been promoted to first sergeant. By May 4, 1863, he received a first lieutenant's commission from Kansas governor Thomas Carney. He was appointed the captain of Company C of the Second Kansas Cavalry on November 1, 1863.[99] After three years of combat command, Barker was familiar with the brutal warfare on the border.

About the time Barker was being warned by his scouts of the advancing Confederates, Gano and Watie were already on the hill, spying on his position. After his scouts reported the Confederate column, their presence did not seem to concern the captain, since the scouts had placed the Confederate strength at only about two hundred.[100] Barker sounded recall and positioned his men in a ravine located to the rear of his camp. He felt it was important to try to guard the hay, which was the only food source the livestock at Fort Gibson would have during the winter months.[101]

Unable to get a clear idea of the enemy's strength, Barker decided to find out for himself. Riding with a small reconnaissance party only about a mile or two from the camp, Barker rode almost straight into skirmishers from Gano's advance force on the move toward the main hay camp.[102] The captain immediately rode back to his troops as he and his men skirmished with the rebels' advance force. Almost cut off from the men in the ravine, he and his mounted troopers fought virtually every step of

Lieutenant Pleasant Porter, First Creek Regiment, CSA. Porter was recognized by Stand Watie in his report for capturing six prisoners at the Battle of Flat Rock, Indian Territory. Years later, Porter was elected chief of the Muscogee (Creek) nation. *Courtesy Smithsonian Institution, Washington, D.C.*

the way back to their camp. He dismounted his soldiers, placing them with the black soldiers already in the ravine, just as the Confederates attacked on the position. After receiving attacks from five different points and holding off three separate Confederate cavalry charges in less than half an hour, and with the enemy infantry less than two hundred yards away, Barker began to contemplate his position as hopeless. He was completely surrounded.

The Union captain then made a command decision, as all military commanders must do when faced with a life-or-death situation. He decided that all cavalrymen who still had their horses would mount up to make a desperate charge at the weakest point in the Confederate line. Barker had noticed that part of Watie's line had become overextended due to the distance and the rapid movement needed for the Indian troops to complete the flanking movement Gano had ordered.[103] Captain Barker picked the extended point in the Indian line for his escape attempt. Someone from his command had to get through and warn Fort Gibson. Lieutenant Sutherland was left in command of the remaining men in the ravine.

Holding on to the reins of his horse and leaning down as far as possible to prevent giving the enemy a clear target, Barker led his mounted men through a hail of gunfire directly toward the predetermined spot in the rebel line. Of the sixty-five men who attempted the charge, only Barker and fourteen others managed to break through to safety. The rest of the mounted men were captured, including two officers.[104]

General Gano ordered Major Stackpole to proceed toward the Union position with a flag of truce to avoid further bloodshed. Stackpole took along a Federal lieutenant who had been captured in the breakout attempt. The two rode toward the ravine, and Stackpole ordered the surrender of the remaining men in the ravine. The black troops, however, fired on the white flag, ignoring the offer.[105] Many of these men had fought against these Confederate units before at the Battle of Poison Springs, Arkansas, the past April. After the enemy had taken possession of the Arkansas field, numerous black soldiers had been murdered after they surrendered. Helpless wounded men had been bayoneted or shot where they lay. Company K had suffered the highest casualties at Poison Springs. Fifteen were killed, including one sergeant and two corporals, and seven men were wounded.[106]

By firing on the Confederate flag of truce, the remaining black soldiers in the ravine had made their decision. They would die fighting. No quarter would be asked. None would be given. The final confrontation with the enemy would be a bloodbath.

Sutherland and his black infantry managed to defend their position for about two hours. To conserve ammunition, they waited until the rebel force had advanced to within close range.[107] The soldiers then fired a volley, reloaded and waited for the next assault. The Confederate force was driven back several times. Gano and Watie realized that the time involved in taking the Union position could not be wasted. Howell's Battery was ordered up to the front of the line, and once unlimbered, its guns began firing. It only took one or two well-directed rounds of grapeshot and canister to stampede the besieged troops in the ravine.[108]

As ordered, the Confederate line advanced toward the Union position. Barker later reported that the whole force of the enemy then charged into my camp, capturing all of the white soldiers remaining there and killing all of the colored soldiers they could find.

When the smoke cleared, more than seventy-three bodies wearing Union blue littered the field. Captain Barker reported his loss as forty killed, wounded and missing. He listed sixty-six men as captured. Out of the thirty-seven black troops with the detachment, only four escaped.[109] Gano reported his loss as three wounded.

Union reports later claimed that black soldiers were also killed after surrendering. These reports survive in the *Official Records*. Previous historians have noted that the Union reports cannot be substantiated, simply because the Confederate commanders did not see it necessary to mention in their reports what actually happened after the Union position at Flat Rock was captured. However, Confederate captain George Grayson, who later became the chief of the Creek nation, wrote in his autobiography that black soldiers were shot down who were hiding under the cover of the high grass of the creek: "The men proceeded to hunt them out much as sportsmen do quails. Some of the black soldiers finding that they were about to be discovered would spring up from the brush and cry out, 'O Master! Spare me!' But the men were in no spirit to spare the wretched unfortunates and shot them down without mercy."[110]

Grayson explained that some of his men captured six or eight black soldiers, but from where he was located on the Confederate line, not one single black soldier was captured. Some of the Union soldiers were found hiding in the creek with their noses barely sticking out of the water. These men were summarily shot, dragged out and thrown on the bank. The victorious Confederates rifled the pockets of the dead, taking anything of value.

Veterans of the battle later recalled that the water of the small creek near the camp turned red with the blood of the black soldiers.[111] The creek was known locally as Nigger Creek until 1990, when R.T. Taylor, a college student from Wagoner, Oklahoma, successfully petitioned the Oklahoma Geological Survey's board of geographic names to change the name of the creek to "Battle Creek" to honor the soldiers killed at the battle of Flat Rock.[112]

Here a student of history might ask how Gano, an experienced commander and a deeply religious man, allowed the outright murder of black soldiers who were surrendering. The answer may be simple. Gano may not have been able to stop the slaughter, even if he had wanted to. Two thousand soldiers bent on revenge and driven by bloodlust are hard to control, even on a modern-day battlefield.

In addition, the Union military command had thrown down the gauntlet earlier that same year. Colonel William A. Phillips's written orders to his

George Washington Grayson as he appeared while serving as chief of the Muscogee (Creek) nation. Captain Grayson served with the First Creek Regiment, CSA, during the Civil War and later wrote about his experiences in his autobiography. *Courtesy Oklahoma Historical Society, Oklahoma City, Oklahoma.*

men dated January 30, 1864, during a raid known by historians today as the Second Union Invasion of Indian Territory, were well known to the Confederate commanders. The soldiers under Phillips's command were not to take prisoners. At the Battle of Middle Boggy, Indian Territory, on February 13, 1864, Union troops had cut the throats of the Confederate wounded.[113]

Grayson wrote that even though the butchery at Flat Rock sickened him—the men acting like wild beasts—he was powerless to stop it. Grayson himself saved the life of a least one white private that day. He ordered his men to take the man prisoner.[114]

Watie's wife, Sarah, had written to him a year before, after learning that their son Saladin had killed a prisoner. She had instructed Watie to tell her boys to always be merciful as they expected God to be merciful to them. She was afraid Saladin would never again value human life.[115]

Years after the war ended, R.M. Peck's column "Wagon Boss and Mule Mechanic" appeared weekly in the *National Tribune*, a veteran's magazine. Peck had served in the U.S. Army before the outbreak of the Civil War. He was hired by the army as a civilian wagon master. In 1904, Peck wrote he was with the Union burial detail from Fort Gibson. The detail found and buried forty-two black soldiers and probably did not find them all. Also, the soldiers found the bodies of white soldiers and civilians but no dead Confederates, which led him to conclude that not one rebel had been killed at Flat Rock.[116] For years afterward, human bones were discovered along the creek and in the prairie, even though the government hired men and teams to collect them and inter them at the Fort Gibson National Cemetery.[117]

Years after the war, J.B. Stroud, a Confederate veteran, recalled that at the Battle of Flat Rock he saw one man take his own brother prisoner. Howard Holland, a private in Howell's Battery, captured his brother, John, a private in Company C of the Second Kansas Cavalry. John Holland was sent to Camp Ford, the Confederate prison in Tyler, Texas, and remained there until the war's end. Stroud also remembered a son in Confederate gray capturing his own father, who was wearing Federal blue. However, he could not remember their names.[118]

Another Confederate veteran, W.T. Sheppard, remembered that it was on the battlefield at Flat Rock where he shed all of the blood he lost during the war. As Sheppard bent over a dead Federal to remove his boots (he had been without any footwear for nearly a year), a fellow soldier named James Yeary, curious as to what was happening, walked up behind him, stepping on one of Sheppard's homemade spurs. Since Sheppard was barefooted, "it shaved off a good slice of the back part of his heel." It was ironic to Sheppard that he later acquired a good pair of boots in the Cabin Creek raid that were just his size, but his wound would keep him from wearing the boots that winter.[119]

Through some of the eighty-five prisoners taken at Federal camp, the rebel commanders learned of the expected wagon train from Fort Scott.[120] It was due any day. The Confederates camped on the battlefield after burning more than three thousand tons of hay, mowing machines and all of the haying equipment. Gano wrote in his report that "the sun witnessed our complete success and its last lingering rays rested upon a field of blood."[121]

Barker reported that he lost all of his company papers, a quantity of ordinance and ordinance stores, twelve U.S. mules and two six-mule wagons and harnesses, all of which had been burned.[122]

That night, one of the black soldiers came out of his hiding place and escaped into the darkness. George Duvall had hidden in the small creek earlier in the day. He had lain there and heard all of the cries for help and mercy. These cries were followed by gunshots. When darkness finally fell, and the Confederate camp quieted down for the night, Duvall slipped through the Southern pickets, carrying his gun with him. Another black soldier jumped into a lagoon of the creek that was deep enough to conceal his body, and he managed by lying on his back to expose enough of his nose above the water under the overhanging willows to breathe freely. Yet another black soldier lay on his back and covered his nose, just out of the water enough to enable him to breathe, with the broad leaves of a water lily. These soldiers also heard the Confederates all around them, frequently only a few yards distant, pursuing and shooting down their comrades in the most heartless manner.[123]

Early the next morning, the main Confederate column headed north on the Texas-Military Road. Gano detailed a small body of men to attack the nearby Hickey place, another Federal haying camp. After a short skirmish with the strongly guarded camp, the Confederates broke off the attack to rejoin the main command.[124]

With all Federal patrols out of the way, the Southern force concentrated on its main objective: the wagon train.

CHAPTER 6

Rollin' Down the Texas-Military Road

The wagon train had departed Fort Scott on Monday, September 12, 1864, en route to Fort Gibson. After a brief stop at Fort Gibson, the train would roll eastward toward its final destination at the military post at Fort Smith, Arkansas. The supply train consisted of 300 wagons driven by six-mule teams. The train included 205 government wagons, 4 government ambulances and 91 sutler wagons.[125] The wagons were loaded with supplies intended for the garrisons at both forts, as well as for Union Indian refugees. When fully in motion, the wagon train stretched out more than four or five miles over the prairie.

The train's escort was under the command of Major Henry Hopkins of the Second Kansas Cavalry. Hopkins, a seasoned veteran at the age of twenty-seven, had been commissioned a captain in the Ninth Kansas Infantry at the beginning of the war.[126] A native of Nottingham, England, his family had traveled to America, where he was orphaned by the time he was seven years of age.[127] The major and his men had been called heroes for capturing an artillery battery at the Battle of Fort Wayne, Indian Territory in 1862. The battery had been captured from the Texans of Howell's Battery, and the battery was named "Hopkins Battery" in his honor. Hopkins and his men had also fought with noted distinction at the Battle of Honey Springs in 1863.[128]

The escort for the train was made up of fifty men mounted and thirty dismounted of the Second Kansas Cavalry, ten mounted men and forty dismounted of the Sixth Kansas Cavalry and sixty mounted and seventy

A Union wagon supply train consisting of 205 government wagons, 4 government ambulances and 91 sutler wagons begins the trip down the Texas-Military Road from Fort Scott, Kansas, to Fort Blunt (Gibson), September 12, 1864. *Courtesy Warren Entertainment.*

dismounted men from the Fourteenth Kansas Cavalry. There were also six hundred unarmed recruits traveling with the wagon train.[129] At Baxter Springs, Kansas, the train was reinforced by one hundred Cherokees led by Captain Talala from the Third Indian Home Guard regiment stationed at Fort Gibson.[130] Major Hopkins had felt it necessary to put all Union army posts between Fort Scott and Fort Gibson on the alert for possible attack by enemy forces even before one wagon started to roll. He had also instructed all station commanders to send reinforcements to protect the wagon train.[131]

When the train reached on the Grand River, Hopkins learned of General Sterling Price's movement between Little Rock and Fort Smith. He immediately sent word to Colonel Stephen H. Wattles at Fort Gibson, requesting more reinforcements. Major Hopkins decided to leave fifty of his men under Lieutenant Waterhouse at Hudson's Crossing to act as a rear guard. With no time to lose, the wagon train continued down the Texas-Military Road.[132]

Captain Henry M. Hopkins. This image was taken in Leavenworth, Kansas, in 1863 before he received his promotion to major of the Second Kansas Cavalry. He was the commander of the ill-fated Union wagon supply train bound from Fort Scott, Kansas, to Fort Gibson, Indian Territory. Years after the war, several of the major's former officers questioned his whereabouts once the Confederate attack began. This is the only known image of Hopkins in uniform. *Author's collection.*

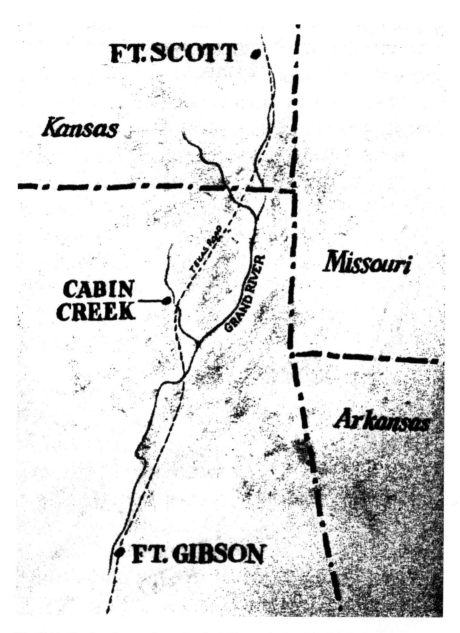

The Cabin Creek station was located at the halfway point between Fort Scott, Kansas, and Fort Gibson, Indian Territory, on the Texas-Military Road. *Courtesy Warren Entertainment.*

Major John A. Foreman and six companies from the Third Indian Home Guard Regiment arrived too late at the Cabin Creek station to rescue the wagon train. Wounded in the First Battle of Cabin Creek, July 1–2, 1863, he carried a piece of a Minié ball in the back of his head for the rest of his life. Because of his ferocity in battle, the Indian soldiers who served under him gave him a name that translates into English as "lion." Foreman Street in El Reno, Oklahoma, was named in his honor. *Courtesy Jess Epple.*

On Saturday night, September 17, while the wagon train was camped at Horse Creek, fifteen miles north of the Cabin Creek station, a courier from the commander at Fort Gibson rode into the Union camp with an urgent dispatch for Hopkins. The message from Colonel Wattles warned of a rebel force of 1,200 to 1,500 men that had been spotted and was heading north. He directed Hopkins to move with all possible haste to the Cabin Creek station. In the note, Wattles assured Hopkins that reinforcements were on the way. He had ordered Major John Foreman of the Third Indian Home Guard regiment, commanding six companies with two mountain howitzers, to march to Cabin Creek.

Reacting swiftly, Hopkins ordered the train to start toward Cabin Creek and the protection of the stockade.[133] The first wagons arrived at the Cabin Creek station at 9:00 a.m., Sunday, September 18. Waiting to reinforce Hopkins's command at the station were 140 Creeks and Cherokees commanded by Lieutenant Benjamin Whitlow of the Third Indian Regiment. These troops were in addition to the garrison force of 170 Union Cherokees commanded by Lieutenant Palmer of the Second Indian Home Guard. Hopkins's force now totaled about 1,000, including 610 armed men. Whitlow and Palmer reported to the major that Whitlow's rearguard had skirmished with the rebels as they came up the Texas Road to Cabin Creek.[134]

Knowing that the Union commander at Fort Gibson was without enough horses and mules to effectively pursue their combined force, Gano and Watie took their time moving up the Texas Road in search of the train. The Confederate column took two days to travel only thirty-five miles, the distance between the hay camp and Cabin Creek.[135] The Southerners moved cautiously, making sure that the train did not get by them. Before leaving the Flat Rock battlefield, Gano sent a polite note through a released prisoner (a civilian—probably one of the hay contractors) to Colonel Wattles to come and bury the Union dead.[136] When the Federal commander realized that the Confederates had advanced up the road after the wagon train, he reported that he tried to help relieve the train, even though he had already sent four hundred of his men to reinforce the escort. Time was of the essence, as the Confederates had a good head start. How could Wattles rush infantry fifty miles up the road in time to help save the train?

Luckily, help was camped nearby. Colonel James M. Williams and his Second Brigade, consisting of four regiments of black soldiers, had marched from Fort Smith Arkansas and were camped between the Big and Little Sallisaw Rivers on the Whiskey Road.[137] These troops included the First Kansas Colored Infantry (now renamed the Seventy-ninth U.S. Colored Volunteers), the Second Kansas Colored Infantry, the Eleventh United States Colored Infantry and the Fifty-fourth United States Colored Infantry. In addition, a section of Parrott guns belonging to the First Arkansas Light Battery had been attached to Williams's command.[138] Williams was the same commander who only a year before had blasted a combined force of Confederate Texans and Indians from their positions at the First Battle of Cabin Creek.[139]

Williams's black soldiers marched into Fort Gibson on Sunday, September 18. After a brief discussion, Williams suggested to Wattles that he should round up as many wagons and mule teams as he could find in order to rush Williams's troops up the Texas Road as fast as possible. A few wagons were found and loaded with ammunition, rations and men. The remaining soldiers had to march at the double-quick in order to reach Cabin Creek in

Colonel Stephen
H. Wattles, First
Indian Home
Guard Regiment,
was in command
of Fort Blunt
(Gibson) at the
time of the
Cabin Creek
raid. His efforts
to relieve the
besieged train
were ineffective.
*Courtesy National
Archives.*

time to save the train. Decades later, Corporal Allen Lynch, Company E of the Seventy-ninth U.S. Colored Volunteer Infantry, recalled his march of eighty miles from Fort Smith to Fort Gibson and on to Pryor's Creek as "the longest walk, I ever took."[140]

About the same time Williams and his troops were arriving at Fort Gibson, the main Confederate force was going into camp on Wolf Creek near present-day Salina, Oklahoma. Gano picked this location so his scouts could watch for the wagon train on the Texas Road, as well as the

Brevet Brigadier General James M. Williams defeated Stand Watie's forces at the First Battle of Cabin Creek, July 1–2, 1863. However, Williams's Second Brigade was unable to recapture the wagon train taken by Confederates at the Second Battle of Cabin Creek a little over a year later. After the war, Williams stayed in the army, but wounds from two Indian arrows cut his career short. His appearances at soldier reunions in Kansas were always gala events, as his former officers and men, both black and white, turned out to honor him. *Courtesy Kansas Historical Society, Topeka, Kansas.*

other branch of the road located east of the Grand River.[141] Confident that the train had not passed, Gano proceeded north up the road with four hundred men and two pieces of artillery to reconnoiter.[142] Seventeen-year-old Richard Martin served as Gano's guide. In a letter written many years after the war, Martin wrote about the condition of his uniform at the time of the Cabin Creek raid:

> *On that occasion my shirt was without a back, but the defect was covered by a friendly gray jacket with buttons of wood. My pants from the pockets down was only represented by the inner part called lining. My shoes were almost soleless with a good slice of the uppers gone. My hat, well, I am not positive whether I had one or not and my garb were about as respectable as many others in our command.*[143]

On Sunday afternoon, September 18, the Texas general found the wagon train parked at the station on Cabin Creek. Major Hopkins, not realizing the danger that was approaching him, had not ordered the teamsters to park the wagons in any type of defensive or corral formation. Instead, the wagons were haphazardly spread a mile and a half to the south of the stockade, parking in open-order style, with each team about thirty feet apart. A group of sutler wagons was also parked on a ridge located on the east side of Cabin Creek, overlooking the ford.[144] Through his field glasses, Gano and his men watched as more than 1,800 mules and horses leisurely grazed on the prairie in front of the stockade. Hopkins had posted a weak, long-stretched guard around the wagons. The Union major's actions indicated that he didn't comprehend the seriousness of the situation or that he refused to believe there was a sizable rebel force in his front threatening his command.

Gano immediately sized up the situation and sent a courier to inform General Watie to bring up the rest of the Confederate force. While waiting for Watie to arrive with the remainder of their troops, Gano and his men camped in a small hollow a few miles south of the Cabin Creek stockade. It was a deep hollow sheltered on the north side by a huge rock formation.[145]

Late Sunday afternoon, Hopkins and Captain Patrick Cosgrove of Company L, Second Kansas Cavalry, led a detail of twenty-five men from the stockade on a scouting mission. Reports from earlier scouting parties had indicated that a rebel force of one hundred men had been encountered. Hopkins and his men found the rebels posted in the hollow only three miles

The Cabin Creek stockade as it appeared on the night of September 18, 1864. This artist's conception is based on actual reports and official records. This view of the stockade looks to the northwest. *Courtesy Warren Entertainment.*

south of the station. They watched one man, whom they identified as an Indian lieutenant, walk toward a larger group of cavalry posted in the timber, but Hopkins could not get close enough to ascertain their approximate size or strength.[146] Hopkins later reported that to counter the threat of a Confederate attack, he doubled his pickets and moved the train in a quarter circle near the rear of the stockade.[147]

In reality, Hopkins had no idea as to the size or the strength of the enemy force that was getting ready to attack the Union position. In his article in the *National Tribune* some forty years later, Peck wrote that Hopkins had time to prepare a defense but did nothing. He had from noon until nightfall to erect defenses and prepare for the anticipated Confederate assault. Instead of taking any measures for the safety of this outfit, he moved through the timber across Cabin Creek, spreading out that huge train on the prairie for camp in the usual open order or park style—extending the camp over a mile and a half to the front, and correspondingly on the flanks, with no other preparations for meeting an attack save for the usual chain of sentinels posted at night outside around the ground occupied.[148] Some of the wagons were parked behind the stockade near the bluffs of the creek.

Dr. George A. Moore was a dentist and businessman who happened to be traveling with the wagon train when Confederate forces attacked the Cabin Creek stockade. Moore served as one of the first regents for Kansas State University. In 1874, Moore moved his family to San Francisco, California. This image (circa 1902–3) was taken when Moore served as the president of the Pacific Mutual Life Insurance Company. In 1914, he wrote his recollections about the battle, published in the *Leavenworth Times*. *Author's collection.*

Alfred Collins, a teamster traveling with the wagon train, later said that "the train was allowed to camp in open order, scattered over all creation. It seemed like as though there wasn't an enemy within one hundred miles of us."[149]

Dr. George A. Moore, a Leavenworth, Kansas dentist traveling with the wagon train, later recalled "the loose disposition of the train wagons certainly indicated a lack of prudence by somebody."[150]

While waiting for word from General Gano, the rest of the Confederate column patiently waited in the darkness at Wolf Creek. The highly superstitious Indian troops, including Captain Martin, encountered a white deer, which they immediately took as a "sign" that foretold of their victory over their Union enemies.[151] The courier from R.M. Gano arrived on Sunday afternoon at about 3:00 p.m. with a dispatch. The wagon train had been found! Gano urged Watie to bring up the rest of the troops as quickly as possible.[152] Without wasting any time, the Cherokee general ordered the Confederate column up the road. At about midnight, Watie and the remainder of the rebel force reached Gano on the field. Richard Martin, who had guided General Gano and the four hundred cavalry troopers to the meeting area, used another ford on Cabin Creek that was located directly to the south and east of his former home.[153]

After a short discussion, the two Confederate generals decided to advance on the Federal position immediately. It would mean fighting at night—a rare Civil War encounter. The lucky omen of the white deer was about to be tested.

CHAPTER 7

A Perfect Cyclone of Excitement

G ano formed his battle line within half a mile of the Federal position. Howell's Battery was placed in the center, with Head's and Glass's companies from Gano's Guards in support. The Thirty-first Texas was posted to the right of the battery. The Twenty-ninth Texas was posted to the extreme right flank. The Thirtieth Texas was posted on Howell's left. Next to the Thirtieth Texas, Watie's brigade was posted in order—First and Second Cherokee Regiments, the Seminole Battalion, with the First and Second Creek Regiments on the extreme left flank. At about 1:00 a.m. on Monday, September 19, 1864, the Confederates moved to within five hundred yards of the Federal stockade.[154]

In the bright moonlight,[155] the Confederates saw the stockade with what appeared to be immense earthworks positioned to the front.[156] The rebel force formed a double line, with cavalry at the front and dismounted troopers fighting as infantry immediately behind. The Confederate line began to move forward.

Captain Cosgrove, in command of the Union advance picket post of twenty-two men, met the intruders. A warning shot rang out from the Union picket line as the dim shapes began to advance toward them.[157] In the darkness, Cosgrove approached the line directly in front of his position. The thirty-four-year-old captain had been the first elected sheriff of Johnson County, Kansas, before the war. Cosgrove and his parents had immigrated to the United States from Ireland in 1844. He had lived in Kansas for only one year before his stint as Johnson County's chief constable. As sheriff,

Cosgrove was used to dealing with the unexpected. He had fought with proslavery forces in 1856 in what was known as "Bloody Kansas," but he tried to be impartial to both sides during his tenure as sheriff.[158] When war broke out in 1861, Cosgrove's decision to remain loyal to the Union cost him many of his old friendships. He had fought for the extension of slavery into the Kansas territory, but he was not a secessionist. He enlisted as a first lieutenant in Company G of the Second Kansas Cavalry. At the time of the Confederate attack on the Cabin Creek stockade, he commanded Company L in the same regiment.

According to several eyewitnesses, the Confederate line advanced to within several yards of Cosgrove's position. Gano was startled to hear a voice with an Irish brogue coming from the darkness. The voice was asking the identity of the advancing line.

Gano: "What are your men?"

Cosgrove: "Federals. And you?"

Gano: "Rebels, by God!"

Cosgrove: "May God damn you, sir! I invite you to come forward."

Gano: "Who is your commander?"

Cosgrove: "A Fed. Who's yours?"

Gano: "A mixture. Will you protect a flag of truce?"

Cosgrove: "I will tell you in five minutes."[159]

Accordingly, Gano's aide handed Cosgrove a written order demanding the surrender of the Union post. Cosgrove reported that he then proceeded to find his commander, Major Hopkins, for an answer. The Confederate commander waited five minutes. Five minutes became ten. Ten minutes became fifteen. While the rebel troops were waiting, they could hear the taunts of the Union soldiers in the stockade. The Confederates assumed that many of the Union troops were drinking, and many of the enemy were apparently drunk when the attack on the stockade commenced. One of the drunk Union men, probably one of the civilian teamsters, took it upon himself to face down the enemy force. "Heaping vile epithets and curses," he started toward the rebel line, never ceasing his curses as he came. He was called to halt, but after being challenged three times, he was shot and all became quiet."[160]

One Confederate later wrote that after the shooting had stopped, they found buckets of whiskey on the battlefield. General Watie warned his Indian troops not to drink the liquor from the buckets, because it might be poisoned. Drunkenness on the battlefield was substantiated when Lieutenant Samuel L. Jennings of Company L, Fourteenth Kansas Cavalry, was captured and reported by his fellow officers as being in a state of beastly intoxication when last seen on the field.[161]

More than fifteen minutes had passed, and still there was no word from the Federal commander. Suddenly, the Confederates heard the sound of several wagons moving toward the stockade. Gano reported that he assumed the movement of wagons was a negative response to his query and ordered his line forward.[162] Later, Union officers claimed that they were not given enough time to answer the surrender demand. One report stated that Major Hopkins directed Captain Cosgrove to receive a flag of truce but that the rebel line advanced, not waiting for an answer.[163] This may have been an obvious slant to mask the truth and protect the military reputation of Hopkins as well as Cosgrove for allowing the entire command to be surprised and flanked by the enemy. Hopkins's report in the *Official Records* does not mention the parlay between Gano and Cosgrove. Instead, Hopkins wrote that at midnight his pickets were driven in and the enemy was reported advancing in force.[164]

The Confederate line slowly began moving forward, and Cosgrove ordered his pickets to open fire. The Texans and Indians answered with small arms fire and a thunderous artillery barrage from Howell's Texas Battery. The roaring sound of the cannons and the explosions of the shells panicked the mule teams still hitched to the wagons. In the blackness behind the stockade, some of the mule teams dragged their wagons off the one-hundred-foot bluffs into the creek below.[165] Gano later reported that he began his advance at 3:00 a.m.; however, he may have been mistaken as to the approximate time he ordered the attack to begin. Although in his report, Watie confirmed the time the attack began as "3 o'clock on the morning on the 19th," one must remember that during the Civil War, no standard time zones had been established.

Hopkins reported that the Confederates began their attack at about 1:00 a.m. with artillery and small arms fire. Dr. Moore recalled the rebel attack also beginning about the same time. After interviewing Union soldiers who survived the battle, Peck estimated that the attack on the stockade began at about 1:30 a.m., even though he also reported Private Alfred Collins's account of the Confederate attack beginning at 2:00 a.m. Collins stated that he heard one of his neighbors who struck a match to look at his watch say that it was 2:00 a.m. Although it is possible that the two Southern generals synchronized watches before the battle began, it is more probable to assume that Gano provided Watie with a copy of the report he wrote from Camp Bragg on September 29. Watie wrote his report to Captain T.B. Heiston from Camp Bragg on October 3. Since there were no standard time zones, it is also possible Gano's watch was set to Texas local time.[166]

The Confederate line closed to within three hundred yards of the Federal position as Howell's six-gun battery continued firing solid shot and exploding shell, creating sheer pandemonium in the Union camp. Peck wrote:

> *Soldiers, teamsters, mules and wagons, in a perfect cyclone of excitement, went flying back towards the timber…some men mounted the unhitched mules, where they could catch them, only to be thrown off again by the frantic animals. Some ran on foot among the wildly rushing torrent of men, wagons and animals, teams and parts of teams dragging their wagons without guidance, crashed into each other as they turned from the rebel fire in their front and raced madly for timber in the rear.*[167]

Without waiting for orders, teamsters—civilians and soldiers alike—hastily grabbed horses and saddle mules to retreat back up the Texas Road in the direction of Fort Scott. They were joined by the mass of six hundred unarmed recruits.

Colonel DeMorse of the Twenty-ninth Texas Cavalry regularly sent letters home to the newspaper he owned in Clarksville, Texas. In a series of letters he

Pandemonium reigns as Confederate artillery pounds Union resistance into the ground during the early morning hours of September 19, 1864. *Courtesy Warren Entertainment.*

Colonel Charles DeMorse, Twenty-ninth Texas Cavalry, wrote letters describing the Second Battle of Cabin Creek to the readers of the *Northern Standard*, the newspaper he owned in Clarksville, Texas. Upon his death, DeMorse would be remembered as the "father of Texas journalism." *Courtesy Harold B. Simpson Confederate Research Center, Hillsboro, Texas.*

wrote, identifying himself only as "private," he vividly described the battle to readers back home: "The bright flashes of musketry along both lines, the white smoke of the bursting bombs, the whistle of the Minnie' ball, accompanied by the guttural sound of Howell's artillery as it belched forth its iron messengers of death, under the brilliant luster of the moon and stars…rendered the scene sublime."[168]

DeMorse, a veteran of the Texas War of Independence from Mexico, survived the war to return to his Clarksville newspaper. After his death in 1887, he would be known as the "father of Texas journalism."

Dr. Moore was in the Cabin Creek stockade that fateful night. He had joined the wagon train at Baxter Springs and was bound for Fort Smith, where his professional services as a dentist had been requested. In an article published in the *Leavenworth Times* in 1914, he recounted the events of that night:

> *Officers and soldiers were running toward the prairie and I followed soon coming to a double line of battle formed upon the open prairie. In the dim distance I could see the dark outline of the Confederates and hear their shouts: but the distance was too great for words to be distinguished. Our soldiers, mistaking the sounds of hoofs of a runaway band of mules for those of a charging body of Confederate cavalry, discharged a volley of musketry and the scene of confusion that followed is indescribable. The teams of mules stampeded and entirely beyond control were running in various directions, and I was in the midst of the tumult. The wild grass was so high that I could not see the teams until they were almost upon me and no sooner did I spring from before one team than I would find myself directly in front of another. It seemed almost miraculous that I escaped injury.* [169]

Private Collins remembered that

> *a little after midnight we would be waked up by the booming of rebel cannon and the crash of the shot and shells through the trees amongst us. It was 2:00 am when the enemy's guns broke in on our peaceful slumber. In a few minutes, some of the stampeding six mule teams came tearing back through our camp, and we didn't know which was the most dangerous, the enemy shot or the runaway teams. For a while, it seemed like the devil was turned loose right there. There seemed to be no effort on the part of Hopkins and his officers so as far as I could judge, to form his soldiers for the defense of the camp or to make any preparation to meet the attack. I could see soldiers, teamsters, and others mounting horses, mules or going afoot and all striking out for the ford of the creek, on a back track towards Fort Scott.* [170]

The maelstrom of fire from Howell's Texas Battery continued. The exploding shells set some of the hay stacked near the stockade on fire, momentarily lighting up a section of the battlefield. The Texas and Indian Confederate soldiers later told stories around their campfires about the unearthly sounds of the crashing wagons and the mixed high-pitched screams of mules and men. On the Federal right, Watie's men found a weak point and drove the Federals from their rifle pit positions, thus leaving a large segment of the train in Confederate hands. The Confederate line was formed in a quarter-circle extending past the Federals' right and left flanks.[171]

The moon, which had shown so brightly at the beginning of the battle, now became covered by clouds and darkened the field, leaving the Confederate generals with no clear idea of the battle's progress. They could only see the flashes of the enemy's muskets to ascertain their position. The Southern commanders decided to break off the attack to wait until daybreak to continue.[172] The rebel force fell back out of musket range, and the gunfire slowly stopped. At one point during the night, the Union force tried to move the remaining wagons across the ford. The Confederate line smartly advanced, fired a few volleys to check the Federal move and then retired once more.[173] Some of the Confederate Cherokees taunted their Union brothers by running up to the stockade walls chanting the ancient turkey gobble call of challenge. The Union Cherokees responded from inside the enclosure with the same turkey gobble challenge.[174]

Daybreak revealed what Gano and Watie had been waiting for—the exact position of the train and its defenders. In the gray early morning light, they realized that what they had mistaken for earthworks in the darkness were in reality only huge hay ricks.[175] The hay ricks were positioned running parallel with the creek to the old home of Greenbrier Joe Martin on the Texas Road.[176] The Union troops had reinforced the stockade fence surrounding the Martin house as well, giving them added protection from small arms fire.

Some of the Confederate Indian soldiers were relying on a magic medicine bag to protect them. First Lieutenant Fixico—or Thomas Benton, as he was called in English—offered the medicine bag to Captain Grayson, who commanded a company in the First Creek Regiment. The educated Grayson loudly scorned his Creeks' superstition and admonished them to dismiss the "magic pouch." He then walked boldly up and down the Creek line under fire to demonstrate that the "magic medicine" had no effect on Yankee bullets and was ridiculous.[177]

Gano rearranged his artillery, moving one section of Howell's Battery to the Federal right flank. This action placed the Southern cannons within one hundred yards of the Union fortification. The First and Second Creek Regiments were ordered to support the battery.[178] The Confederates continued the bombardment of the stockade with shot and shell. The battery's movement pinned down the Federal troops in a murderous artillery crossfire, pounding their resistance into the ground. Seizing the advantage, Watie sent Colonel C.N. Vann with two Cherokee regiments across the creek to capture any retreating wagons and to prevent further escape by fleeing Union soldiers. Vann returned without any wagons but had captured eighteen prisoners.[179]

Meanwhile, Gano personally led a bold charge of the Thirtieth Texas (Gurley's) Cavalry, but the entrenched Federals repulsed the attack from a gully full of troopers of the Fourteenth Kansas Cavalry, which had not yet seen action.[180] The rebel cavalry retired and reformed back behind the line of Confederate infantry.

Union private D.O. Crane of the Fifth Kansas Cavalry had been detached from his unit while he was going on furlough. In 1882, he wrote his eyewitness account of the fight at the Cabin Creek stockade for the *Osage City Press*:

> *About 1 am, we were formed in a line of battle in front of the train. The teamsters had been ordered to hitch up. At about 2 am, the Rebels opened their fire with artillery and all the mules stampeded; some going over the high bank; leaving us with a handful of men out in the prairie with no protection. Soon a charge was made by the Rebels. We were lying flat and when the command was given a deadly fire was opened upon them. They answered, but overshot and did no damage. They retreated in disorder. We fell back several yards and awaited results. I am sorry to say that several of our soldiers and officers put spurs to their horses toward Fort Scott at the first fire.*

Captain Howell's six-gun battery continuously fired round after round of canister, grapeshot, Parrott shells, spherical case shot and solid shot projectiles at the Union position. The Parrott projectiles were fired from the two rifled guns that also made up part of the Confederate battery. The effect of the canister and grapeshot was devastating and demoralizing to the Federal defenders. It can be described as a huge shotgun blast—lead and iron balls, some up to 1.5 inches in diameter, are hurled toward an enemy at a range of two hundred to four hundred yards.[181] Under this type of fire, Captain Henry Ledger of the Sixth Kansas Cavalry led one of the most daring feats of the day. With twelve Federal cavalrymen, he charged one rebel battery as a "dernier resort," a last resort to silence the cannons. Ledger's charge failed, and he fell only fifteen feet from the mouth of one of the cannons—his horse riddled with balls. Thought to be dead, Ledger later surprised everyone at the Fifteenth Kansas Cavalry headquarters at Osage Mission, Kansas, when he and some of his men walked in alive and well.[182]

At the beginning of the battle, the Union line faced directly south. After several hours of bombardment from Howell's Battery, it faced due west.[183]

Gano decided to press his advantage with one final charge. He ordered Lieutenant Colonel Welch commanding the Twenty-ninth Texas Cavalry, Captain Strayhorn and the Thirtieth Texas along with Major Mayrant and Martin's Regiment to the opposite end of the Confederate line to sweep around and flank the Federal right.[184] Meanwhile, Colonel John Jumper's Creek and Seminole troops, who had retired to replenish their ammunition, returned to the front line. Volley after volley was fired from the Seminole muskets at the Union defenders. The rebel yell, mixed with Indian war whoops, reverberated up and down the Confederate line as it began its final charge on the Union position.

With no hope for reinforcements, the remaining Union troops tried to escape along the brushy creek bottom. The Southern troops charged through the encampment and pursued the retreating Federals for several miles, capturing some and killing those who put up a fight. Private Crane later recalled, "At about 6 a.m., the Rebels opened a tremendous fire with artillery and kept it up till 8 a.m. We concluded to save ourselves from prison or death if possible. After getting back about 5 miles, we encountered about 50 Rebels who tried to stay our retreat, but we continued on."[185] Back in the stockade, a white flag had been raised.

In his report to General Cooper, Gano wrote, "Crash after crash of shell swept Yankees, Negroes and mules away from the land of the living and the Confederates, with a loud shout, rushed onto victory, driving their enemy beyond their fortification, from where they fled in wild confusion into densely timbered bottoms."[186]

Collins, serving as a teamster with the wagon train, told a remarkable story to his brother-in-law, Peck, who published the account in the *National Tribune* several years later. The account was lost to historians until it was featured in the television documentary *Last Raid at Cabin Creek* in 1992.[187]

Collins recalled:

> *When the shooting started the cannon shells and musket balls were flying pretty thick through the trees. I concluded I had better get behind a tree that*

Postwar image of Lieutenant Colonel John Jumper, who commanded the Seminole Battalion in Watie's Indian Brigade at the Second Battle of Cabin Creek. After the war, Jumper became a Baptist preacher and the chief of the Seminole nation. On the back of the carte de viste is written, "Rev. John Jumper, Chief of the Seminole Nation and Pastor of a church of 100 members, converted 1858. A good farmer." *Author's collection.*

stood alongside my wagon and wait till the shower of shot slackened up. By and by the enemy's firing slackened and when I looked around everyone was gone. I was alone. I was starting off a foot when a soldier's horse...bridled and saddle but without a rider came galloping past me. I lunged out and grabbed the bridle and hung on to him and quickly climbed into the saddle. The horse had been shot in two or three places and the saddle was bloody

Two of the wagon train's teamsters ride a mule, frantically trying to get away from the battle, in this illustration captioned as "A heavy load for old Whitey" from R.M. Peck's column "Wagon Boss and Mule Mechanic: Incidents of My Experiences and Observation in the late Civil War," which appeared in the *National Tribune*, November 10, 1904. *Author's collection.*

indicating the former rider had been shot and had fallen off. I tried to turn the horse north back towards Fort Scott, but instead the horse made a mad run at the Rebel line. Unable to turn the horse around, I decided to take a gamble and bluff my way through the Confederate lines. The only problem was that I was wearing a blue Federal overcoat, which might give me away. However, the moon has gone down so I thought I might not be discovered.

Illustration from R.M. Peck's column "Wagon Boss and Mule Mechanic." Pictured is Alfred Collins, Peck's brother-in-law, attempting to stop a runaway mount. Collins kept his head under fire, rode through the Confederate lines and escaped. *Author's collection.*

The bold ruse worked as the horse slowed down and trotted through the Southern men, who mistook the Union teamster for one of their own:

I heard one of them say "There goes the General's aide…going to bring up the artillery I reckon." This gave me a cue to act like the General's aide if I were confronted by anyone. As I rode on through the rebel lines, I noticed that many of the mounted Southern men are wearing blue overcoats like the one I had on. This gave me confidence that I would not be detected. Just as I managed to get to the gap between the mounted men and infantry, an officer approached on horseback to find out who I was and where I was going. Thinking fast, I called out to the officer. "Where's that battery? The General wants it moved up to the front," he yelled as I continued toward the Confederate rear. On nearing two guns of a battery, he noticed another mounted officer and yelled to him. "Captain, the General wants you to move your guns up nearer to the front, where he is, in the direction of those hay stacks over there." I immediately proceeded to use my horse to indicate the direction to place the guns. As I reached the edge of the timber, I distinctly heard the Captain give the order to "Limber up." Riding on, I also encountered a few rebel stragglers who I told to "hurry up" because we had the Yankees on the run. [188]

Collins rode on to Fort Gibson without any further mishap. He was one of the few Union soldiers at Cabin Creek who kept his head under fire and lived to tell about it.

CHAPTER 8

The Spoils of War

By 9:00 a.m. on Monday, September 19, 1864, the Second Battle of Cabin Creek was over. The Confederates were victorious. They had complete control of the field and the wagon train. General Watie galloped into the stockade shouting, "Hurrah for General Gee-No!" and was quickly joined in the cheer by both Texans and Indians.[189] In their haste to escape, the Union soldiers left both their dead and their wounded on the battlefield.

Casualties were few on both sides considering the number of troops involved in the engagement. In his report, Major Hopkins wrote, "I lost in killed, wounded, and missing [did] not exceed 35 men." Gano, however, claimed in his report that he captured twenty-six Union prisoners. He wrote, "The killed of the enemy at Cabin Creek numbered about 23. The wounded not known; captured 26. The jaded condition of our already weak horses prevented us from capturing as many as we might have done. Our loss was 6 killed, 48 wounded—3 mortally." He later amended the number of killed to seven and the number of wounded to thirty-eight.[190]

Private T.S. Bell of Company E of the Thirtieth Texas wrote a letter home on September 30, 1864, and included the names of the men from his company killed and wounded in the Cabin Creek raid. Those killed were Lieutenant G.W. Chitwood and James Killough. The wounded included H.C. Powell and W.H. Richardson.[191]

Watie reported two men killed, including Lieutenant D.R. Patterson, the adjutant of the Seminole Regiment. He also wrote that the Indian brigade's wounded included Major Vann, who was shot severely through the neck;

Captain Taylor, shot dangerously through the thigh; and Captain Shannon, shot slightly in the breast. Also included were all of the Second Cherokee Regiment and Lieutenant Richard Carter, Company C, First Cherokee Regiment, slightly.[192]

Burial details were hastily assembled to bury the Southern dead. The wounded were cared for as the remaining rebel troops quickly gathered the serviceable wagons for the return trip south. Out of the 300 wagons in the train, 130 wagons and 740 mules survived the battle.[193] The other wagons and the mule teams were too damaged either from the sustained artillery barrage or the wild stampede that followed.

As the Confederate soldiers rifled through the wagons, they found all types of foodstuffs and provisions, firearms and ammunition. The sutler goods and government supplies in the captured train were later estimated by Gano to be worth more than $1.5 million in U.S. currency.[194] The official Union tally of horses, mules and equipment captured at Cabin Creek listed 202 wagons, 5 ambulances, 40 artillery horses (which were quickly acquired by Howell's Battery) and 1,253 mules.[195]

The spoils included new Federal uniforms and other clothing, which the Confederates gleefully exchanged for their uniforms of rags.[196] Although the new uniforms were of Union blue, the Texas and Indian soldiers welcomed any type of clothes. The Confederate commanders detailed men to complete the task of destruction. Anything not salvageable was burned or destroyed. This included any remaining supplies that the Southern force could not take with it. One by one, the damaged wagons that could not be moved were set on fire. Damaged wagons still able to be managed by hand were rolled over the high Cabin Creek bluffs to crash into the creek below. Richard Martin also recalled "rolling sutler wagons off of the ridge on the east side of Cabin Creek."[197]

Among the items the Texas and Indian soldiers found in the wagons was a trunk full of "Lincoln money." The "greenbacks," as they were called by the Confederates, were on the way to the army paymaster at Fort Gibson. One Texas soldier later recalled the trunk full of money that they were "foolish enough to despise."[198]

Adding to the embarrassment of Hopkins, all of his personal correspondence was captured, along with his returns for government property and his commissions promoting him to captain and major, as well as all muster rolls.[199]

One question still remains. During the Confederate onslaught, where was Major Hopkins? In his official report, Hopkins stated that he tried to rally

A Union wagon supply train at Brandy Station, Virginia, in 1864. This photo gives a perspective of the supply train of 300 wagons captured by Confederate forces at the Second Battle of Cabin Creek on September 19, 1864. After the battle, the Confederates were able to salvage 130 wagons filled with supplies. *Courtesy Library of Congress.*

the teamsters in order to get the rest of the wagons under control. However, several eyewitnesses later reported that he was nowhere to be found after the firefight started. Dr. Moore went on record, writing, "Major Hopkins placed me in command of a small company of Indian soldiers and informed me that he would immediately make an attempt to meet and hasten the coming reinforcements, said to be but a few miles distant."[200]

According to Moore's account, Hopkins left before daylight toward the Grand River, three miles away. Did Hopkins lie about his actions in his written report? He was not to be found on the battlefield, so he could not have ordered a retreat once the Confederates began their final advance.

Another eyewitness, Captain Nathaniel B. Lucas of the Sixth Kansas Cavalry, commanded a company under Hopkins. Many years later, at a Grand Army of the Republic Encampment in Long Beach, California, Lucas told R.M. Peck:

> *You are wrong in stating that the train's escort made no defense. We did form a line of battle, and did some firing; but with the frantic stampeding teams rushing through our line, soon became demoralized and broke. Soon*

after the attack was begun by the rebels, and the teams were rushing wildly back towards the timber, I heard officers asking anxiously, "Where's Major Hopkins? Who's in command?" Hopkins was nowhere to be found. He had abandoned the outfit and struck out for the Grand River on his way to Fort Gibson. With the victorious rebels coming on yelling and firing, stampeding teams and single horses and mules running back towards the creek, hell seemed turned loose right there and then; and with no commanding officer, what could the soldiers be expected to do, but break to the rear and try to save themselves the best they could. Oh it was shameful!

Peck wrote that Captain Lucas's eyes filled with tears at the thought of his long-ago humiliation.[201]

Captain Cosgrove later reported to his commanding officer that he did not know where Hopkins was at the time the attack first started but thought that the major had been cut off from his command.[202]

As the Confederates had found buckets of whiskey on the battlefield, they also found barrels of intoxicating liquor in several of the wagons. Once the alcohol was discovered, it proved to be too big a temptation for some of the rebels to resist, and many became intoxicated. Captain William Welch, in command of Gano's Guards, was one of the revelers. By the time the battle ended, it was reported that Captain Welch was in a state of "delicate health" and was "physically exhausted" after being up all night on picket duty. The night air had been very cold, and the captain had not eaten in more than twenty-four hours. The liquor's effect on Welch was instantaneous. As the members of the Howell's Battery were making preparations to return south, an unfortunate incident occurred. As Welch approached with revolver in hand, a single shot rang out. When the smoke cleared, Private Samuel Henderson lay crumpled on the ground in a pool of blood. The shot from the pistol had struck him square in the head, killing him instantly. Subsequently, Welch was charged with disorderly conduct to the prejudice of good order and military discipline.[203]

The Union stockade was also put to the torch, along with three thousand tons of hay and all the equipment. Union reports later accused some drunken Confederate soldiers of killing and mutilating Federal wounded belonging to the Second Indian Home Guard Regiment. The rebel soldiers then proceeded to see what was of value in the Union hospital. However, upon the humanitarian request of the station's surgeon, Dr. A.S. Ritchie, the hospital and its stores were spared.[204] Dr. Ritchie's surgical instruments, however, were taken by the Confederates,

Captain Nathaniel B. Lucas, Sixth Kansas Cavalry. Lucas was assigned to protect the wagon train and was in the Cabin Creek stockade during the battle. Years later, he told R.M. Peck of the *National Tribune* that during the battle, Major Hopkins was nowhere to be found. *Courtesy U.S. Army Military Institute, Carlisle Barracks, Carlisle, Pennsylvania.*

and he later had to amputate one man's arm without them. Others among the wounded who needed legs amputated decided to wait and have the procedure done at Fort Scott instead.[205]

Forty women who were on their way to visit friends and relatives serving in the Union army found themselves among the prisoners. General Gano assigned guards to protect them and generously offered to send the women north, but they would not go. The women were loaded up in the wagons with the rest of the captured supplies.[206] Also discovered traveling with the wagon train was another group of black women and children. They did not receive any offers of being returned to Kansas. Instead, Gano instructed one of his officers that they would likely be sold as confiscated contraband—and, if so, to buy one woman for him.[207]

Chapter 9

Gano's Bold Ruse at Pryor's Creek

Gano and Watie had their prize. Capturing the large wagon train had been one problem they had solved together. Now they faced an even larger tactical problem. The Southern force was about one hundred miles behind enemy lines. There could be no possibility of concealment as they would have to travel in open country. They could not travel on the main roads, since Union patrols would be looking for them. The Confederates would have to blaze their own trail on which to travel. Their men would have to cut down trees and push up hill by hand the wagons laden with supplies plus the six artillery pieces. To add to their predicament, three rivers—the Verdigris, the Arkansas and the Canadian—would have to be crossed. In addition, there would be no reinforcements from Confederate headquarters sent to help them bring in the wagon train. On top of all of these problems, the column would be hotly pursued by Union troops from Forts Gibson and Smith. The Confederate commanders would not be able to draw an easy breath until the column was safely in Southern-held territory.

By 11:00 a.m., as the last of the 130 serviceable wagons were driven into line to begin the slow trek south down the Texas Road, Gano's advance guard came into contact with skirmishers of Williams's Second Brigade north of Pryor's Creek.[208] According to one account, the Confederate scouts had earlier come into contact with a group of Quantrill's men, mistaking them for Yankees and almost firing on them.[209]

After the initial contact with the Union troops, the Confederate advance guard drove them back three and a half miles, where the black infantry

George Washington Trout (1850–1933) was a Confederate soldier who served in Watie's Indian Brigade. After the Second Battle of Cabin Creek, he was chosen to drive one of the captured wagons. After the war, he settled in Big Cabin, Oklahoma, where some of his descendants still live today. *Courtesy Warren Entertainment.*

formed a battle line. The two lines were about a mile apart in open prairie, with the timber of Pryor's Creek near the rebels' right and Williams's left.[210] Williams was confident that his men could win the fight. His men had been trained well for the job, and their weapons were far superior to the rebels' weapons. But he was also aware of the weakened condition of his troops after so strenuous a march. With no cavalry for support, Colonel Williams decided to assume the defensive and draw the Confederates into attacking. As Gano's brigade watched from a distance, the Second Brigade smartly moved into battle formation.[211]

Leaving a small guard covering the wagons, Gano formed his troops into a double line for battle. Skirmishers advanced to keep the Union troops at a distance. Williams's force advanced, with skirmishers in double ranks, and exchanged a few volleys with the rebels. The Federal colonel hoped that this demonstration would draw the Southern force into an attack across the open prairie. The plan seemed to work, as Gano and Watie attacked. However, this time it was the Confederates who felt the thunder of Union artillery.

At 4:30 p.m., an artillery duel began between the two forces when the rebels came into range of Williams's six Parrott guns.[212] From Williams's rear area and on his flanks, his gunners fired Hotchkiss and Parrott shells at the advancing Confederates.[213] The rebel line continued forward, but its advance soon withered as the men were pelted with Yankee shells and clumps of prairie sod. Howell's Battery was quickly unlimbered and answered the Federal cannons, shot for shot.[214] The artillery duel continued until darkness fell. Meanwhile, Colonel Williams decided against a direct frontal assault because his men were exhausted after the fifty-mile forced march. It proved to be a costly decision.

As night cloaked the battleground, perhaps Gano remembered the biblical story of Gideon and thought the plan usable in the situation. He ordered his soldiers to build and light campfires on a small ridge in plain sight of Williams's troops. Gano also ordered a small line of men to stand on the ridge, silhouetted against the darkening sky. He then ordered one of the wagons emptied and driven repeatedly over the rocky ground. This gave the Union pickets the impression that the wagon train was being corralled and that the Confederate troops were going to camp for the night. For two hours, while the empty wagon nosily circled a small patch of ground, the actual wagon train slipped away in the cover of darkness to the northwest.[215] The Confederate column crossed Pryor's Creek at a ford that it discovered on its right flank. The train traveled all night and the next day, arriving at the Verdigris River, where it crossed beside Claremore Mound that evening.[216] Watie, along with a few of his Indian companies, acted as a rear guard for the captured wagon train. His small force left the Pryor's Creek battlefield well before daylight.[217]

Seeing the lighted campfires from a distance, the Federal commander was assured that a firefight would begin after sunup. He ordered his troops to bivouac in the battle line. The next morning, the black soldiers awoke to find one lone, empty wagon and dozens of smoldering campfires. The wagon train they were after was gone.[218] It had disappeared into the night. Due to his soldiers' weakened condition, Williams reported he could not pursue the rebel force. He claimed that his men were exhausted after marching eighty-two miles in forty-six hours. However, instead of resting the troops at Pryor's Creek, Williams marched his command back to the hay camp at Flat Rock.[219]

In a letter to his wife, Captain John K. Graton of Company C, First Kansas Colored Infantry (now renamed the Seventy-ninth U.S. Colored Volunteers), described the scene at Pryor's Creek:

Color Sergeant William T. Gass of Howell's Texas Battery, CSA, displays his old unit's flag in this photograph for the *Confederate Veteran* magazine. Cass was wounded several times during the war, receiving his first wound at the Battle of Fort Wayne, Indian Territory. He was also wounded by a shell fragment at the Battle of Pryor's Creek. The fragment that wounded him in the shoulder also ripped a hole in the flag he is holding. *Courtesy Curtis Payne.*

Upon the arrival of Col. Williams, we immediately started in pursuit, but were nearly 2 days behind. When we got within 15 miles of Cabin Creek, our old battleground, we learned that the enemy had taken the train and were advancing on the road to meet us. We immediately formed a line of battle and waited for them. When they got within a mile of us, they halted and did not seem anxious to attack. Col. Williams ordered a few shots to be thrown from our rifled pieces at what appeared to be a rebel battery. The second shot from our guns struck right in front of theirs. You had better believe there was some scampering to get away from there. They tried some shots at us, but they could not reach us, while a few shots from our guns completely broke up their lines. Our men being very much exhausted from hard marching without rest, prevented us from pursuing the advantage. The next morning, they had got the train beyond our reach.[220]

Williams reported no Union casualties at the Pryor's Creek battle. The only known Confederate casualty to occur during the long-range artillery duel was when William T. Gass, Howell's Texas Battery's color sergeant, was seriously wounded by a shell fragment. The fragment hit him in the shoulder and then tore through the company flag. Along with the hole made by the artillery fragment, Gass counted thirteen bullet holes in the battle-scarred flag.[221]

Major John Foreman and his relief force sent from Fort Gibson were the first Union troops to arrive on the scene at Cabin Creek.[222] He reported to his superiors that "the destruction is complete." His men found quartermaster and commissary stores from the wagons strewn along the Texas for miles. The Union dead had been left on the battlefield. Foreman also reported the discovery of two fresh graves of rebels at Wolf Creek. He believed them to have been killed in the artillery duel.[223] Since no casualties were reported by either Gano or Watie at the Pryor's Creek skirmish, the graves may have been two soldiers who were severely wounded in the Cabin Creek fight and may have died as the captured train headed south on the Texas Road. Their comrades stopped only long enough to give them a hurried yet decent burial.

Foreman found that the Confederates had spared the old Martin house, which was occupied by sick and wounded soldiers. A few sound mules were also found to have escaped the rebels' observation. One six-mule team was found fully rigged, reined and hitched to a wagon containing a full load of flour. The wagon, only lacking a driver, was found wandering about on the prairie about three miles away from the stockade. The wagon tracks showed that the mule team had run away from the field during the night stampede and had crossed without accident several ravines where it would have been difficult for an even skillful driver to have steered them through safely in daylight.[224]

Foreman's command gathered up all of the scattered harnesses, along with some other supplies and government property, storing them in the old house. They buried the Union dead and loaded up the wounded into wagons for the return trip to Fort Gibson. As the Union column began its journey back down the road, a lone mounted rebel approached the column. The Confederate rode alongside the battalion of Indians with so much indifference that he was at first mistaken for one of their own men. He soon began to talk wildly, asking for "the commander of this—outfit," saying that he had come to kill him. It was evident to the Union Indians that the rebel was drunk. He had probably drank some of the liquor found in the captured train, filled up on it, fell asleep and was left by his retreating comrades… and he was still drunk. When Major Foreman was told that the stranger declared his mission was to kill the commander of our men, he told some of his Indians to disarm him, take him back to the rear and "take care of him." The rebel was taken off to a ravine and left there.[225]

Christian H. Isley of the Second Kansas Cavalry visited the Cabin Creek station one month to the day after the battle.[226] Isley was on detached service escorting a refugee wagon train from Fort Smith. It took the train six days to travel from Fort Smith to Fort Gibson. Then the train headed north from Fort Gibson bound for Fort Scott. While camped at Horse Creek, he wrote a letter to his wife, Eliza, describing what he saw. "For miles the disastrous effects of the Confederate raid were seen along the road. One buried man was dug up by wolves and the flesh eaten off, broken and gone, cracker boxes, beans, rice, & were scattered all of the Prairie & along the road." Isley also wrote that the soldiers and refugees had not eaten any bread for two days. When they arrived at Cabin Creek, they were given some of the foodstuffs that soldiers had collected on the prairie a few days after the raid.[227]

CHAPTER 10

The Thanks of the Confederate Congress

The Confederate raiders did not sleep for the next three days and nights as they raced for the safety of the Arkansas River. General Gano wrote in his report about the days the Texas and Indian troops spent blazing their own trail. "Our boys were without sleep except as such that they could snatch in the saddle or at watering places. They dug down banks, cut out trees, rolled wagons and artillery up hills and banks by hand, kept cheerful and never wearied in the good cause and came into camp rejoicing."[228]

The Southern column crossed the Verdigris River at Claremore Mound near Captain Clem Rogers's ranch.[229] Rogers, a scout for Watie, would be the father of the world-renowned humorist Will Rogers. The elder Rogers would also become well known in Oklahoma state politics, being one of the framers of the Oklahoma state constitution. Rogers County, Oklahoma, was named in his honor. Visitors may tour the Will Rogers home place at the Dog Iron Ranch located east of the town of Oologah, Oklahoma.

Upon his arrival at the Confederate camp near Claremore Mound, General Watie found several of his men drunk after imbibing of the whiskey in the Federal wagons. Worried about the performance of his men, Watie ordered three wagonloads of whiskey barrels captured in the raid emptied into the Verdigris River.[230] S.H. Mayes, who later served as the chief of the Cherokee nation, vividly recalled assisting in the unusual task of hauling these barrels to the river, tapping the heads and watching the whiskey mingle its fiery liquid with the clear waters of the stream.[231]

Postwar photograph of Clem Rogers, who served as a captain of scouts in Watie's Indian Brigade. After the war, Rogers rebuilt his Dog Iron Ranch near Oologah, Indian Territory, and became prosperous in the businesses of banking and cattle. Rogers's son was the world famous humorist Will Rogers. The elder Rogers served as one of five Oklahoma statehood delegates elected from Indian Territory. He was also one of the framers of the Oklahoma state constitution. Rogers County in Oklahoma was named for him. *Courtesy Oklahoma Historical Society, Oklahoma City, Oklahoma.*

The Confederate column continued on to Tulsey Town, where the wagon train crossed the Arkansas River at a place still known today as Gano's Crossing. One of the captured wagons was left by the Southerners in the quicksands of the Arkansas River.[232] When the river is low, the crossing can be still seen just north of the Eleventh Street Bridge on the Arkansas River in Tulsa, Oklahoma. The trail that the Confederate troops blazed was called the Gano Trail for years afterward and was frequently used by locals.[233]

Two prisoners from the Second Kansas Cavalry who were captured at Flat Rock, James M. Carlton of Company C and Louis Hammer of Company G, escaped from the Confederate column when it crossed the Arkansas River.[234] Other Union soldiers who had escaped capture at Cabin Creek made their way north on the Texas Road to safety. Men were still coming in at least a week after the battle. Master Sergeant Septimus Stevenson of Company H, Third Wisconsin Cavalry, wrote in his small pocket diary on Thursday, September 22, 1864, that "four men came in from the wagon train. The men reported not so many killed as first reported."[235]

Once safely across the river, the rest of the Southern troops who had not received one of the captured Federal uniforms were outfitted. Grayson later placed this camp's location near present-day Okmulgee, Oklahoma. He wrote that this was their first camp after the long three-day forced march. Richard Martin wrote, "The first of October found us safe on our side of the deadline (Ark River) where a division of the goods took place. And then had Uncle Sam come upon us, he would have claimed is for his soldiers as everyone of the 2,200 men and officers was arrayed in bright blue uniforms with bright shining buttons."[236]

Apparently, not all of the Confederate soldiers received new uniforms. Private Jefferson P. Baze of Company G of the Thirteenth Texas (Partisan Rangers) remembered, "There was not enough clothing to go around, so we drew for it. An overcoat fell to me."[237]

The ragtag Confederate force had accomplished its mission. Gano wrote in his official report to his superiors:

> *We were out fourteen days, marched over 400 miles, killed 97, wounded many, captured 111 prisoners, burned 6,000 tons of hay and all the reapers or mowers.*

Gano also praised Watie and all of his officers:

> *The officers and men behaved gallantly. General Watie was by my side at Cabin Creek, cool and brave as ever. Lieutenant-Colonel Welch, commanding*

Twenty-ninth; Major Mayrant, commanding Martin's regiment; Major Looscan, commanding Thirty-first; Captain Strayhorn, commanding Thirtieth; Captain Welch, commanding Gano Guards; Colonel Vann and Major Vann, commanding Cherokees, Colonel Jumper, of the Seminoles and Creeks, deserve great praise. Besides captains and lieutenants, many were noticed by me of whom I cannot now speak, for space and time will not allow. Captain Howell and lieutenants of the battery deserve special mention for gallantry and efficiency. Captains Nicholson and Matthews, Lieutenants Wall and Gano, Adams and Smoot, Majors Stackpole, Eakins, Captain Pulliam and Doctor Sears, of my staff, all were there and did their part well. Also Major Scales and Lieutenant Watie, of General Watie's staff, did nobly. I wish I could name all. The men all did well and laid up for themselves imperishable honors. They fought as the brave patriot fights. Our cause is dear to their hearts, and to say they were in the Cabin Creek fight of the 19th is honor. While all did their duty, let us give God the praise and thank him that the victory is ours.[238]

The news of the captured wagon train traveled quickly. Headlines along with official dispatches appeared in the Tuesday, September 27, 1864 edition of the *New York Times*: "From Fort Scott—Government Train Captured and Burned at Cabin Creek—Stand Watie in Strong Force Moving North—Loss 2 Million."[239]

The *Times* told its readers that Watie did not command the Confederate force of 1,500 men. However, the paper did not know the name of the general who was in command of the Southern troops. Few men were killed or hurt, the newspaper reported. In a follow-up story the next day, the *Times* reported that none of the forces guarding the train were killed or taken prisoner and that few were wounded.[240]

After the train was safely in Confederate territory, the rest of the spoils were divided throughout the hungry army. Watie refused to take any of the captured supplies, but his men realized the need of his family, loaded a wagon with food and clothing and sent it to Mrs. Watie in Texas.[241] The Confederate column then continued its journey to Perryville, Indian Territory.

So, just how much material did the Confederates capture at Cabin Creek? During the Civil War, horse-drawn wagons were not standardized, so the effective load a wagon could carry was not accurately measured as the loads in modern-day semi-trailer trucks can be measured today. Francis T. Miller's *Photographic History of the Civil War* gives the dimensions of a Civil War supply wagon: "The dimensions of the box of these useful vehicles were as follows:

A Union supply wagon with a four-mule team near City Point, Virginia, in 1865. *Courtesy Library of Congress.*

Length (inside), 120 inches; width (inside) 43 inches; height, 22 inches. Such a wagon could carry a load weighing about 2536 pounds, or 1500 rations of hard bread, coffee, sugar and salt. Each wagon was drawn by a team of four horses or six mules."[242]

In his memoirs, General William Tecumseh Sherman, who knew a few things about supplying an army in the field, wrote, "An ordinary army-wagon drawn by six mules may be counted on to carry three thousand pounds net, equal to the food of a full regiment for one day."[243]

U.S. Army Center of Military History historian Ted Ballard backed up Sherman's estimate in his book *Staff Ride Guide: The Battle of Ball's Bluff*: "An Army wagon, drawn by four horses over good roads, could carry 2,800 pounds. A good six-mule team, in the best season of the year, could haul 4,000 pounds. In practice, wagons seldom hauled such loads because of poor roads."[244]

The U.S. Army frequently used the Texas-Military Road in order to transport supplies from Fort Scott to Fort Gibson. It was well known and must have been in pretty good shape considering the number of wagon trains mentioned in the *Official Records* that frequently used it.

Taking all of these statements into consideration, it can be estimated each of the 130 supply wagons captured at Cabin Creek carried between 3,000 and 4,000 pounds of material. It is therefore probable to assume that Gano and Watie's men returned to their base at Fort Towson with between 390,000 to 520,000 pounds (or 195 to 260 tons) of supplies.

In a letter dated, September 30, 1864, from the Perryville hospital, Wesley Walk Bradly, a soldier in Randolph's Company of the Texas Partisan Rangers, wrote to his wife, Nancy, about his experiences on a "heavy scout" from which he had just returned. He was at the hospital helping with the wounded from the Cabin Creek raid. Bradly told his wife that his take of the spoils was a hat, an overcoat, pants, a shirt, drawers, shoes, two pairs of socks and ten yards of nice bolt linen. He also received one ligee of domestics and one pair of shoes for her. His horse, he wrote, had "nearly give out."[245]

The unlucky Union prisoners who were captured at Flat Rock and Cabin Creek still had some traveling to do. They were sent to Camp Ford, the Confederate prison located just outside of Tyler, Texas. In command of the guard detachment from the Thirtieth Texas Cavalry was Second Lieutenant James Rumsey of Company A. In a letter to his father, Lieutenant Rumsey wrote that the Union prisoners arrived at the prison stockade on October 24, 1864.[246] They remained there until the war ended. A few lucky ones, including some officers, were exchanged in late March 1865. The rest were not released until May 22, 1865.

Some of the lucky Confederate soldiers received two mules as part of their share of the loot from the wagon train. Lime was used to obliterate the U.S. brand or sutler brand on the animals, in case Federal troops happened to visit their homes and farms. It took off not only the brand but also the hair and hide, almost to the bone. As long as the mules lived, they had bald spots where the brands had been.[247] Those soldiers who received an empty supply wagon made sure that they did a little work on them, changing their appearance, so they wouldn't look like army wagons to passing Federal soldiers.

Wesley Walk Bradly fought in the Second Battle of Cabin Creek as a private in Randolph's Company of Texas Partisan Rangers. He wrote to his wife, Nancy, about his experiences, including his share of the spoils from the "heavy scout" from which he had just returned. *Courtesy Truitt Bradly.*

Many mules and horses from the Cabin Creek raid were "freed" by many of the Confederate enlisted men of Gano's Brigade on the march from Perryville, Indian Territory, to Bonham, Texas. It was reported that some men of the command left without permission and drove off the mules captured from the enemy.[248]

DeMorse wrote another letter to his editor at the *Northern Standard*, again signing his name as "Private." Appearing on October 10, 1864, he wrote, "To the indomitable energy of Gen. Watie and Col. Gano, the country is indebted for this victory. They were everywhere in the hottest action, now gallantly leading the charge; again encouraging the men to their utmost exertions."[249]

Gano presented General Maxey with two bolts of calico, five dozen star candles and cans of pineapple and oysters taken from one of the wagons in the Cabin Creek raid. He also sent a bolt of calico from the captured wagon train to Mrs. Edmund Kirby Smith.[250] Gano only kept one item from the raid for his personal use. It was a small sorrel saddle mare that he named "Bird" because she was swift and alert.[251] While in the heat of battle just a short time after he had the horse, a shell burst over her head, and the blood ran from her ears—from which time she was totally deaf. He continued to ride her until the war ended. He took Bird home with him, and she became a great pet with the family, never being used except that some of his children learned how to ride on horseback on her. She was cared for as though she was a member of the family and lived to be very, very old.[252]

It has appeared in more than one source that Gano was wounded in the Second Battle of Cabin Creek. However, some historians have confused this fact. In reality, the Confederate brigadier general had been wounded six months earlier on April 14, 1864, in a skirmish near Munn's Mills on the Moscow-Camden Road before the Battle of Poison Springs, Arkansas. One of Gano's aides, James R. Wilmeth of the Thirty-first Texas Cavalry, described the event in his diary:

> *They (the enemy) broke in different directions, but most of them found it too late and surrendered. The others were pursued hotly by different squads. General Gano ran onto one on the left—an Indian—but the Indian shot him through the left elbow. The Indian heeded no calls to surrender, but kept trying to shoot the general. At this crisis, Lt. John T. Gano came up and gave the Indian a deadly shot. John T. Gano was the general's son. We crossed an open field while several shots were being fired after the wounded Indian, but he escaped. The general's wound became very painful and we had to stop occasionally on account of it. He, however, kept his saddle and*

*gave commands to the column. A courier was dispatched to the command
for an ambulance. We were met by the same, accompanied by Dr. Pierce, in
good time and the general was conveyed in this, just in front of the prisoners.
The general's wound incapacitated him for duty.*[253]

Out of seventy-nine engagements with the enemy, having five horses shot
out from under him and holes shot through his clothing, Gano was wounded
only this once, in the left elbow.[254]

The captured train gave a much-needed boost to the low morale of the
Trans-Mississippi Department. Maxey had three general orders printed
in pamphlet form, so the soldiers could send them home to their families
as souvenirs:

CIRCULAR

*HEAD QUARTERS, DIST. IND. TER'Y
Fort Towson, C.N. October 17th, 1864*

*There having been many applications within the last few days for copies of
Gen'l Orders No. 61, current series from these Head Quarters, the Major
General Commanding this military District has ordered that another supply
embracing General Orders No. 81 current series from Head Quarters
Trans-Mississippi Department, and General Orders No. 26 current series
from Gen'l Cooper's Head Quarters, be printed for the use of the troops of
this District, to enable them to furnish copies to their friends at home.*

*By Order of MAJOR GEN'L MAXEY
T.M. Scott, A.A. Gen'l*[255]

*HEAD QUARTERS INDIAN DIVISION
Camp Bragg. Sept. 30th, 1864.*

GENERAL ORDERS
No. 26

*I. The thanks of this command are hereby tendered to the gallant officers
and men, of Gano's & Watie's Brigades and Howell's Battery, for the
signal successes they have gained over the enemy within his lines, and in
rear of his fortifications, north of the Arkansas River by destroying his
Forage Camps and capturing a magnificent train of 255 loaded wagons*

and other property (valued at one and one half millions of dollars in U.S. currency) a large proportion of which they secured and brought out, marching 300 miles in fourteen days, engaging the enemy victoriously four time, with small loss on our side in numbers. We mourn the death of the honored few, among them the promising young soldier Adj. D.R. Patterson of the Seminole Regiment whose career of usefulness was suddenly terminated at Cabin Creek, while at the side of gallant Chieftain John Jumper charging the enemy's right. The enemy lost 97 killed, many wounded and 111 prisoners. The brilliancy and completeness of this expedition has not been excelled in the history of war. Firm, brave and confident, the officers had but to order and the men cheerfully executed. The whole having been conducted, with perfect harmony between the war-worn veterans Stand Watie, the chivalrous Gano and their respective commands, ending with the universal expression that they may again participate in like enterprises. The commanding Genl. hopes that they, and the rest of the command may soon have an opportunity to gather fresh laurels on other fields.

II. In the departure of Genl. Gano he takes the best wishes of the Comdg. Gen'l. and it is a matter of pride to record, in General Orders, the gallant bearing, energy and promptness which has characterized that officer in the execution of every order and instruction—from his brilliant dash at Diamond Grove, to the splendid achievement at Cabin Creek. While the circumstances attending require his immediate transfer, the Comdg. Gen'l. hopes that it may be of short duration.

By command of BRIG. GEN'L. D.H. COOPER
T.B. HEISTON, Capt. A.A. Gen'l.

HEAD QUARTERS, DIST. IND. TER'Y.
Fort Towson C.N., Oct. 7th, 1864

GENERAL ORDERS
No. 61

The Major General Commanding announces with pride and pleasure the series of brilliant victories on the 16th, 17th, 19th and 20th ultimo, north of the Arkansas River, by the Troops under the leadership of the gallant and chivalrous Gano, and the noble old hero Stand Watie, accompanied by Howell's Battery.

Of this expedition Gen. Gano in his official Report says:

"For three days and nights our boys were without sleep, except such as they could snatch in the saddle or at watering places."

"They dug down banks, cut out trees, rolled wagons and Artillery up hill and down by hand, kept cheerful and never wearied in the good cause, and came into Camps, all rejoicing on the 28ᵗʰ."

"We were out fourteen days, marched over four hundred miles, killed ninety-seven, wounded many, and captured one hundred and eleven prisoners, burned six thousand tons of hay, and all the reapers and mowers, destroyed all together (from the Federals) one and one-half millions of dollars worth of property, bringing it safely into our lines nearly one third of that amount estimated in Green Back."

Officers and men behaved gallantly. Of Gen. Watie, he says: "Gen. Watie was by my side, cool and brave as ever."

Of the whole command he says: "The men all did their duty and laid up for themselves imperishable honors."

Throughout the expedition I am rejoiced to say perfect harmony and good will prevailed between the white and indian troops, all striving for the common good of our beloved country.

For gallantry, energy, enterprise, dash, and judgment, and completeness of success, this raid has not been surpassed during the war.

The Major General Commanding deems this a fit occasion to say that not the least of the glorious results of this splendid achievement is the increased cheerfulness and the confidence of all in their prowess, and ability to whip anything like equal numbers. Throughout the year, the MORALE *of the command has been steadily on the increase. For the Troops of the Indian Territory, this has been a year of brilliant success.*

Your Arkansas campaign is part of the recorded history of the country.

Since your return, almost every part of the command has been engaged.

A steamboat laden with valuable stores has been captured, a regiment has been almost demolished in the sight of the guns of Fort Smith, the survivors captured and the camp destroyed.

Many guns and pistols have been taken,—mail after mail has been captured,—hay camps almost without number have been destroyed and the hay burned; horses, mules, and cattle have been wrested from the enemy and driven into our lines. Vast amounts of Sutlers Stores have been captured. Wagons have been burned in gun shot of Fort Smith; the enemy has been virtually locked up in his Forts, and your successes have culminated in this most glorious victory, over which the Telegraph informs us the enemy is now wailing.

In our rejoicings let us not forget our gallant comrades in arms who have offered up their lives upon their country's altar of Freedom, priceless sacrifices to their country's redemption. If there be widows and orphans of these gallant men seek them out and deliver this poor tribute to their worth.

And let us remember the sufferings of our wounded, and offer them tears of sympathy.

Soldiers! There is a cruel enemy still cursing your country. There is still work to do. You have proven what you can do.

—Remember that strict and cheerful obedience to orders, strict discipline, and thorough drill, will render you still more efficient as solders of the holy cause. Your Commanding General has every confidence in your ability and willingness to take and perform any part you may yet have in the ensuing campaign.

II. It is ordered that his order be read at the head of every regiment and battalion, and company of artillery, and at every post in this District.

III. A copy will be forwarded of this order and the commendatory order of Brig. Gen. D.H. Cooper, to the Head Quarters Trans-Mississippi Department.

S.B. MAXEY   Maj. Gen'l. Comdg.
Official,
M.L. BELL   A.A. Gen'l.

Trans-Mississippi Department commander General Edmund Kirby Smith published his own congratulatory order from his headquarters in Shreveport, Louisiana:

HEAD QUARTERS, TRANS-MISSISSIPPI DEPARTMENT.
Shreveport, La., Oct. 12, 1864
General Orders.
No. 81.

The General commanding announces to the army the complete success of one of the most brilliant raids of the war. The expedition under Brigadier Generals Gano and Stand Watie, penetrating far within the enemy's lines, has captured his forage camp and train, destroyed five thousand tons of hay, and brought out one hundred and thirty captured wagons, loaded with stores, after destroying as many more which were disabled in the action.

These, with one hundred and thirty-five prisoners and more than two hundred of the enemy killed and wounded, attest the success of the expedition.

The Thanks of the Confederate Congress

The celebrity of the movement, the dash of the attack and their entire success, entitle the commands engaged to the thanks of the country.

By command of General E. Kirby Smith.
S.S. Anderson,
Assistant Adjutant General[256]

On January 19, 1865, a joint resolution passed both houses of the Confederate Congress commending Gano and Watie on their daring and skill in the capture of the wagon train on September 19, 1864:

Resolved by the Congress of the Confederate States of America, That the thanks of Congress are due, and hereby tendered, to General Stand Watie, Colonel Gano, and the officers and men under the command for the daring and skill exhibited in the capture of over two hundred and fifty loaded wagons from the enemy, in the Cherokee Nation, on the nineteenth day of September, eighteen hundred and sixty-four, and for the brilliant and successful services in the Indian Territory.[257]

President Jefferson Davis signed it.

Just as the capture of the wagon train boosted Southern morale in Indian Territory, it also put fear into the hearts of the people of Kansas and Missouri. Rebels seemed to behind every tree and bush. When one reads the *Official Records*, it's clear that Federal officers jumped to conclusions based on mere rumors concerning possible Confederate attacks rather than relying on intelligence about possible enemy troop movements.

On September 22, 1864, General John M. Thayer, Federal district commander of the area including Indian Territory, ordered all wagon trains stopped. On October 18, Thayer ordered Colonel Wattles at Fort Gibson to be ready to evacuate Gibson and fall back to Fort Smith, destroying any equipment he could not bring with him.[258] Rumors continued to fly. Stand Watie was reported to be attacking several places at once. General Edward S. Canby recommended to his superiors that all of Indian Territory be abandoned and all of the Union forces be pulled back into Kansas. Writing from the Union trenches at Petersburg, Virginia, Lieutenant General Ulysses S. Grant participated in the discussions and believed Fort Smith should be retained as a military post.[259]

The Second Battle of Cabin Creek was the last major engagement of the Civil War in Indian Territory. The final battle in the territory was a

Lieutenant General Edmund Kirby Smith, CSA, ordered Stand Watie and Richard M. Gano to launch their planned raid at the same time of Major General Sterling Price's raid into Missouri. In his official congratulatory message dated October 12, 1864, Kirby Smith called the Cabin Creek raid "one of the most brilliant and daring raids of the war." *Courtesy Harold B. Simpson Confederate Research Center, Hillsboro, Texas.*

Confederate victory, even though rebel forces had been plagued by shortages, disappointments and defeats throughout the war. Following the Cabin Creek battle, another wagon train filled with supplies slowly made its way down the Texas Road to Fort Gibson. This time, however, there was a notable difference. The wagons were pulled by wild steers, gathered up and trained to work as oxen. This was the only means of transportation the Union's Army of the Frontier had at its disposal. The rebels, it seemed, had cleaned them out of horses and mules.[260]

CHAPTER 11

With Malice Toward None

The Union army's juggernaut continued onward. The war ended in the East seven months later. Even as the Army of Northern Virginia was laying down its weapons and furling battle flags for the last time, Watie was planning yet another raid.[261] The continued shortage of arms and equipment stopped the Indian general from mounting yet another raid north of the Arkansas River. However, successful guerrilla operations by the Confederate Indians allowed them to hold out for another two months after General Robert E. Lee surrendered to Grant at Appomattox Court House in Virginia. On June 23, 1865, near the town of Doaksville, Choctaw nation, Watie formally and officially ceased hostilities.[262] With the stroke of a pen, Watie signed his name to the surrender document. He was the last Confederate general in the field to surrender. Lieutenant Colonel Asa C. Matthews of the Ninety-ninth Illinois Volunteer Infantry received and accepted Watie's surrender on behalf of the Union army.[263]

Upon hearing the news of Watie's surrender, DeMorse wrote to his readers in Clarksville, Texas, "Huzza for the Red Men! They have been true to the last."[264]

Doaksville, the one-time capital of the Choctaw nation, has disappeared. No buildings remain. Near the center of what was the main street, the Oklahoma Historical Society erected a marker to honor Stand Watie's surrender site.

After the war, Watie tried to return to the life of gentleman farmer and Cherokee politician. In 1867, attorney Perry Fuller wrote to the former

Lieutenant Colonel Asa C. Mathews of the Ninety-ninth Illinois was sent by General Canby to accept Stand Watie's surrender on June 23, 1865. He also accepted the surrender of the Choctaw nation by Governor Peter Pitchlynn, which was the last Confederate community. After the war, he went into politics, serving as Speaker of the Illinois House of Representatives. Under President Benjamin Harrison, he served the comptroller of the United States Treasury Department and later was a judge in the Illinois Circuit Court. *Courtesy Oklahoma Historical Society, Oklahoma City, Oklahoma.*

Confederate brigadier general and asked him to go to Washington, D.C., to consult with H.E. McKee and Company (the owners of some of the goods in the wagons he had helped purloin at Cabin Creek) to prove the time and the manner of the capture of the U.S. and sutler train in 1864.[265] Watie received an all-expense-paid trip to the reunited nation's capital. While there, he tried to secure permission to raise a battalion of Cherokee volunteers to fight the Plains Indians who were raiding along the Santa Fe Trail. Watie thought he might receive a commission in the U.S. Army to lead the battalion. Government officials, however, denied his request.[266]

The rough years of campaigning took their toll on Watie's health, and he died in 1871. He is buried in the Polson Cemetery near the Oklahoma-Arkansas state line, surrounded by his family. A monument to him stands next to his grave, and a large granite monument placed by the Oklahoma Historical Society stands outside the cemetery's entrance.[267]

Near the end of the war, Gano was reassigned to Richmond, Virginia. After Lee's surrender at Appomattox, Gano was approached by several ex-Confederate leaders wanting to continue the Confederate cause in Mexico. He declined to join them. Years later, he was told both by Davis and Lee that he had been commissioned a major general in the Confederate army. Both men had signed the commission papers. Unfortunately, the commission never reached him. Although requested by Davis and Lee to accept the honor, Gano never accepted the title.[268]

He returned to his native state of Kentucky following the war to recoup his fortune, taking his family with him. While there, he completed his study of the ministry of the Christian Church, preaching his first sermon at Leesburg, Kentucky, in July 1866.

Later that same year, he was seriously injured in the explosion of the steamer *W.R. Carter* at Vicksburg. He quickly recovered, to the astonishment of his doctor. In the early 1870s, he and his family returned to Dallas. The man, who was once a warrior, faithfully served as an ordained minister of the Churches of Christ/Christian Church for forty-five years. He established many churches and reportedly baptized more than sixteen thousand people during the course of his ministry.[269]

Gano participated in a signal event for Dallas: the arrival of the Houston and Texas Central Railroad in 1872. It was the city's first railroad. As one of the principal speakers at the celebration, he shared the platform with John Neely Bryan, Dallas's founder. In May 1875, Gano was the principal speaker at a dinner given in Dallas to honor Jefferson Davis. In 1879, he petitioned the Texas state legislature for a bill granting assistance to found a colony of sixty Kentucky families in the uninhabited western regions of the state. The bill was passed on first reading but was withdrawn by Gano when advised by the governor that it would be vetoed if passed. The former Confederate brigadier general also made a speaking tour across Texas during the prohibition campaign of 1887 to promote a Texas prohibition amendment.[270]

Gano and his family prospered in the Dallas area. The general and his brother, John Allen Gano, engaged in the business of importing and selling short horn cattle and blood trotting horses from Kentucky. On November 15, 1873, the following article and ad appeared in the *Fort Worth Weekly Democrat*:

> *The Rev. R.M. Gano, one of the most eminent ministers of the Christian Church has located in Dallas. His brother and himself have a fine lot of short horns and thoroughbred horses for sale, which are advertised in another column. We hope to see Gen. Gano in our city ere long, and hear him preach.*

> *R.M. Gano   J. Allen Gano, Jr.*
> *General R.M. Gano & Bro. of Bourbon Co., Ky.*

> *Would respectfully announce to the stockman of Texas that they have imported from the Blue Grass region of Kentucky, 60 head of choice thorough bred Short-horns and pedigreed trotting horse stock, descendants of some of the best families in that famed fine stock State. They have located near Dallas, Texas, and will be pleased to show their Short-Horns and Trotters to all. Enquiries by letter, address Gano Bros., Dallas, Texas.*

> *Catalogues of stock furnished on application.*

Besides his horse farm in Kentucky, Gano, along with his sons John T. and Clarence W., owned and operated R.M. Gano and Sons in Dallas, a land and cattle company.[271] The general also served as the vice-president of the Estado Land and Cattle Company, which handled all of the ranching activities in the Big Bend area. In what is now the Big Bend National Park, he and his sons owned fifty-five thousand acres of land which was known as the G4 Ranch.[272] The land is located in the southern part of Brewster County, in Block G4, and this is how the G4 Ranch got its name.[273] The G4 was the largest ranch in the area in the late 1880s and early 1890s.

Years after the war, General Gano sat for a photo with some of his children. *Left to right, back row*: Lee, Sid, W.B. and Maurie. *Left to right, front row*: Emma, Gano and Kate. *Courtesy Claire Witham.*

By 1891, the G4 herd was estimated to be at thirty thousand head. All of these successful ventures provided the former Confederate brigadier now turned evangelist with an ample income, making him a millionaire. This family tradition was carried on and improved on by Gano's great-grandson, billionaire Howard Hughes.[274]

Gano was also instrumental in the formation of the United Confederate Veterans organization in Texas. He served as the commander of the Texas division of the UCV and also held the office of chaplain general. He was the featured speaker at several Confederate reunions, including the 1899 reunion held at Austin.

The former Confederate brigadier general turned evangelist, land developer and cattleman died at his daughter Emma's house surrounded by his children and grandchildren on March 27, 1913, at the age of eighty-three. His funeral was held the next day at the First Christian Church, which was located on Bryan and North Pearl Streets.[275] He was buried in Dallas's

Oakland Cemetery. The small town of Gano, Texas, was named in his honor.[276] Gano Street in Dallas was also named for the former Confederate general, rancher and preacher. The street borders the old City Park, where his restored dogtrot house, moved from its original Grapevine, Texas site, is on display along with other historic houses and buildings from Dallas's colorful past.

Almost one month to the day after the capture of his wagon train at Cabin Creek, Major Henry Hopkins asked to be mustered out when his troops' enlistments were completed.[277] He resigned his commission, citing his service since the beginning of the war in 1861. Before leaving the army, however, Hopkins saw action at the Battle of Mine Creek, Kansas. He was officially mustered out on January 19, 1865. He went home to his wife, Florence, at Leavenworth, Kansas. He tried the mercantile business for a few years, even having his own establishment of Hopkins & Hark, later known as Hopkins & Company, in Leavenworth.[278] Selling his business after one year, he went to work for Colonel J.L. Abernathy. In March 1867, he was appointed deputy warden of the Kansas State Penitentiary. In 1870, he was appointed warden by Kansas governor Harvey.[279] He served as warden at the Kansas prison for thirteen years. He planned and oversaw the construction of all of the buildings at the state prison.

Hopkins is credited with instituting many reforms at the prison. In 1872, he began to insist that the state should make reform the number one policy of the prison. He became convinced that the state should reclaim rather than punish the criminal. Hopkins went on record about his belief, stating publicly, "I intend to use every man here so that I shall not be ashamed to meet him in this world or at the judgment bar of God."[280]

One day, while opening his mail in the Warden's Office, Hopkins was surprised to find a reply to a note he had mailed a few days earlier:

Wichita, September 9, 1871
Major Henry Hopkins, Warden State Penitentiary,
Leavenworth, Kansas

Dear Sir—Your note, bearing date of September 5th has been received. I send you the papers by my friend, Mr. Charles R. Miller. I obtained them from one of my men on the occasion of a little dispute concerning the right of possession of one certain wagon train at Cabin Creek, Cherokee Nation, in the late difficulty about state's rights. I had several applications for them during my late residence in the nation by parties representing themselves

Postwar photo of Henry Hopkins taken while he was the warden of the Kansas State Prison in Lansing. Hopkins died in 1886 at the age of forty-six. His wife, Florence, later wrote that the former Union major died as a result of malaria. His friends said that he died from overwork. *Courtesy Kansas Historical Society, Topeka, Kansas.*

friends of yours, but I refused to give them up to parties I was unacquainted with, hoping to be able to return them directly to you some time.

Very respectfully,
A.B. Barnes, Captain, C.S.A.

Also enclosed in the envelope were Hopkins's very much-soiled and travel-stained major's and captain's commissions.[281]

Hopkins resigned the warden's job when appointed a commissioner for the Kansas Railroad Commission in April 1883. He died on December 18, 1883, at the age of forty-six.[282] The cause of death was listed as "overwork." The Union Pacific Railroad provided a special train for state officials in Topeka to attend his funeral in Leavenworth. His obituary in the Leavenworth paper listed his gallant service in the war but left out the humiliating defeat at Cabin Creek. Florence Hopkins wrote a longer article on Major Hopkins's life that was published by the Kansas State Historical Society. In the 1903–4 prison notes published in the collections of the Kansas State Historical Society, it highlighted the fact that "the good work of Warden Hopkins continued to bear excellent results."[283]

R.M. Peck wrote in 1904 that he noticed Wiley Britton's book, *The Civil War on the Border*, gave the Cabin Creek affair a generous coat of whitewash:

> *But I have talked with officers, soldiers, wagon masters, teamsters, sutlers, and others who were in that unfortunate "mix-up," and they all nearly attribute the disaster to Major Hopkins mismanagement, but no one has ever charged him with cowardice. The loss of this train was about the worst blow the rebels struck us in this part of the country, but Britton implies there is no one to blame. The author of "The Civil War on the Border" wields a facile whitewash brush; and his object seems to have been to write a book that would be popular with the officers and soldiers who served in the Federal forces in that part of the country and their friends: for he has scattered bouquets among them with a lavish hand. He has probably succeeded in making a popular book, but at the expense of recorded history. One who undertakes to write historical events should tell the literal truth, "no matter whose corns are tread on."*[284]

An undated, handwritten statement by Private Allen Ross, who served in Company I of the Third Indian Home Guard Regiment, found in the Special Collections Department of the University of Tulsa's McFarlin Library, tells a interesting story:

At the time Col. Phillips was put under arrest and had gone to Fort Smith and Col. Wattles was in command at Fort Gibson—there was a large train on the road to Fort Gibson from Fort Leavenworth, and there was a large Rebel force on the way to intercept the train—Col. Wattles had ordered Major Foreman with a company from Gibson to go up on this side of the river and meet the train—and when the command had got near the Grand Saline—the command received an order from Col. Wattles ordering the regiment to return to Flat Rock and cross the river and go upon the other side—causing a delay of two days or more in reaching the train, and there was a large Rebel force between the command and the train.

One night between 12 and one o'clock Lieut. Parsons came over to where I slept—and told me Col. Wattles wanted to see me, as I had charge of the Magazine at the time. Lieut. Brown (Ordnance officer) had gone to Kansas and left me in charge. When I arrived at Col. Wattles quarters, he ordered me to go into the magazine and get out a large amount of ammunition for the Howitzers to send up to the command—I went into the magazine where (I found) a cracked lamp and powder scattered all over the floor. If a spark had ignited I would never have known what became of me. I remained in the magazine about an hour, getting the right kind of ammunition needed, and it was sent off that night—I never thought of the danger I was in until after it was all over—the train was lost on account of Col. Wattles bad management.[285]

Luckily for all of the Federal officers involved, there was never an official U.S. government inquiry into how the wagon train was captured.

Captain Joe Martin received a promotion to major before the war was over. Martin returned to his home at Dian in 1866. Finding someone occupying his old house, he invited the stranger to go hunting with him and his boys. The stranger never returned, and Martin took possession of the place.[286] Life would never be the same for the Martin family. All that they once had was gone.

Martin and his family would never again live in his old home at Cabin Creek, and no trace of it remains today. What happened to the Martin house at Cabin Creek? Union forces supposedly burned it to the ground after the Second Battle of Cabin Creek, but this claim has never been substantiated. Christian Isley wrote in 1864 that Union troops continued to use the old Martin house as a storage facility for tack and harness. Perhaps the answer of what happened to the old structure lies in an interview conducted for the Works Progress Administration's Indian-Pioneer Papers project in the

1930s. Lula Poole Kelley of Vinita, Oklahoma, was personally interviewed by a WPA field researcher about her life. She told the interviewer about an "old Army post" that was built before the Civil War and where she and her family lived after the war. Kelley described the old house as having three large rooms, with the house positioned east–west and an "L" portion of the house running south. Chimneys were located at each end of the house, and it had a well of fine water out back. The old Texas Road ran right in front of the house, and hundreds of people stopped there on their way from Texas to Fort Scott.

Kelley said that her mother sold the old house in 1895 to a man named Henry Hill after living there for twenty-five years. While Hill still owned the property, the old house burned to the ground. Kelley recalled that the house burned down in 1908.[287]

In April 1904, a tornado described as a "cyclone" (and as the worst storm in the history of Indian Territory) destroyed Martin's old Greenbrier home. Martin's widow, Jennie, went to live with one of her daughters.[288] According to family history, from 1865 to 1867, Federal troops harassed the Martins, destroying any improvements the family made to their property. Richard Martin told his grandchildren that the family had to literally "live off of the land" during that time.[289]

In his golden years, Joe Martin wrote many articles for the *Cherokee Advocate*, the *Vinita Chieftain* and other newspapers under the pen name of "Greenbrier Joe."[290] He, like many others who had fought for the Confederacy, had seen his home, his prosperity and his way of life vanish, never to return. Martin died of pneumonia on November 9, 1891, at the old family home at Greenbrier.[291] Many people throughout the Cherokee nation grieved at his passing. Some of his family and friends recalled that "Uncle Joe" died of a broken heart.[292] For most of his life, he had lived in a time of wealth and luxury. The war took away all that he had, and he died in poverty.

Martin's obituary published in Salina's *Cherokee News* on November 14, 1891, perhaps gave the best summary of his life: "He was one of the few connecting links, uniting the present with the past history of our country and but one or two others could claim intimate acquaintance with the historic past. Perhaps no other living or dead Cherokee had such a faculty of entertaining with anecdote and word pictures of long ago."

Tahlequah's *Cherokee Advocate* newspaper featured Martin's obituary, and the editor wrote that he was "brilliant, genial and good, he was one of nature's noblemen; modest, he never sought place; charitable, he lived poor, and honest, he died without fear."[293]

The Richard Martin family poses for a photograph at the Rock Creek plantation in about 1900. The house still stands just west of the Big Cabin Creek Bridge on Oklahoma Highway 28A, a few miles west of Pensacola, Oklahoma. Richard can be seen sitting on the porch and petting the dog. His wife, Flora, holds a small child in her lap, which members of the Martin family believe is D.E. "Bill" Martin. *Courtesy Rod Martin.*

Greenbrier Joe Martin was laid to rest at the burial site he had selected. He had loved the Grand River all of his life, and he was buried only twenty-five yards from it. His grave was later relocated to the old Ross-Mayes Cemetery near Salina when Lake Hudson was constructed.[294]

Richard Martin inherited his father's Rock Creek plantation and built a house just west of Big Cabin Creek in 1880.[295] The house still stands today. Richard (or "Dick," as he was known to friends) continued in the livestock business.

In 1907, Richard Martin tried to file a claim against the federal government for the destruction of the Martin Ranch at Cabin Creek. The following letter cut that claim short:

Law Offices of Kappler and Merillat
Washington, D.C. May 28, 1907
Mr. Richard L. Martin,
Adair, Indian Territory

Dear Sir:
We have your letter in reference to a claim you have made against the Government for property taken during the War. If you can prove that your people were loyal to the North, and that General Blunt and the United States Army destroyed property of yourself or your family during the War, you may be able to make recovery, provided you have witnesses as to the value of the property and the circumstances under which it was taken. Unless we know the full details we cannot tell you anything further than this.

Some of these claims are good and some not, and in which class yours falls, it is not possible, of course, at this moment to say in absence of the full facts.

Yours very truly,
Kappler & Merillat[296]

A few years later, Martin made the front-page news of several newspapers around Indian Territory. The August 17, 1911 edition of the *Adair Weekly Ledger* reported murder and suicide as Richard L. Martin shot his wife and took his life with the same gun.[297] Before the shooting, Martin and his wife, Flora, had been estranged for some time. According to family history, Martin shot his wife as she was coming home after a night spent with her lover. He had secreted himself in a closet in their store in Pensacola. When Flora came into the store, Richard shot her. The bullet having penetrated her side, she raced out the door with Martin following her. He shot her again in the head. Calmly, he walked into a backroom, where another shot rang out a few moments later. Family members peered through a window to see Martin slumped in a chair with the pistol on the floor. Flora was buried in Adair. Richard was buried near Spavinaw.[298]

Colonel James M. Williams, the man who couldn't stop the Confederate force made up of Texans and Indians and rescue the wagon train captured at Cabin Creek, was brevetted a brigadier general of volunteers. After the war, he remained in the regular army and was renowned for his daring exploits as an Indian fighter. Two arrows cut his army career short, and in 1873, he retired from the army and moved to Washington, D.C. Upon visiting the War Department, Williams found that no reports had been filed on some of the battles in which the First Kansas Colored regiment was engaged. He corrected this error, submitting reports on the action at Island Mound, Missouri, where the First Kansas became the first organized black unit to ever fight in the service of the United States Army, as well as reports on the Battles of Poison Springs and Jenkins Ferry, Arkansas.

On October 17, 1890, Williams returned to a hero's welcome in Leavenworth, Kansas, at a grand reunion and mass meeting of veterans, black and white, from his old brigade. He died on February 15, 1907, and was buried at Arlington National Cemetery.[299]

Following the war, Sam Maxey returned to Texas to practice law. He finally succeeded in getting a presidential pardon in 1867 after asking his old West Point classmate Ulysses S. Grant for help. Grant wrote to President Andrew Johnson asking him to pardon Maxey, "I knew him [Maxey] well as a cadet at West Point and afterwards as a lieutenant in the Mexican War. I believe him to be well worth of executive clemency and heartily recommend it." Maxey received his presidential pardon on July 20, 1867.[300] He was elected to the United States Senate in 1874 and served as a U.S. senator from the state of Texas for twelve years.[301] Maxey died on August 16, 1895, at the age of seventy in Eureka Springs, Arkansas, where he had gone for treatment of gastrointestinal disease. He was buried in Paris, Texas.[302] The Maxey home in Paris, a two-story frame residence completed in 1868, is a combination of Greek Revival and High Victorian Italianate styling. It was listed on the National Register of Historic Places in 1971.[303] Today, Maxey's home is a Texas state historic site.

Captain Edgar Barker resigned from the U.S. Army on May 23, 1865, at Fort Gibson.[304] He returned to his home at Junction City, Kansas. In 1867, he answered the call of his country again to fight Indians. He was

After the war, Maxey served two terms as a U.S. senator from Texas. Senator Maxey was visiting New York when this photograph was taken. His home in Paris, Texas, is now a Texas State Historic Site. *Author's collection.*

appointed captain of Company B in the Eighteenth Kansas Cavalry.[305] After his noted service under the command of George Armstrong Custer, Barker was mustered out of the regiment and faded into obscurity. In his military service file located in the National Archives, there is a short note written in longhand on telegraph sheet. The note, dated March 21, 1870, shows that Barker was due a balance of $156.70 for a horse under claim no. 9587, which he filed for Friday, September 16, 1864—the day of the battle at Flat Rock.[306]

First Lieutenant David M. Sutherland, who had been in command of the detachment of black soldiers in the ravine near the hay camp, was among the few soldiers captured at the battle of Flat Rock. He and the other prisoners were forced to march to Camp Ford, Texas, where they remained for the rest of the war. He was exchanged on March 27, 1865. He was discharged at Fort Leavenworth, Kansas, on October 1, 1865. In the years following the war, he worked for the Kansas Pacific Railroad guiding cattle trail herds from central Texas to Abilene, Kansas. Sutherland was also hired by the railroad to map the Great Texas Cattle Trail from Sewell's Landing, Texas, to Abilene. This trail stretched more than five hundred miles. He was made a life member of the Andersonville Survivors Association in May 1879 for his incarceration at Camp Ford.

In later years, Sutherland moved to Alamogordo, New Mexico, where he owned a large ranch near White Sands. He was well educated for his day and had a library in his house. He liked poetry, especially Rudyard Kipling. He was fond of his children and grandchildren and entertained them with stories about the Old West. One of his grandchildren later recalled seeing a cribbage board that Sutherland told them he had made out of matches while a prisoner at Camp Ford. Sheriff Pat Garrett, the man who shot and killed Billy the Kid, was counted among Sutherland's friends. His last house, which was built in La Luz, New Mexico, in 1909, is still used as a residence today. Sutherland applied for a Union veteran's pension in 1912 and received a small monthly stipend from the federal government. He died of heart problems on December 8, 1932, after contracting influenza while working a mining claim in the White Mountains. He was eighty-nine years old. The local American Legion Post supplied the American flag to drape his casket at his funeral. He was buried in the Monte Vista Cemetery in Alamogordo.[307]

Captain William Welch was finally brought before a general court-martial at the headquarters of Gano's Brigade in early February 1865. Welch pled not guilty to the charge of "disorderly conduct to the prejudice of good order

Many years after the war, First Lieutenant David M. Sutherland (standing right) posed for a photograph with his son. He and his detachment of black soldiers were left in the ravine when Confederates attacked the hay camp at Flat Rock, Indian Territory. Sutherland spent the remainder of the war as a prisoner at Camp Ford near Tyler, Texas. After the war, he was a cattle trail guide for the Kansas Pacific Railroad, driving herds to Abilene. Among his friends was Pat Garrett, the man who killed Billy the Kid. Sutherland died in 1932 at the age of eighty-nine. *Courtesy Pat Sutherland Mittelsteadt.*

and military discipline" that led to the accidental shooting and the death of Private Samuel Henderson. He was found guilty of the charge by the court and sentenced to be dismissed from the service of the Confederate States. There were three witnesses for the prosecution, including Private Shepley of Howell's Battery. Before the sentence could be carried out, though, the court held a second hearing. Due to Welch's previous good character and the lack of any evil intent, plus the performance of his duty in the capture of the wagon train, the court unanimously recommended and granted Captain Welch clemency. He was released and restored to active duty. There is no doubt that the court's reversal of the verdict was in a large part due to the influence of his father, Lieutenant Colonel Otis G. Welch, who presided over the hearing.[308]

With the war over, Captain Patrick Cosgrove returned to Olathe, Kansas, to till the soil on his farm north of Olathe for the rest of his life. He and his wife, Amanda, settled down to raise crops and their children.[309] He was

Private Thomas M. Cass of Company E, Second Kansas Cavalry, was assigned to escort duty with the wagon train at Fort Scott, Kansas. He was in the Cabin Creek stockade when the Confederates attacked and managed to escape capture. After the war, he made his living as a farmer and a stonemason. In his later years, he lived at the National Home for Disabled Volunteer Soldiers in Leavenworth. When he died in September 1930 at the age of ninety-four, he was buried in his uniform at the Leavenworth National Cemetery. *Author's collection.*

a member of Franklin Post No. 68 of the Grand Army of the Republic. There's no doubt that the old post room echoed with Cosgrove's stories about the night the wagon train was captured at Cabin Creek. He died on Sunday, July 8, 1916, at the National Soldiers Home in Leavenworth, where he had been living the past five years. He was eighty-six years old. Cosgrove and his wife were buried side by side at the Olathe Memorial Cemetery.[310]

Dr. George A. Moore, the unlucky dentist who was traveling with the wagon train when it was attacked, was appointed to the Leavenworth Board of Education in 1864 when it was established and was appointed as one of the first regents at Kansas State University. He was listed as a businessman from Leavenworth rather than a dentist.[311] In 1874, he and his family moved to San Francisco, California, where he became the president of the Pacific Mutual Life Insurance Company.[312] Moore's account of the Confederate attack was published in the *Leavenworth Times* in 1914.

Major John A. Foreman, who arrived too late with reinforcements to save the besieged wagon train, became a successful businessman. He was an early resident of Muskogee, Oklahoma, and was the first president of the Indian International Fair Association, organized in 1874. He served as steward of the Cherokee Asylum for the Deaf, Dumb and Blind before becoming a contractor for the Missouri, Kansas and Texas Railroad. He also owned and operated a mill and a cotton gin in Muskogee. In the Land Run of April 22, 1889, he claimed a tract of land for his homestead on which part of the city of El Reno, Oklahoma, now stands. Working for the Rock Island Railroad, Foreman became very prosperous, building one of the largest homes in the territory. Foreman Street in El Reno was named in his honor. He died in 1929 at the ripe old age of ninety-five and was buried in the El Reno Cemetery. Foreman carried a small memento from the First Battle of Cabin Creek to his grave. He had suffered a bullet wound to the back of his head, and the lead bullet remained there for the rest of his life.[313]

CHAPTER 12

The Veterans and Their Recollections

Over the years, the Cabin Creek engagement of September 19, 1864, has been steeped in folklore. On April 2, 1882, a thirty-six-year-old farmer named Richard M. Roark hobbled into the Polk County, Missouri clerk's office and applied for a government pension. He had served in the Fourteenth Kansas Cavalry during the war. His pension papers read in part: "While in service received a gunshot wound in the knee while escorting a supply train from Fort Scott, Kansas at Cabin Creek, Cherokee Nation which incapacitated me. Unable to perform manual labor because of which I pray for a pension."[314] When he received his wound, Roark was eighteen years old and had been in the army a little more than one month. He was awarded his pension for military service at the rate of eighteen dollars per month.[315]

In 1930, Confederate veteran George W. Trout of Big Cabin, Oklahoma, sat down at a table to write down his reminiscences of the First and Second Battles of Cabin Creek. The Vinita newspaper published the eighty-three-year-old man's account shortly after his death in 1933. After receiving his Cherokee allotment in 1892, Trout went into the mercantile business in the town of Big Cabin. Today, the Big Cabin School is located on part of the land that made up Trout's allotment.[316]

Trout's son, Henry, related an incident that was told to him by his father. Following the Second Battle of Cabin Creek, Trout and his friend Dave McGhee helped bury some of the Confederate soldiers killed in the battle. They were assigned as aides to Stand Watie. When they had completed their task, Watie told Trout and McGhee to go get their horses as they were getting ready to leave. Reaching the place where their horses were staked on the edge of the prairie, they discovered two Mexicans in the act of stealing their horses. They had already caught one horse and were trying to catch the other. Trout was barefoot, and McGhee noticed the Mexicans were wearing new shoes. He asked, "George, what size of shoes do you wear?" "Most any size would beat what I have on," Trout replied, "whereupon McGhee pulled down on one of the Mexicans and shot him dead. He ordered the other Mexican to remove his comrade's shoes, which he gave to my father. McGhee then shot the other one. The horse thieves were left on the ground without burial."[317]

Henry Trout also recalled that the town of Big Cabin was the home to a lot of old Civil War veterans. He wrote that these old men didn't do anything but meet up in town and fight over the battles they had gone through in their youths so many years before. Trout remembered that "sometimes you would think they were going to have a sure enough battle, as some of them would get pretty hot under the collar."[318]

In 1929, Thomas Hendricks, a ninety-year-old Union veteran of the Cabin Creek battle, spoke of his Civil War experiences in an interview with the *Tulsa World*. Hendricks recalled one of the "hottest places" he was ever in was at the camp ground at Cabin Creek, Cherokee nation, on September 19, 1864.[319] Following the publication of the article, a letter to the editor soon appeared from Caleb P. Wright of Stillwell, Oklahoma, He had read Hendricks's reminiscences and noted the accuracy with which he recounted his experiences. Wright wrote, "Although at that time he wore the blue and I wore the gray, and were flying at each other's throats, as it were, he is now and has been for a long time one of my best friends." Wright also added an item not found in the *Official Records*. Apparently, when a Federal officer (probably Captain Cosgrove) was parlaying with General Gano, Wright recalled that the Federal officer found out that Stand Watie was with the Confederate force, commanding a brigade. He remembered that the officer shouted, "Come ahead, God damn you! That is the fellow I have been waiting to meet a long time!"[320]

Wright was wounded in the thigh during the Cabin Creek fight and was carried from the field. He probably expressed the feelings of most of the veterans of the battle when he wrote, "There is no more hard feeling between us today than if we had both worn the blue or both worn the gray. We feel that it all turned out for the best, and we cherish no enmity whatsoever."[321]

Decades after the end of the Civil War, veterans of both sides paid honor to their former commanders. The United Confederate Veterans in Oklahoma named some of its local camps after former Indian Territory generals and officers. Camp Douglas Cooper No. 576 was located at Antlers. Oklahoma camps named after Stand Watie included No. 1442, Wilburton; No. 1007, Berwyn; No. 514, Muldrow; No. 573, Chelsea; and No. 1717, located at Hugo. Sam Cheocote was the name of No. 897 at Muskogee. The name of R.M. Gano proudly adorned No. 1408 in Sulpher.[322]

Near the end of March 1924, the Oklahoma UCV camps were saddened to learn of the death of Elbert W. Kirkpatrick of McKinney, Texas.[323] Kirkpatrick had been serving as lieutenant general, commanding the Trans-Mississippi Department for the Confederate association. In his obituary in the *Confederate Veteran* magazine, Kirkpatrick was described as being one of the most constructive citizens of the great state of Texas.[324] A veteran of many battles, Kirkpatrick had served with Company I (Martin's Regiment), Gano's Texas Brigade. He had been wounded in the neck at Cabin Creek. As his regiment was always camped without shelter, he recalled on one occasion that more than one hundred of the regiment's horses froze to death in a single night.[325]

In Stafford, Kansas, the name of Henry Hopkins adorned Post No. 301 of Grand Army of the Republic, the group of local Union veterans. Organized on January 26, 1884, not one of the original members who signed the application for the post's charter served under Major Hopkins. Only one of the original "comrades" served in a Kansas regiment during the war (the Tenth Kansas Infantry).[326] The post's officers were officially installed with a public installation at the GAR Post room, which included entertainment from the church choir and a fifteen-piece brass band. R.M. Blair, the editor and publisher of the *Stafford Herald*, served as the first post commander.[327] The post thrived and over its fifty-year life had 179 members on its muster rolls. On December 31, 1934, eighty-eight-year-old Asa O. Gere submitted the final muster roll of Post No. 301. He was the only member of the post still alive. Gere also noted that he was the only living Civil War veteran in the county. The rest were "all gone."[328]

The city of Vinita, Oklahoma, also had a GAR Post filled with feisty Union veterans. They named their post Cabin Creek in honor of the battlefield located just a few miles south of their city. Even though the battlefield saw both Union and Confederate victories, the veterans, it seemed, wanted to honor the memory of all who fought and died there.[329]

There is a small cemetery a few miles northeast of Cabin Creek Battlefield named the Military Cemetery. Its origin is also shrouded in the stories of the battles of Cabin Creek. Amateur researchers Connie Schofield and Mary

Two former members of the Indian Home Guard pose for a photograph at a Grand Army of the Republic encampment at Mount Vernon, Ohio, in 1925. The Native Americans from Oklahoma surprised everyone with their attendance. *Author's collection.*

Oakley shared a story with the author that was told to them by Ted Price, a local resident, whose grandfather-in-law was Henry Trout. Trout told Price that the cemetery had been laid out to follow the first graves located in what is now the west end of the cemetery. Price said Trout told him that the first bodies buried at the site were of twelve Confederate soldiers killed in one of the battles of Cabin Creek. Hence the cemetery's "Military" name.[330]

Today, all traces of the first graves are gone, but the cemetery, dotted with both old and new tombstones, remains. It is interesting to note that the old Texas-Military Road passes by the cemetery in a small draw to the south. Could this be the final resting place of some of the Confederates killed in the battles of Cabin Creek? Further research may one day solve the mystery.

CHAPTER 13

The Legend

The Lost Cannon in Cabin Creek

A legend lives on today around Cabin Creek that in local folklore rivals stories of Bigfoot and the Loch Ness monster. It is the tale of a cannon said to have been pushed off of the Cabin Creek bluff during one of the many battles there. On different occasions, the author had the opportunity to speak with several employees of the Oklahoma Historical Society on this issue, including Whit Edwards, Chris Morgan (Fort Gibson site manager) and Ralph "Rocky" Jones, former superintendent of the Honey Springs Battlefield Park. These historians basically repeated the same answer. "In the history business," they said, "there's not a fort without a secret passage or a cannon in a creek. It makes for a good story."[331]

But is it just a story? Over the past several decades, many people who were raised around the battlefield and who swam in the creek claimed that they saw a cannon. As children, they claimed that they played on it during the long, hot summer days, even diving off of one of the cannon's large wheels. During the Civil War Centennial in the early 1960s, Mary Elizabeth Good wrote a series of articles on the Civil War in Indian Territory for the *Tulsa World*. Good's husband, Lee, helped with the research for the articles. In an interview with the author in 1991, Mr. Good related the search for the facts about the "cannon in the creek" story. He and his wife had interviewed several of these "eyewitnesses." After reviewing all of the evidence, they concluded that the "cannon in Cabin Creek" story was just a story—probably made up by some old men in Adair while playing dominos.[332]

D.E. "Bill" Martin and his wife, Jennie, pose for a photo taken by the author in 1991. The Cabin Creek stockade once stood in the field directly behind them. As a Federal Bureau of Investigation agent, Bill was assigned to the White House to protect President Harry S. Truman. Jennie once rode in a biplane with the world-famous pilot Wiley Post at the controls. She also claimed to have seen a huge relic of the Civil War in Cabin Creek: a cannon still on its carriage in the old swimming hole. *Author's collection.*

Stella Crouch of Vinita, Oklahoma, told a WPA interviewer in 1938 that many historically minded people in recent years had searched Big Cabin Creek in an effort to find a cannon that, tradition says, rests on the bottom, buried in the accumulated silt of seventy-four years.[333]

While doing research for the television documentary *Last Raid at Cabin Creek*, the author became acquainted with D.E. "Bill" Martin, his wife, Jennie, and their son, Rod. Rod served as the technical director and history consultant on the ninety-minute program. Over the course of many different videotaped interviews, the Martins told many interesting and detailed stories about their ancestors.

One of these stories, told to the author in the presence of the director Rick Harding and the art director Royce Fitzgerald, was how Mrs. Martin had come upon the cannon in Cabin Creek while taking her sons, Doug and Rod, swimming at the old swimming hole. Her father-in-law, Emory Martin (Richard Martin's son), was also with the group.

The Legend

In an affidavit signed on March 14, 1994, Mrs. Martin described what she saw:

I, Jennie Martin do hereby swear and affirm that during the summer of 1939 or 1940, the following event took place at Cabin Creek, three and one-half miles north of Pensacola, Oklahoma on what is now near the property of Herman Stinnett. My sons, Doug and Rod wanted to go swimming. It was summertime, good and hot. Daddy Martin told me "that there was a good swimming hole up on Cabin Creek and I'll go with you." So we went north past Pat Nugent's place and got out of the car and started west along the creek. We were on the low side. On the other side was a rather high embankment and there were depressions every so often in the embankment. We had had a drought and the creek was way down. I was walking along with the kids and Daddy Martin looking down at the creek. All at once, I looked up and said, "Daddy Martin, There's a cannon!" He said, "Oh yes, that's just one of those old Civil War cannons." And I said, "You knew it and you haven't taken it out of here?" He said, "Well, who wants it?" I said, "I do. Let's get help and take it up and put it in the yard." There was about three inches of water over the left wheel and almost none on the right. It leaned just a little to the left. The spout was sticking up. The whole cannon was in view. I never could get any help to get that cannon. I begged for years. Daddy Martin told me that every one of those depressions had held a cannon.

When I saw the cannon, I was looking at it from the side. It was pointing towards the west, parallel with the creek. The whole cannon was exposed and it was intact. It looked as if it had just been fired. The snout was pointing upward slightly. The whole carriage was there. The wheels were there. The whole thing was there. You could see every bit of it. The tube was a dull bronze in color. It was sitting at the base of the embankment on the creek. Then there were these indentations up above me on the high side of the creek. There were three of them from what I could see, about three or four feet apart—one to the left of the cannon, the center one near the cannon and the other indentation on the right of it. Daddy Martin explained that during the war each one of these held a cannon to guard against attack. He said the South had owned this cannon. It appeared that the cannon fell out or off of the embankment since it was near the bank. It makes me sick that I couldn't get anyone to help me retrieve the cannon or at least take a picture of it. But no one in the family would help me. I guess its still there to this day as I heard of no one getting it out. The cannon is probably still there, lying under a ton of mud.[334]

Artist Royce Fitzgerald's conception of the lost cannon in Cabin Creek based on Jennie Martin's account of seeing a cannon in the creek during the summer of 1939 or 1940. Mrs. Martin helped with and approved of this sketch. She signed an affidavit to what she saw in 1994. *Courtesy Royce Fitzgerald.*

An undated article from the *Tulsa Tribune* found in the Tulsa City-County Library in the Oklahoma history files, revealed that in August 1959 or 1960, Dr. T.L. Ballenger, professor emeritus of history at Northeastern State College in Tahlequah, Oklahoma, led a small expedition to Cabin Creek in search of the cannon. Armed with an underwater metal detector, an 1851 model Colt pistol for snakes and insect repellant, the group searched the creek's old swimming hole but found nothing. A report by seventy-five-year-old Bill Sparks, an area farmer who claimed that when he was a boy he used to stand on the high wheels of the cannon and dive into the creek, boosted the hopes of the searchers.[335]

In 1964, Orval Neal of Vinita was fishing in Cabin Creek when he looked down in the water and found a Civil War musket. It was later identified as a Suhl musket. In a story that appeared on the front page of the January 23, 1964 edition of the *Tulsa World*, Neal said, "We sure need some place to preserve everything that's been found. I guess we've found thousands of rifle and Minnie balls over the years, but somehow, they just get away." Neal made sure that his musket wouldn't get away. He donated it and other relics from Cabin Creek to the Vinita–Craig County Historical Society. The musket can be seen today in a display at Vinita's Eastern Trails Museum.[336]

Two views of a cannon reportedly found in Cabin Creek that was recovered by a family
living in the area. It was restored by Steve Cox. Known as a "walking stick," the barrel was
poured in 1821 at the Fort Pitt, Pennsylvania foundry. The trunnions are marked "McC
Pitt 1821," and the letters "U.S." are engraved on top of the barrel. The gun's carriage
is marked "#66 Model 1837, Watervliet Arsenal." It is one of only four known carriages.
Courtesy Steve Cox.

In the late 1980s, local Cabin Creek landowner Herman Stinnett and Civil War relic hunter Jack Mullen searched for the cannon in the creek. Using a metal detector, Mullen tried to pinpoint the cannon's location without success. A skilled diver, Stinnett dove along the bottom of the area of the old swimming hole. Visibility was poor, and Stinnett had to rely only on touch and feel. The pair reported that the only "find" they made while searching the creek was the hood of what they believed to be old Ford Model T.[337]

Steve Cox of Van Buren, Arkansas, has his own "cannon in Cabin Creek" story. He even has the cannon to prove it. Cox acquired the cannon from a gentleman whose family reportedly pulled the cannon from Cabin Creek shortly after the war. According to Cox, the cannon stood as a silent sentinel for many years near the shores of Grand Lake in Langley, Oklahoma. Cox restored the cannon, which was a Model 1819, six-pounder field gun with an iron tube. This type of gun was known as a "Walking Stick." Upon starting the restoration process, Cox said that he found the gun loaded and spiked, with the barrel jammed full of iron, projectile fragments, rocks and wood. Cox's research about the cannon revealed some interesting facts. The barrel was poured in 1821 at the Fort Pitt, Pennsylvania foundry. The barrel weight of the gun is 742 pounds, and the serial number is also still on the barrel. The trunnions are marked "McC Pitt 1821," and the letters "U.S." are engraved on top of the barrel. According to Cox, there were only thirty-one of these types of guns recorded. The gun's carriage is marked "66 Model 1837, Watervliet Arsenal." It is one of only four known carriages to have survived to the present day.[338]

Is this the lost cannon of Cabin Creek? The only evidence Cox has tying the cannon to Cabin Creek is one family's story. Upon examination, the *Official Records* reveal no historical mention concerning the loss of a cannon or cannons at Cabin Creek. However, there may be other evidence. In a 1937 interview, Josephine Spence told a WPA interviewer that her father, William W. Williams, served in Company I of the First Iowa Cavalry during the Civil War. He was part of a detachment that camped at Cabin Creek. During the night, the troops were surprised and attacked by Confederate troops. According to Spence's story, the Federal mules and artillery were pushed into the creek, and the entire Union force was either killed or captured, except Williams and two or three other men.[339]

At least part of Spence's story is true. William W. Williams from Martinsburg, Iowa, enlisted in the Union army on August 16, 1862, as a private. He was mustered into Company I of the First Iowa Cavalry. He was discharged for disability on November 17, 1863, at Little Rock, Arkansas.[340]

What if the other part of her story is true?

CHAPTER 14

May the Spirits Keep Watch

Today, the guns are silent at Cabin Creek. Instead of the sounds of cannons and musketry, one hears only the birds and the wind. Those who died and were buried on the battlefield are forgotten. The location of the Confederate graves said to have been located near the bluff has been lost.[341]

One Confederate soldier reported killed during the second battle was Private William J. Candler of Company F of Martin's regiment of the Fifth Texas Partisan Rangers. Candler was born in Russell County, Virginia, in 1836. He enlisted in the Confederate army at Farmersville, Texas. Many years after the war, his comrade Tom Howard wrote:

> *Bill Candler was not a talker, but when he was called on or when volunteers were called for, he stepped to the front without a word and was ready for duty. He was the only man killed in the Cabin Creek fight. He was wounded in the bowels and we put him on a litter and started to carry him off the field. We had gone but a short distance when he said he was dying and was soon gone. We dug his grave as best we could with our big knives, and as his blanket was bloody, I wrapped him in my own. He was buried near where he fell. Such was the fate of many a good man. May the Spirits keep watch over his lonely resting place.*[342]

Contractors working for the U.S. government after the war removed the bodies of Federal dead from several Indian Territory battlefields and reinterred them at the Fort Gibson National Cemetery in 1867. Sixteen

Union soldiers who died at Cabin Creek and twelve Union dead from Flat Rock now lie side by side at rest in the soil they fought to defend. Only grave numbers mark their final resting place.[343] Our country honors them and the thousands of other soldiers buried at the cemetery by flying the American flag at half-mast. As President Abraham Lincoln said during his Gettysburg Address, "they here gave the last full measure of devotion."

Monuments to the memory of Stand Watie and his Confederate Indian soldiers also stand on the grounds of the old Cherokee nation capitol in Tahlequah, Oklahoma. Another monument dedicated to the memory of the Confederate soldiers of Indian Territory also guards the front of the Bryant County Courthouse in Durant.

Watie's men could not forget him either. In 1915, George W. Grayson wrote:

> *Watie's presence about an active firing line, always inspired confidence in the boys that fired the guns. We would win because Watie was with us. Let me say here: that whatever else the Indians of old Indian Territory may lose in the shock and crash of time, be it property, land or name; let it be so provided now in song and story that the name of General Stand Watie may never fade away. Let his memory and fame stand forth as proud monuments to the virtues of patriotism and devotion to duty as exemplified in his life, as long as the grass flows and the flowers bloom.*[344]

Another Confederate veteran, D.W. Vann, perhaps best summed up the feeling of all of the veterans of Watie's Indian brigade when he wrote, "At the age of sixteen years I joined General Stand Watie's command and served under him until the close of the War Between the States. I was with him at Pea Ridge, Cabin Creek, Honey Springs and other battles. He was a great man and a brave soldier. On going into battle he always said, 'Come on boys.' He never said, 'Go boys,' but always led. And we were always glad and willing to follow."[345]

Twenty-one years after the Cabin Creek raid, General Gano spoke for most of his comrades when he observed, "I may forget things of last week, but the memory of those who fought in the times that tried men's souls shall never be forgotten."[346]

Appendix I

General Gano's War Memoirs

This manuscript was typed from the original memoirs of Brigadier General Richard M. Gano, CSA. Unfortunately, not all of the pages from his diary have survived. This part of his diary highlights his service with General John Hunt Morgan in Gano's native state of Kentucky. Missing are the pages that concern his service in the Trans-Mississippi Department, including Arkansas, Indian Territory and Texas. This information appears courtesy of Claire Witham and Mrs. Gene Rain, both direct descendants of General Gano, who compiled this document. Please note that for some reason, the general always speaks in the third person, calling himself "Gano," "R.M. Gano" or "Dr. Gano." It is presented as it was from the original. The numbers given in the text in parentheses are the page numbers in the original. Various sections are missing, and this text begins on page 30 of the original.

WAR RECORD OF BRIGADIER GENERAL RICHARD MONTGOMERY GANO
COPIED FROM THE ORIGINAL MEMOIRS WRITTEN OR DICTATED BY GENERAL
RICHARD M. GANO

Gano had become thoroughly satisfied with his trip over Texas. Texas being a great stock raising country, in which he especially delighted. He thought it very poor farming country and subject to droughts, and indeed, some man told him that he couldn't raise any crops...nothing but grass...not even a garden. The state has since developed into a very fine farming country, also, good fruits and vegetables, and, as he could purchase good land in Texas from four to ten dollars per acre, and could sell his land in Kentucky at one

Lieutenant Colonel Richard M. Gano, Company A. Gano's Squadron Texas Cavalry and Seventh Kentucky Regiment, Morgan's Division, CSA. In this half-plate ambrotype, circa 1862, Gano wears a double-breasted frock coat with his rank insignia on the collar. His tri-cornered hat is adorned with a fancy feather plume, with a gold bullion tassel hanging from one corner. He's wearing a Nashville Plow Works sword. Gano and his Texans fought gallantly under Morgan before he and his men were transferred to Indian Territory in December 1863. *Courtesy Steve Mullinax.*

hundred per acre, and also, having a growing family and needing a warmer climate for his health, he decided to move to Texas, against remonstrances of many friends. He moved by wagon and carriage with his brother-in-law, Dr. Welch, and his brother, Frank Gano, also, his servants and some horses, to Northern Texas. He stopped at Dallas, Texas, and inspected the country around, and located on the North end of Grapevine Prairie, which he purchases from Judge J.T. Morehead with improvements on the place and 60 acres in cultifation, for $10.00 per acre. He had left his family in Kentucky to come out with his father-in-law, Dr. Welch.

His family landed about a month after he did, and, as they were driving up to the Grapevine home, and were within a mile and a half of the place, they passed a house and stopped for a drink of water. They told the old lady who they were, and where they were going, when she remarked, "you have got a fine home; there is a dining room in the house," from which one might infer that dining rooms were uncommon in that country.

They all landed in Texas late in the fall, in the year 1856, Dr. Gano having retired from the practice of medicine when he removed to Texas and engaged in stock raising, 23 miles northwest of Dallas. His farm was located in the Northeast corner of Tarrant County. Another son was born to him on March 15, 1858, and they named him Clarence Welch Gano, for his Grandmother.

One day when Dr. Gano was riding out on the prairie, looking after his stock, he saw a horseman coming galloping from the west, who exclaimed to him, "Oh, sir, get the neighbors together as quickly as you can and come to the frontier and help us drive back the Indians, for they are murdering our women and children." Gano rode leisurely home and commenced to prepare for a trip to the West. His wife, moved to tears, said to him, "You won't leave us here on the frontier so far from our kindred, and go out to fight the Indians?" He replied, "Mattie, it tries my soul to do this and nearly breaks my heart, but our lives and our property are protected by these frontier people, living west of us, and it behooves us to go to them while they are in jeopardy. I will leave you for a few days with the children, surrounded by good neighbors, friends and servants."

He started with a few of his neighbors to the frontier, and at Fort Worth, they found a lawyer on the stump lecturing an audience on the subject of frontier protection. With this lawyer, they mustered up twenty-six men and moved on westward.

Frank Gano, brother of Dr. Gano, reached home after his brother had left and he determined, also, to go, but he had nothing but a mule to ride. His sister-in-law, Mrs. Gano, provided him with some biscuits and meat and he put them in his saddle bags for the trip and started out to overtake his brother, who was some 30 miles ahead. But as soon as he got out on the prairie, his mule became alarmed at the rattling of the saddle bags and began to plunge and pitch, as only a Texas mule knows how. He kept it up until he had scattered all of Frank's biscuits and lunch over the prairie, and piled up Frank and his saddle bags in a lump, and ran away with his saddle, so that Frank never overtook the company of defendants.

The company of 26 men, after leaving Fort Worth, selected the lawyer, who had made such a grand speech, as their captain. General Jno. R. Baylor out with several hundred men to drive the Indians away. Before they reached General Baylor, they passed a house with only a little girl in it, the father, and mother, grandfather and grandmother having been murdered by the Indians, and their dead bodies left in the cabin. The little girl who had hid in the bushes said that the Indians, after killing her parents and grandparents, had carried away her little brother on a horse, the little fellow crying at the top of his voice, "Oh! Father, grandfather, save me! "They reached Baylor's camp, which was then about four miles from the Indians and reported with their company to Baylor, for duty. Baylor told them to stake out their horses to grass, get some dinner, and they would soon be ready to move on the Redskins, and that we would teach them how to come in and murder our women and children. While preparing for dinner, the lawyer, the captain of our company, called Dr. Gano to one side and, seated on a log, inquired of him what he thought of this. Gano asked…"of what?" He replied, "Of putting up your body as a target to be shot at by the Indians. Gano replied," That is not a pleasant thing to be talking about. Get your dinner, and when we get in action we won't have so much time to think about it. The captain said, "I can't fight; I am scared half to death right now; I am going home." Gano replied, "You can't go home. We have reported to Baylor for duty and I don't know what his rules are, but if you were to desert and start home, he would probably have you shot, so you had just as well, or better, take your chances with us fighting the Indians." The Captain said, "What shall I do then? I can't fight." Gano said, "Go down there to Baylor's headquarters and tell him all about it and see what he will say." He did so, and returned and called Gano out and told him that he had told Baylor that he was scared and couldn't fight and wanted to go home, and that Baylor had cursed him and told him to go, that he didn't want any of that sort in his command, and the captain said, "I am going." Gano replied, "You can't go home; don't you know that the Indians are now on the hilltops all around here watching us? If you were to start home, they would run you down and scalp you in less than six miles." "Well," he said, "what can I do?" Gano said, "The best thing for you to do, is to ride along behind our command and follow, but follow far enough behind to be out of danger if we were to get into a fight, but close enough that if we should be attacked in the rear, you could ride to the front."

While they were talking an officer came along with several prisoners who had been selling whiskey to the Indians, and he was taking them back to Ft. Worth…and needing some help to get them there, we gave him our captain.

Gano then remarked to the company to select an old Baptist preacher, V.J. Hutton, who had a thick back head and whom he thought would fight, so we chose him as captain, and as we rode along in the evening in the direction of the Indians, some Indians from a hilltop fired upon us from the right, shooting one of our men through the breast. His name was Thomas J. Melton. Our captain dashed away like a wild man to the top of the hill, shouting to his men to charge them. The Indians ran away from the hills and disappeared into the timber. The company finding that our captain, though not afraid to fight, had no ability to command nor presence of mind to direct the company's movements, so when the captain came back he said, "Now boys, you see I have no sense to command a company, select some man who has sense enough to command a company and fight, besides." They selected Dr. Gano as their captain. They moved on, carrying their woulded man, Melton, with them to Marlin's Ranch. Baylor, with his men, stopped at the ranch house; Gano, with his men at the school house about 100 yards to the left. Gano got down under the shade of a tree and was dressing Melton's wounds, when Melton remarked, "It is pitiful for a man to die way out here away from his wife and two little children." But Gano replied, "Melton, it is not every man that dies when shot through the lungs and we hope that you will recover, but if you should die, I will promise you one thing: your wife and two little children shall be cared for." While dressing the wounds of Melton, a terrific yell was raised from the Indians who were attacking us in the rear and numbering about twice as many as we. Gano was fighting at the school house on the inside, while some of his soldiers were outside, some behind the school house and some under cover of the oak trees on the east side. A man by the name of Washburn was in the school house with Gano and he told him that the Indians had murdered his father and mother, and he intended to spend his life killing them.

While the firing was going on, Washburn stepped in front of the door to discharge his rifle and a bullet passed through his breast. He laid down on the floor and said, "boys, I am a dead man." In less than twenty minutes he was dead. The Indians, feeling sure that they could take the school house away from us, charged down upon it, but we used our six shooters and drove them off. Two of our men, Melton and Washburn, were killed and several were wounded. About a dozen dead Indians were left upon the ground, and Some were carried away on their horses by the retreating Indians. After the fight was over, Baylor was heard to say that he believed that the young Doctor from Kentucky did the best fighting of any man on the ground, to which old Major Whitton, who belonged to Gano's command said,

"Baylor, if you say that, I will present him with a handsome sword." Baylor said, "I said it because I believe it." The command was called out on dress parade and Gano, who knew not what the movement meant, was asked to step out four paces in front of the line, then he was informed that Capt. Throckmorton, who was afterwards governor of the state, would make an address and deliver him a sword as a testimony of his valor in the fight. Gano, replying to Throckmorton, said, "I have no knowledge that I deserve any reward; there are old Indian fighters here, while I am but a novice, but I always try to do my best when I undertake anything, and there was no chance here for anybody to surrender, even if he had been inclined to do so…it was simply a fight to the death." Mr. Throckmorton presented to Dr. Gano as a compliment of his valor in the fight the handsome sword, which was afterwards lost in the battle of Chicamauga. Mr. Whitton served under Gano during the Civil War.

They all returned to their homes. Gano with his command passing down together, however, with two ranges of hills on either side of him. Some Indians looked down on them, and presently one of Gano's soldiers from Grapevine, a man by the name of Holland, rode up by the side of Captain Gano and said, "Captain, did you see those Indians on the hill look at us?" Gano said, "Yes." He said, "We will all be killed." Gano replied, "You fall back into your place, I don't see that you are in any great danger." Soon after, one of the soldiers rode up to Gano and asked, "Did you know that Holland has gone crazy?" Gano replied that he did not. "Well," the soldier said, "he is as crazy as a loon." "He is riding along with a loaded gun." Gano rode down to the side of Holland and saw that he was indeed mentally unbalanced. Gano asked Holland if he felt well. Holland replied, "I know that you are going to have me killed, but I haven't done anything worthy of death." "Yet," he said, "I know you are going to have me killed." Gano had his gun taken away from him and two men placed as guards over him, so it required two men to take care of him. Holland, when he got in sight of home, recovered his mental balances immediately.

He and another man named Clark were left to guard an old man who had been arrested on the prairie one night, and they murdered him. Both of these men, Holland and Clark, died a violent death. The son of the murdered man killing Holland, and a man by the name of Morgan killing Clark at Witts mill.

Dr. Gano attended a large barbecue about four miles north of his residence in Denton County, and Dr. Hines, practitioner of medicine, attended the same barbecue. Hines had married a Miss Lusk and separated from her, and having been drinking some at the barbecue, he happened to lean his arm, in the crowd, on the shoulder of one of the Lusk boys, who looked around, and, seeing that it was Hines, cursed him. Hines went over to where Gano was standing and asked him to loan him a pistol. Gano replied, "Hines, I wouldn't loan you a pistol if I had one; I wouldn't loan it to you in a crowd like this, for if you were to get to shooting, a good many innocent people might get killed. Wait until you get out by yourselves and settle this difficulty." But Hines went off and borrowed a pistol and came back. The two Lusk boys attacked him and Hines shot one of them, Newton Lusk, through the thigh, but the other one shot Hines through the back, being behind him, killing him instantly. The neighborhood thereby losing their physician, the people, knowing that Gano was a physician, urged upon him to practice. Gano consented to do so, until they could get another doctor in the neighborhood, as he didn't wish to resume practicing.

A young doctor came to the neighborhood and settled down to practice, but soon proved himself incompetent and left. Another physician came to the neighborhood, but as he was incompetent also, the people didn't advise him to stay. Dr. Gano then told them that if they didn't employ a physician, that he would quit, and leave them without a doctor, that he didn't care to permanently resume the practice. Dr. Lipscomb then came into the neighborhood, a good physician and a Christian gentleman. Dr. Gano turned his practice over to him.

About this time there was a good deal of excitement on politics and the people of Tarrant County requested Gano to run for the Legislature. His opponent in the race was Julius Smith, a lawyer of Ft. Worth; they had quite an animated discussion over the country, but Gano was elected a little over two to one. He served, acceptably, the people of Tarrant County until Texas went out of the Union. They had quite a rousing discussion in the year 1861 on the subject of frontier protection, and upon several other questions, one of which was the railroads of Eastern Texas.

(38) Gano was elected to the Legislature in the same year that Abraham Lincoln was elected president of the United States, and served in the Legislature during the year 1861.

Samuel Gano, the fourth son, was born to Dr. Gano, in Tarrant County, November 24, 1857, and died while on a visit to relatives in Kentucky, November 26, 1860.

General Terry, a very estimable gentleman of Fort Worth, but an extreme secessionest, canvassed Tarrant County in favor of secession, and telling the people in public speeches that the South might secede and that there wouldn't be blood enough shed to stain his pocket handkerchief. Gano replied to his speech and told the people not to be deceived, that if the government was to divide, there would be a great war, and many, many lives sacrificed in the North and South. He told the people of the South to try to secure their rights in the Union, but when the state of Texas went out, passing the ordinance of secession, Gano espoused the cause of the South, and fought for her through the war. But Julias Smith, who canvassed the country against Gano and made bitter secession speeches, and proclaimed from the stump how the South could whip the North, never took up arms for his state.

In January 1862, Gano resigned his seat in the Legislature, receiving an order from General Albert Sidney Johnson to organize two companies of Texas Cavalry and bring them out and report to him for duty at Bowling Green, Kentucky, where he was then stationed. General Johnson had known Gano and his family in Kentucky, and, although he knew that Gano had never had any military education, he believed that he was the man he wanted to command his Headquarter scouts.

Gano immediately set to work and organized two companies from Dallas, Tarrant, Collin and some of the adjoining counties. They numbered 180 men. Gano told them to select their officers. They selected him as captain of Company A, and senior captain commanding both companies.

(39) John R. Huffman as captain of Company B. The officers of the squadron in addition, were E.R. Nicholson, adjt., E.M. Stackpole as quartermaster. The first lieutenant of Company A was Robt. Spears; second lieutenant, W.A. Kendall; third lieutenant, _____. First lieutenant of Company B was _____. Second Lieutenant, _____; Third lieutenant, _____.

They were all mounted and equipped with guns and pistols when they started out to report to General Albert Sidney Johnson, who, in the meantime, had left Bowling Green and was moving in the direction of Fort Donelson. Gano moved with his command after a touching farewell to his dear wife and little boys. Crossing the Red River at Shrevesport, La., they camped at Monroe, La., where a Frenchman by the name of Frank Pargoud came down from his plantation, having ordered and received from France several hundred very elegant sabers, and he made a present of 180 of those sabers to Gano's squadron, so that every soldier had, buckled on his saddle, one of those fine sabers; and each fellow felt proud that he would be enabled to accomplish some valiant work with his sabre. But strange to relate, no man was ever killed by one of those sabers, as far as we remember. It might be true that some soldier got to use his sabre in some little hot contested fight, but it was never reported to Captain Gano, and after getting into a number of brush fights with the Federal Cavalry and finding the sabers a great incumbrance, they began to leave them, lose them, and make away with them, until, finally, they were all gone.

Gano's method of fighting with his two companies was to charge down on the enemy, emptying their shotguns and then making a pistol fight, as his soldiers were much more capable with six-shooters than with sabers, and could do quicker fighting than if they had long range guns.

General Albert Sidney Johnson, having gone with his army to Shiloh, Capt. Gano proceeded to try to meet him there, but the day before he reached Shiloh, the famous battle of Shiloh took place, and Albert Sidney Johnson was killed. He made the enemy retreat toward the river, and, had he lived two hours longer, he would have capture Grant and his army.

(40) Gano, not being able now to report to General Johnson on May 15, 1862, desired to be placed on outpost duty, but General Beauregard now had assumed command of the army and resolved to put all the cavalry under General Beale of Arkansas. Gano, failing to secure outpost work, reported the fact to his soldiers that night, and they were a sad, down-hearted body of men. Gano went up that night to General J.C. Brackenridge's headquarters, and had quite a lengthy chat with him, he being from the same congressional district in Kentucky, and being personally acquainted with Captain Gano and his father's family. When Gano had related to General Brackenridge his disappointment at not being put on outpost duty, Brackenridge said, "Gano, when you get your breakfast in the morning, come down to headquarters and I will go with you over to General Beauregard's headquarters and see if we can't accomplish your wishes." So next morning they rode together down to General Beauregard's headquarters, passing by General Bragg's headquarters, where they tried to secure his assistance, but he declined to have anything to do with it. Gano thought that Bragg was wounded in feelings because he had not been placed in command of Johnson's army instead of General Beauregard. They rode up to General Beauregard's headquarters and after the usual salutations, General Beauregard remarked, "General Brackenridge, what can I do for you?" Brackenridge replied, "I have a special request to make of you and you will confer a lasting favor by granting it. My young friend, Captain Gano, with his squad of cavalry, desires to be placed on outpost duty, and not be consolidated with the Grand Army Cavalry, and if you will grant this request, I will be under great obligations to you." General Beauregrd replied, "I would be greatly

pleased to grant this favor, but I have determined to consolidate the Cavalry under General Beale and will have to carry out my former intentions." General Brackenridge replied, "General Beauregard, Captain Gano and his command are active Texas Cavalrymen, and they are suited for outpost duty, [41] and can accomplish more good there than elsewhere; they don't mind marching or fighting, but they don't like to be cooped up in camp, and I believe they can do more valuable service in the position Gano desires than in any other, and if you will grant this request, you will place me under lasting obligations to you, and Gano and his men will ever remember you with gratitude." Beauregard, turning to Gano, inquired, "Where do you wish to go?" And Gano replied, "Anywhere that we are most needed; we don't mind long marching; we don't object to fighting, and we will serve our country to the best of our ability; but we don't want to be cooped up in the Grand Army of Cavalry." Beauregard inquired, "How would you like to report to J.H. Morgan for duty, who is now at Chattanooga?" Gano replied, "Very well, for I am personally acquainted with Morgan; we are both from Brackenridge district, and old Ashland district of Kentucky, and with him we can lead very active lives, such as we desire." Turning to his Adjutant, General Beauregard said, "Write an order to Captain Gano to report to General Morgan at Chattanooga." Gano was afraid that Beauregard might rescind that order, so inside of thirty minutes, he and his men were out of Shiloh on the march up the Tennessee River toward Chattanooga. He had the good fortune to fall in with Colonel Basil Duke with a few of his men from Morgan's command, and so they had his company. While marching along near the river, they discovered, in the little town over on the north side of the river, a lot of Federal Cavalry marching up and down from a boat that they had prepared at the river. Gano concluded that they intended to cross the river and march out a large public road in front of where he and his men were, so he hid his men down in a thicket between which (it and the public road) lay a cornfield. Gano took his position where he could view them when they moved out on the road. Sure enough, they came and marched out the public road, passing by the cornfield. As soon as they were out of sight, Gano galloped his men across the field, had them take down the fence (42) and took after the cavalry. Turning a bend of the road where they came into view of the cavalry, they raised the Texas yell and charged down the road in pursuit of them. Instead of turning for a fight, they took to flight, so terrific was the yell of the Texans, they imagined that Gano's forces were superior in numbers. Down the road they went until coming to the forks of the road; the cavalry divided; a little over one half of them taking the right-hand road; the balance, the left. Gano pursued the right-hand road and chased them into a wheat field where some little fighting occurred. The Federals fell down in the wheat. Gano's men rode through the wheat field and captured them, and Gano, himself, rode up on a tall man about six feet and six inches high, with a tremendous tall stove pipe hat. When he rose up to surrender, he looked almost as tall standing on foot as Gano did on horseback. But he had an ague upon him and his knees were smote together. Gano said, "Don't be alarmed, sir, you will be treated as a prisoner of war."

Stopping that day at a cotton gin where several planters had gathered, one of them, looking at Gano's tall fellow, remarked, "There is that rascal now." His knees shook as they had done before. Gano asked what he had done. The men replied, "He insulted a young lady down here who lives with her mother, a plantress." Gano took this tall man and another one who looked as near like him as he had in his command, and with the two and two soldiers and the man who informed him of the tall man's conduct, they rode out to this lady's residence and called her out. She came out to the style block, and Capt. Gano inquired of her whether or not her daughter was at home. She replied that she was, and called her out. Gano asked if she had ever seen either of those men before. She said she had seen the one with the tall stove pipe hat. She said with tears in her eyes, "He came here one day with some other soldiers and insulted me at my mother's house." Gano returned to the cotton gin and the planters requested him to give them that man. Gano replied, "No, he is a prisoner of war and if punished for his (43) crimes, it must be done by court martial. I will send my prisoner up to General Kirby Smith, and will send up any charges you write out against him." After Gano reached Morgan he sent his prisoners on up to Kirby Smith with the charges, but never heard what became of them afterwards.

(44, 45, 45 and 47) Gano with the assistance of Colonel Duke and a few of his men, reached J.H. Morgan at Chattanooga, turning over the prisoners that he had captured on the way up. Morgan said, "Gano, you are a strange fellow to come up here with 180 soldiers and nearly twice as many prisoners." Gano replied, "I didn't capture them all in one fight." After staying around Chattanooga several days preparing for movement, General Morgan added two Tennessee Companies to Gano's two Texas Companies. They moved out of Chattanooga in the middle of the evening, General Morgan ordering Gano, with a guide that knew the country, to take the road running to Tompkinsville, and he (Morgan) would precede along another road, for Gano to march all night and strike Thompkinsville on the east and he on the south, just at the break of day, as soon as it was light enough to see how to fire a gun, they would attack to Federal Cavalry, who were in heavy force at that place.

After midnight, Gano's forces were passing a large brick residence on the right hand side of the road. The night was so dark the residence was scarcely visible, and just as the head of his companies were passing the residence, the door opened, it was brilliantly lighted inside, although the windows had all been shaded with blankets and comforts, so that no light could be seen until the door was opened. One of the ladies put her head out the door and said, "Go on boys, we are all in here praying for you," and the door closed. The words that she said were passed back down the line of men, and no doubt it helped many in the hard-fought battle the next morning. Gano, up to this time, had never been in a hard-fought battle, and, knowing that they were to meet a superior force, he thought he would probably be killed the following morning, and finding that they were getting along too rapidly on the road, and would reach Thompkinsville before daylight, he stopped his men in the road and let them dismount and rest a while, while he got over a pair of bars and walked down into an old orchard, running up against a wagon that had no bed on it; he walked in between the wheels and, kneeling down by the coupling pole, prayed to God, and especially (48) if he should be called away the next morning to care for his wife and little children. Then they moved on and ran upon Federal Pickets just about three-quarters of a mile from where a large wing of the Federal Cavalry was camped in an orchard north of Thompkinsville. The pickets fired and ran back into their command, so that when Gano reached the edge of the timber, the orchard and a small field of corn, he discovered the camp all in a stir. He dismounted his men and leaving the horses in the edge of the timber, he moved his men to the front. The Federals formed a line of battle on horseback and moved into the cornfield opposite Gano's lines and opened fire upon them. Gano's men returned the fire, although it was not light enough to see how to take aim well. The Federals continued to advance and fire, Gano returning the fire. Morgan and his men had not yet appeared and Gano was anxiously expecting them, when suddenly Morgan opened up with two pieces of artillery, and, looking off to the south we could see his men coming up over the turn of the hill. Gano and his men thought that the artillery was beautiful music and they were delighted to see Morgan's men coming. The Federals turned back to camp, and, with little more firing, beat a retreat, contrary to Gano's expectation, down the road toward Burksville, Kentucky.

Gano had purchased just a few days before, a fine race horse, not knowing that he had been run on the track…when Gano and his men began running down the road in pursuit of the Federals toward Burksville, his horse ran away with him. Gano tried in vain to stop his horse, cutting his mouth with the bits so that the blood flew back on his pants as he ran. There were no fences on either side of the road, but Gano didn't dare to run his horse into the woods, for the down-wood and the trees would have endangered his life, so he kept right in the center of the road. Turning a bend suddenly in the road, he came in view of the rear guard commanded by Major Jorden of Pennsylvania; they stopped in the road to await his coming to surrender, but they didn't have time to turn their horses in the road before Captain Gano reached them. His horse, striking across the shoulders of the Federal Cavalryman's horse, knocked him down into a ditch and fell on top of the rider, who called for help. They demanded of Gano to surrender. He told them he would not. They began to shoot at him with pistols; every shot endangering the lives of their own men as they entirely surrounded Gano. Major Jorden, seeing this, said, "Cease firing, you are killing our own men! Kill him with your sabers!" They then began to draw their sabers out of their metallic scabbards, which was a rather harsh sound for a man who was to be carved up. Gano, with his pistols, was firing to keep the sabre men off, when suddenly about 100 guns were turned loose and bullets rained down the road. Gano's men had come in sight and turned loose upon them. Jorden with his command of 75 men retreated down the road rapidly except six or seven who had been killed in the attempt to kill Gano. The first man of Gano's command that came up by his side was Joe Nail from Piano, Texas. Gano said, "Now Joe, we will take all those fellows in," and away Gano and his men dashed in pursuit of the Federals. Gano ran up by the side of Major Jorden, presented his pistol and demanded him to surrender. Jorden said, "Yes!, Yes! I'll surrender, don't shoot!" Gano and his men captured the whole posse, and riding back down the road by the side of Major Jorden, Major Jorden remarked, "What command are you?" Gano said, "We are Texas Rangers." Jorden said, "I thought so, for you can outrun the devil." When they got back where they had shot at Gano in the road, among the dead on the ground was a Federal Captain from Pennsylvania. He was resting upon his elbow, with his head upon his hand. Gano dismounted, and asked if he could do anything for him. He said, "Yes, I want some water." Gano raised his head and gave him some water. He then asked him his name. He opened his mouth to speak, but sank back down and died without another word. One of his men, riding up, said, "That was my Captain from Pennsylvania, and he is engaged to be married; that is his engagement ring on his finger." Gano stooped down and took the heavy gold finger ring off his finger, and on the inside of it was the name of the young lady who was to marry him.

Gano said, "Do you know that young lady?" The soldier replied, "Yes, sir." "Will you take this note and ring to her if I will parole you?" The soldier replied, "Yes, sir," appearing very glad to get off so light. Gano wrote a note stating that the captain was killed on the Tompkinsville and Burksville road, giving the date and stating how he was killed, and that the ring was taken off his finger after he was dead, and then sealed the note up, putting the ring on the inside. He then paroled the soldier, and sent the note to the young lady in care of him. Gano never heard of the soldier again, so never knew whether or not the note was delivered to the young lady, as he wasn't keeping a diary at the time, and didn't remember the young lady's name.

(51, 52, 53 and 54) They moved on into Thompkinsville July 9, 1862, where the ladies and some of the old men who were not in the army, asked Major Gano to give them Major Jorden. The day previous, while Major Jorden was in the town, he told the women standing the doors to go to work and cook plenty of provisions for his men and to have it ready in one hour. Some of the ladies, bolder than the rest, replied, "Our pantries and meat houses are open, cook your own provisions, we are not in the habit of cooking for soldiers." Jorden replied, "If you don't go to work and have plenty cooked for my men in one hour, I will turn my command loose on the town and will not be responsible for what they do." The ladies thought his threat was intended for them. Gano told them that he couldn't give them Major Jorden…that he was a prisoner of war and if punished for his doings it would have to be done by court martial, that he would send him up to General Kirby Smith, and if they had any charges to make against him that he would send them up and let them try him by court martial. Jorden assured Gano, however, that he only intended to scare them into cooking provisions, which he did, and that he didn't intend to harm them.

Moving on from Thompkinsville in the direction of Harrodsburg, Kentucky, they came to the town of Lebanon, July 10. Gano's horse became so lame that he didn't dare ride him and was compelled to get another, so he told Morgan to ride on with his command and he would overtake him. He went out to a farmer near by, who let him have a horse, and traded for his lame one, but he had to have him shod before he could proceed. By the time he got his horse shod, it was getting late, but Gano pushed on, trying to overtake Morgan's command, knowing that they were going through the town of Perryville, ten miles this side of Harrodsburg. Gano fell in with a countryman who was going in pursuit of Morgan's command to try to recover a horse that had been taken from his farm by some of the soldiers, and was taking a good serviceable horse to exchange for the one they had taken, which he prized very highly (55). Gano told the man who he was, and promised to assist him in recovering his horse and they rode on together. Gano had never before been in a land of bushwhackers. Suddenly in the dark they heard guns cock and a man said, "Halt! Who goes there?" The farmer replied, "I, a farmer living near Lebanon, going down to Morgan's command to try to recover a horse they have taken from me." The bushwhackers inquired, "Who is that with you?" "This is a man going with me to help me recover my horse," the farmer replied. They allowed them to pass on. Again, in the darkness of the night, some miles further on, the same thing occurred, and the same answers were given. They were again allowed to pass on. By daylight in the morning they reached Perryville and Gano was still alive, all due to the fact that he had fallen in with that countryman, and it was so dark that they couldn't see his uniform. Gano never stayed behind his command in the night to get his horse shod again. Morgan called Gano to him and said, "Major, we are now within 10 miles of Harrodsburg, and will take dinner there today. I want you to take your four companies and try to beat us there an hour or more and tell the people there to prepare dinner for us on the Graham Grounds, the noted watering place." Gano proceeded with his men, capturing a few bush-whackers and getting several recruits. He crossed Salt River about one mile from Harrodsburg. When about half way between Salt River and Harrodsburg he met two gentlemen. It was Sunday morning and they begged him not to go into Harrodsburg with his command, because the Federals were in possession of the town, and had the houses all along the street, that they had every advantage and swore that they would fight till the streets ran with blood before they would give up the town. Gano thanked these men for their kindness, but told them that he and Morgan's men were going to dine there that day and moved on, until, when within less than a quarter of a mile of town, there was a sudden bend in the road which brought them in sight of the town; there they met two other gentlemen, both known by Major Gano. One was old Dr. Smedley, a Union man, and the other (56) was a Confederate; both of them were begging and requesting Gano not to go into the town, that the Federals had the advantage and declared that they would fight to the bitter end, and that they thought that he would suffer considerably if he should go. Gano thanked them for their kindness, but told them that he was going to go on into town, and moved on, knowing that the troops were of the home guard type, and not well-trained soldiers. He marched into the town July 12, 1862, at about 11:30, while the people were assembling at the churches, rode down in front of the old Burton Hotel just across the street on the south side of the Court House, and not a gun was fired. The people had come from out of the churches into the court house yard until there was a large crowd. Gano stood up in his saddle and made them a speech, telling them that they were not going to trouble citizens whatever their political views might be, unless they took up arms against them. He inquired, "Where are those brave men who were going to fight me until the streets ran with blood?" Some one said, "When they heard that you were in one half mile of here they took to their heels and ran out of town across the fields and gardens eight miles away to the Kentucky river. There is no one here to fight you." Gano said, "We are going to take dinner on the Graham Spring Grounds and we want you all, Federal Men and Southern men to get up plenty of provisions and take it down to the grounds," to which they all consented and started for home, and a more plentiful dinner was scarcely ever prepared and partaken of with greater relish by soldiers. One lady, while Gano was seated on his horse in front of the hotel, caught hold of his stirrup leather, weeping as if her heart would break, and said, "They sent my husband off north to prison. (She was a Mrs. Line.) Oh! If you could drive them all out of the state I would be so glad."

After enjoying their dinner, and being greeted by 100 ladies and the Southern men of the country, they decided to move to Lexington. Morgan said, "Gano, take your command and move on so as to tap the Cincinnati and Lexington Railroad between Cynthiana and Paris. A train heavily laden with infantry is coming up that road early tomorrow night to reinforce Lexington, and I want you to capture them." Gano moved out on the road toward Lexington. Some man in Harrodsburg filled one of the soldier's canteen with whiskey and he got drunk, so some of the soldiers found it out and reported it to Major Gano. Major Gano, thinking that some of the others might have whiskey, had his men dressed out in line along the side of the turnpike road and then sent an officer down the line to empty every canteen in the line, telling them that if they only had water in their canteens he would refill them at the next spring they came to. When the officer came to the man who had the whiskey in his canteen, he said, "What are you going to do?" The officer replied, "We are going to empty your canteen." "Why man," he said, "You are pouring out some of the finest old Bourbon you ever saw," and he tried to put his mouth under the stream while the officer was pouring it in the road. Gano had no drunken man in his command that day. About ten o'clock next day, they landed at the farm of John F. Payne, July 13, three miles from Georgetown. Gano camped his men in Payne's woods, who was a Southern man, and proceeded to the house where a colored woman, the cook, informed him that Mr. Payne was in Georgetown, and that Mrs. Payne was visiting a nearby neighbor by the name of West. Mr. Gano sent a message to Mrs. Payne to come home.

In the meantime, the old colored woman sent word to her that the Federals were camped in the woods. Mrs. Payne immediately sent word to her husband at Georgetown to come home at once that the Federal Cavalry was camped in the woods. When Mrs. Payne arrived and saw that it was the Confederates under Major Gano, she said, "Oh, Mr. Gano, what shall I do? I sent word to my husband that the Federals were camped in the woods near here." Gano replied, "That is all right, I would just as soon you had sent that message as any other." Mrs. Payne had an elegant dinner prepared, of which Major Gano partook. In the meantime, Stoddard Johnson, Jr. Payne, (58) Mr. Kelly and several others, all true Southern men, called in at Mr. Payne's residence to meet Major Gano. Major Gano intended that no one should know that he knew which was a Southern man or which was a Northern man, so he took them all as prisoners and put them in the parlor. In the meantime, John Payne, having heard that the Cavalry had camped at his house, had a Provost Marshall to ride out in his buggy and protect his premises. The Provost Marshall was Alec Long, an old school-mate of Gano's, but a Union man. Mr. Payne took the Major to one side and asked him not to trouble Long in any way, that he came here to protect his premises. Gano said, "I will not, but you and Long come into the parlor, I have quite a number of prisoners in there." Just then a young man by the name of Oliver Gaines, the son of Old Oliver Gaines, the livery stable man of Georgetown, came driving up the house in a fine buggy and a pair of horses. He had also been a schoolmate of Major Gano's and Gano knew him well. He drove right up in front of Major Gano without looking up and asked, "Who commands this Cavalry?" Major Gano replied, "I do sir." Gaines said, "I have a written order here for you." Major stepped up and took the order from him and read it. It said, "Officer commanding the cavalry camped at John Payne's residence will proceed with his command down to where the turnpike joins the Frankfort Turnpike, one mile from Georgetown and intercept J.H. Morgan who will bring his command up that road. We will meet him there with all the forces we can muster from Georgetown to help him drive back

Morgan." This order was signed by Stephen F. Gano, Major Gano's uncle. Oliver Gaines, with a startled expression on his face, said, "Why this is Dr. Gano from Texas." Gano replied, "It was Dr. Gano, but Major Gano now." "Well," said Gaines, "how does it happen that you are commanding Federal Cavalry?" Gano replied, "We are not Federals; we are what you call Rebels." By this time Gaines eyes looked about double size and he exclaimed, "What shall I do?" Gano said, "Hitch your horses to that rack and go into the parlor, (59) you will find plenty of company." Gaines said, "Well, if I must, I must," and hitched his horses and went into the parlor. Gano then went into the parlor and said to the room nearly full of men, "You must all take an oath or go with me as prisoners of war." They replied, "What oath do you require of us?" "I require that you shall swear that you will not tell who I am, what kind of troops I am commanding, what number of troops I am commanding, or anything about me." They said, "We will take the oath." Gano made them all stand up in a row in the room and swore them, then told them that they could go. Alec Long and Oliver Gaines went out in the yard and while they were out there Alec Long said, "Oliver, let me ride back to town with you." Oliver said, "Did he say we could go back to town?" and went back to the house and asked Major Gano whether he said he had said that they could go back to town or not. Gano replied, "Yes, you can go anywhere you want to." "And can I take my buggy and horses?" Gano replied, "Yes, Take anything you have except that note." They got into the buggy and rode off at once, and at the toll gate on the Frankfort turnpike they met a body of men who were coming out to reenforce the supposed Federal Cavalry at Paynes residence commanded by Dr. Stephen Gano, an uncle of Major Gano, and Captain Jackson. When Oliver Gaines drove up to the command at the tollgate, Dr. Gano inquired, "Who commands the cavalry at John Payne's residence?" Oliver never opened his mouth, but tried to drive through the command at the gate. Captain Jackson said, "Didn't you hear what Dr. Gano said to you?" He said, "Who commands the cavalry camped at John Payne's residence? Why don't you answer him?" Oliver never spoke one word, still trying to drive through the command, when someone said, "You had just as well let Oliver Gaines alone, he is under oath."

Gano moved down the road to a place called Domereil on the Georgetown and Lexington road. At Domereil he met Henry Moore, an old school teacher to whom he had gone to school when a boy. Moore inquired, "Why, Gano, (60) what are you doing here?" Gano replied, "I am commanding some Confederate Cavalry," Mr. Moore said, "Do you know that your uncle and Captain Jackson are raising all the soldiers they can get in Georgetown to come out here and capture you?" Gano said "Yes, and here they come now up the turnpike from Georgetown." They had gone to Georgetown to put on a show of doing something. They concluded that we were following the Lexington and Georgetown roads, not dreaming that our forces had moved over to Domereil. Gano said to Henry Moore, "I have a message to leave with you for my Uncle." Moore said, "I will deliver it verbatim." "You tell him when he gets here at Domereil, who I am and that I am commanding some Texas Cavalry, that I am not hunting a fight with him, and for him to turn around and go to his home in Georgetown and stay there, and that if he follows me 100 yards from Domereil, and where I am, we will have a battle." "Tell him that I will be over here in the Herndon Woods looking at him. When they reached Domereil, Gano was over in the Herndon Woods. Henry Moore delivered the message to Dr. Gano, telling him who commanded the Confederate Cavalry, and that if they followed him he would ship them, that he was up in the Herndon Woods watching them. Dr. Gano said, "Captain Jackson, what do you say about it?" Captain Jackson replied, "If they are Texas Troops, they know how to fight; they have good horses and good arms. Our forces are mostly home guards, badly mounted, badly armed. If they attack our men, half of them will be killed running through these stake and rider fences, so I think we had better go back, so they turned back to their homes." Major Gano proceeded through the woods from Herndon's Place to Old Dr. Robert Brackenridge's farm, a strong Union Man, the father of Colonel W.C.P. Brackenridge, who afterwards joined the Southern Army. At Dr. Brackenridge's front yard, between his house and the turnpike was a large fine spring.

(61) Gano told his men to dismount and go to the spring and get a drink of water. While they were getting a drink, Gano was sitting on his horse on the turnpike with several other soldiers. Three ladies started from the house and were coming down to the spring to see whether the soldiers were Federals or Confederates. One was Mrs. Brackenridge, wife of W.C.P. Brackenridge, and the other two were daughters of old Dr. Brackenridge. Gano remarked to Lieutenant Murchinson, "Those ladies will recognize me unless I keep my face from them, so I will sit with my face to the opposite side of the road and you do the talking." So when the ladies came, Mrs. Will Brackenridge, formerly a Desha, walked up near the soldiers, rested her arms on the fence, and asked, "What soldiers are these?" Mr. Murchinson replied, "They are our soldiers." "Which side are they on?" "Our side," "Which is your side?" "The right side." She laughed and said, "I believe you are on the right side." She was intensively Southern and the young ladies reported, when they went

back to the house, that Mrs. Brackenridge and the soldiers had some secret signs by which they made known that they were Confederates. But there was no truth in this, as she only guessed at it.

Gano then proceeded with his command down the turnpike road toward Newton until they came to a toll-gate where an Irish woman dashed out and said, "You can't go through here until you pay your toll!" Gano said, "I will pay you with what money I have." She said, "You must give me good money or you can't go through this gate." Gano said, "Don't multiply words, but open the gate! We are going through!" She dashed off into the house. Gano said, "Boys, throw open the gate." Two of the soldiers jumped down and broke the padlock that fastened the pole to the gate, twisting the pole around and splitting the black to which the pole rested, and threw the pole down by the side of the fence in the road. The old toll-gate woman dashed out of the house with a key in her hand, (62) saying, "Why did you break my gate down? Didn't you know I went into the house to get a key?" Gano said, "You should have told me!" During all this conversation there was a man sitting in his buggy at the side of the road, by the name of James Offutt, who was a director of that turnpike road, and a Union Man. One word from him would have passed the soldiers through the gate, but he never opened his mouth. Gano told two of his soldiers to go and take that man as a prisoner. He said, "Put him right behind the command and tell him to follow on, and if he asks where we are going to take him, tell him that you reckon that your commander will take him south. Don't let him come up to me, but keep him right behind the command. In the town of Newton there is a turnpike turning off to the left, which leads to Offutt's home. When you get there, tell him that Major Gano says he may go." When they got there they gave him the message, and he went up the turnpike in a hurry.

Gano moved on about three miles further with his command and stopped in at his father's residence, ordering his men to camp at the big spring where Major Gano got his first drink after he was born. Seated in the yard at Gano's father's residence was his father, grandfather, Dr. Hopson, a minister of the gospel, and Thomas M. All, a minister and a strong Union man. The others were all Southern men. Mr. Hopson had been threatened with arrest by the Federals, and when they saw Major Gano riding down toward the house with his soldiers, Dr. Hopson said, "They are coming to arrest me." Allen said, "Don't you do any talking, let me do all of it." When Major Gano got up in calling distance, he said, "How are you?" His grandfather, the blindest one in the crowd, recognized his voice first and said, "It is Richard."

Major Gano took supper with them, and when about to leave, his mother said, "My son, the Federals are in Georgetown on the west, in Lexington on the south, in Paris on the east and in Cynthiana on the north. You have no chance of escaping; let me (63) hide you away." "Mother," he said, "Don't distress yourself, I came in here with my men and I can go out; we can whip any cavalry command our size and under, and any great big force we can ride around. So have no fears. I didn't come in here to hide, and expect to be seen here on many occasions."

Major Gano was about to proceed down to the Keyser Depot to capture the train as directed by Morgan when a neighbor by the name of Andy Carrol, a stammerer and an intense Southerner, rode up to Major Gano and asked, "Wh-a wha-t, what can I do for you?" Gano said, "Andy, I want some spirits of turpentine." Andy said, "Y-y-you shall have it." Gano said, "Meet me with it on the road to Keyser Station." Andy departed. Gano proceeded with his command and when about half way to Keyser Station, Andy Carrol rode out from under a mulberry tree in the night and said, "H-h-here it is," and delivered two large jugs of spirits of turpentine. Gano proceeded down to the Keyser Station and got there about an hour and a half ahead of the train, had the turpentine poured upon the railroad bridge and set fire to it. The bridge was across an immensely deep ravine. Down in the bottom of that ravine was Keyser's distillery, about 50 yards from the bridge, containing a great many barrels of fine old whiskey. There was a west wind blowing, which blew some of the fire over onto the distillery, and, when the fire reached the whiskey, there was a fire indeed, flames seeming to reach 150 feet into the air. Gano then sent two men with a crow bar down the railroad far enough so that when the train passed they could tear up some of the rails of the road so that the train couldn't back. When the train, loaded with soldiers, stopped at the bridge, Gano demanded a surrender. They had about 400 infantry on the train. One of the officers stuck his head out of the car window and asked, "Whose command is this?" Major Gano replied, "J.H. Morgan's." He heard the officer say to his men, "Johnnie Morgan has got us at last." The engineer tried to back his train, when Gano told them to surrender. Gano said, "Don't do that; the track (64) is torn up; you will upset your train down the embankment and kill all your passengers." The fire had burned somewhat low; the night was very dark.

The soldiers were marched out of the train, stacked their arms on the ground, and then marched down into the woods, where Major Gano paroled them and sent them back to Cincinnati, a distance of about 60 miles, afoot. An officer asked how many soldiers he had. Gano replied, "A hundred and eighty." The officer then began swearing, for he had 400. Gano then moved on with his command toward Georgetown, through the neighborhood where he was born, meeting quite a lot of his Southern friends. They reached the woodland of Dr. Elliot about noon July 15th and camped in Elliots pasture. A poor man from Denton County, Texas, whose mother, when he joined Gano's command had said, "Captain, be sure and bring my boy back," was with them. Gano had replied to his mother, "Mrs. Tannehill (his name was Robert Tannehill), I won't promise to do that; we are going into dangers where life is uncertain, but this I will promise you: If he gets sick or wounded, we will do the very best we can for him." In Elliotts Woods Tannehill had staked his horse out to grass and stood his gun up by the tree and lay down on his blanket to rest. The horse, eating grass, knocked his gun down with his nose. The hammer struck the root of the tree and one barrel of the double barrel gun went off, twelve buckshot passing through Tannehill's lungs. He raised up on his elbow and said, "Oh! God!" and died. Gano sat down beside him on the grass, not able to speak a word of comfort nor to lend him any assistance, and, with tears in his eyes, thought over all the dear mother had said to him. He was buried in the Elliot's Woods. After the war was over, several Confederate Soldiers were gathered up from the neighborhood around and were buried in the Confederate Burial Grounds in the Georgetown Cemetery.

A large crowd had assembled and Colonel W.C.P. Brackenridge was to deliver an address that day, but he didn't get there. General R.M. Gano was elected to deliver the address and did so, paying a beautiful tribute to his old friends and soldiers and Bob Tannehill. The neighbors all around Dr. Elliot's place, together with his family (65) brought food that day, ample provisions to feed all of Gano's men.

In the meantime, Dr. Stephen Gano, Major's Gano's uncle, and Captain Jackson made up their minds to disband their troops and let them go home. Dr. Gano had not informed his men of his and Captain Jackson's intentions not to fight, but ordered them to form in line on the streets in Georgetown near the court house. The men hung back from lining up and said "Dr. Gano, we are not able to fight those men." Dr. Gano replied, "I have determined not to fight and I am going to disband you, but form in line and make a showing." The men formed and then were disbanded. Dr. Stephen Gano retreated to Lexington on horseback. Most of the soldiers struck down the Cincinnati Pike toward Eagle Creek where most of them lived. Some of the Confederates reached Georgetown in time to give pursuit about a mile in the rear down the Cincinnati Pike. The Federal men, not having enough horses to go around, some had to ride behind, making two on one horse and when the Confederates began to chase them some of them fell off, the Confederates thereby capturing several.

J.H. Morgan was coming up the Frankfort pike to George town with his command, and Gano was coming in from Elliot's Farm to meet him. Gano got there first.

As the Southern Soldiers passed the Birch Residence about two miles from Georgetown, a little boy named Milton Birch was sitting upon the front yard fence and when he saw the Confederates pursuing the Federals, he shouted to them, "Go on boys, you will catch them every one."

That night Major Gano camped with his men on the farm of his Uncle, Dr. Stephen F. Gano for the purpose of giving the family better protection that they would otherwise have had. And he slept that night in his uncle's house at the request of his aunt, Mrs. Gano. Before Gano reached the house, some of the soldiers had got around the house and asked for some sugar. Mrs. Gano was giving them sugar out of a barrel in the pantry which was about half full, but hoping to get rid of them, as she had another barrel (66) which had never been opened, she said with a liberal air, "Roll the barrel out here and let them have it all." Just then and old soldier saw through the pantry door another barrel that hadn't been opened, and remarked, "There is another barrel full of sugar in there," Mrs. Gano thought then that all of her sugar was gone, but just then protection came and she was not troubled any more.

(67) The next morning, General J.H. Morgan asked Colonel Gano, as he knew well all the country around Georgetown, if he didn't think that he could capture Sam Thompson, a Federal Officer who had been in command of the soldiers at Georgetown, and had given the Southern sympathizers considerable trouble. Colonel Gano told him that he thought he could, so he took some soldiers and went in pursuit of him. He was acquainted with Mr. Thompson and his wife. She and Colonel Gano were members of the same church. He also knew Thompson's two cousins, Press and Sam Thompson, both of whom were good Southern men, living about one mile from Georgetown. Colonel Gano supposed that the commander, Sam Thompson, would flee to the house of his cousins, and ask the protection of them, hoping that he wouldn't be found there. The Colonel rode up to the house of Press Thompson and, after greeting him, said, "Press, I have a question to ask of you. Is Sam Thompson in your house? If you say yes, I will let you bring him out to me, and I will take him as a prisoner of war, but if you say no, I will search your house and every room and closet in

it." Press Thompson replied, "He is here." "Bring him out," said Colonel Gano. Which he did, and turned him over as a prisoner. Col. Gano took him to town and put him under guard of two of his Texas soldiers. The next morning, his wife, Mrs. Thompson, said, with tears in her eyes, "Brother Gano, I have a request to make of you. You have placed my husband under some Texas soldiers; I am afraid they will kill him, and I want you to take him away from them and put him under Kentucky soldiers." Colonel Gano replied, "I can't grant your request, and if you knew what you were asking, you wouldn't want me to. The Texas soldiers have no prejudice against your husband and will treat him just as directed. The Kentuckians have been persecuted by him and would probably like some excuse to shoot him." She said, "Let the Texas soldiers keep him then."

(68) Morgan with his entire command moved off toward Cynthiana for the purpose of attacking the Federals at that place. Some young men in the neighborhood, Gaines, Hill, Roswell and others had started out to join Colonel Gano's Command, but, not knowing where the Federal's lines were, they ran upon a picked named Smith. He ordered them to halt, and they, thinking that he was a Federal Picket, charged him and while firing at him they killed his horse. Smith fought with desperation, and one of the boys, young Roswell, took to his heels and ran back home. The other boys, finding out that Smith was a Confederate, went with him into Morgan's command and joined them and went on into the Cynthiana fight with them, not yet being attached with Gano's men, but moving along with Morgan's command. When they were within a mile and a half of Cynthiana, Morgan said to Colonel Gano, "Take your command and go up the Licking River to the ford and cross there, one mile and a half above the town, and attack Cynthiana on the east, while I will go down on the Lexington Road, cross the bridge just at the edge of Cynthiana and attack the Federals on the South." The Federals had their artillery stationed at the court house. Colonel Gano went around as directed, crossed the river at the ford, capturing half a dozen pickets that were stationed out there, moved over on to the Millersburg pike and entered Cynthiana on the east. Just as he got to the edge of the town on the top of a high place in the street which overlooked the street from there to the court house, nearly half a mile distant, the firing commenced. Colonel Grenfell, an adjutant of General Morgan's, came dashing through the city to Gano to bring some orders. Gano received the (69) orders and noticed some blood on the back of Grenfell's neck. Gano said, "Colonel, you are wounded on the back of the neck." He put his hand up and rubbed the blood off on his hand and remarked, "It's only a scratch," and went on

back to his commander. Colonel Gano was fighting down the main street in the direction of the court house when he saw a command with its officers waving white hankerchiefs at him. He began to think he had been firing at his own men. Firing ceased and the men with the white handkerchiefs ran rapidly up the street to Gano. He waited until they were within probably about 75 yards of him, when the officer said, "You are firing on our own men." Gano said, "Which side are you on?" He replied, "We are Federals." Gano said, "We are Confederates; lay down your guns! Surrender." Instead of surrendering they threw their guns down and beat a hasty retreat to their command. They laid down their arms, but didn't lay them down in good style. Gano and his command continued firing as they were scampering down the street as fast as they could go. We will let Ben Huffman, who was a schoolmate of Col. Gano's and a warm southerner, describe the fight. Ben happened to be in town on business, when the Federal Authority issued a command that every man in the town should take up arms and help defend the city. Ben said to himself, "I will never fire on Southern men," but they put a gun in his hands and told him to take it and use it. Ben ran into a hardware store and went upstairs where he could watch the fight. About this time the artillery at the court house opened fire upon Gano and his men to drive them back. Ben said, after the fight was all over and he went home, that those Texican Deranges could do the best fighting of any men in the country. He said as they went down the main street in Cynthiana, while he was sitting in the window upstairs in the hardware store, that every time (70) the Federals would fire the cannons at Gano's men, they would divide and let the balls pass, and then close up and got to fighting again. Ben Huffman said, "I didn't know that a Texas fellow that went to school with me could ever put up such a fight as that."

The Confederates captured so many men that they filled the court house to overflowing with prisoners, captured all their artillery and horses. Colonel Gano saw a Federal Colonel dash down the street in a southeasterly direction toward Paris. He gave pursuit and chased the Federal officer out to the edge of town where he saw that his horse could outrun the Colonel's, and was sure that he would capture him, but coming to a fence at the edge of the field, the colonel's horse leaped the fence, and Gano's horse wouldn't try to jump it, but stopped. Gano fired his pistol at the colonel and saw him throw up his right hand as if the ball had struck him, but continued running, making his escape. Gano went on back to town. Gano had a cousin living in Cynthiana, a man of considerable influence, but a Union man. His name was Thomas Ware. He was taking no part in the war, but when they ordered every man in town to take up arms and defend the city, Ware took his gun and went down to the railroad depot, went upstairs where some other Federal soldiers were stationed to fire through the windows when the Confederates came through that part of the town. Several Confederate soldiers hid behind some cars close to the depot and were fired at by the men in the second story window of the depot. The Confederate soldiers fired up at the man in the windows and a ball hit Thomas Ware, fracturing his jaw and going up through his brain and out the top of his head, which killed him. Ware was carried up to his home and laid out in the parlor. Gano went up to his residence and saw his wife and four daughters. He told them how much he regretted that his cousin had been killed. They said he had no business taking a gun; he was not a soldier. Gano told them that he was not in that part of the town when he (71) was killed, and that a husband and a father had no business going into the fight that he was not in the difficulty. They said, "We know that you were not to blame." Thomas Ware had a son-in-law in the city who was a lawyer, and was captured in the fight and locked up in the court house. Gano went down to the court house, it was densely packed, and called loudly, "Mr. Ward." Ward answered over in the dense crown. Colonel Gano said, "Press through the crowd and come out the door." He did so. Gano told him that his father-in-law had been killed and that the family needed his assistance. "I am going to parole you and let you go home and protect the family," which Gano did, and he also placed several soldiers around their home to keep anyone from molesting them in their sorrow.

Before the town was captured, while Morgan and his men were pressing across the bridge in the face of the heavy firing, Gaines, Hill, and some of the new recruits got in an old blacksmith shop in the street and were firing through the windows. J.H. Morgan rode up to the door of the blacksmith shop and said angrily "Come out of there every one of you, and press on toward the court house." They all came out and fought their way. Gaines said afterwards that he didn't know which was going to kill him, Morgan or the Yankees. The following day, Morgan and his command moved on toward Paris, the County seat of Bourbon County, Kentucky. In Paris, Colonel Gano met Dr. Hopson, who had dressed the wounded hand of the Colonel whom Gano had shot when his horse jumped the fence. After the war was over that wounded colonel joined the Christian Church of which Gano was a member and had been ordained a minister. He wrote to Gano and asked him to come there and hold a protracted meeting.

Morgan and his men moved on from Paris to Winchester. (71)

There were some Confederate Prisoners in the second story of the Court House, one of them was Will Webb, a young lawyer, and he was guarded by another lawyer, who was a Union Man. Webb saw through the court house windows the Confederates coming in, and he said to the lawyer who held him prisoner, "You had better give me that gun and let me guard you awhile." The man on guard had not seen the Confederates, so he said, "What do you mean?" Webb replied, "The Confederates are in town and I want your gun." The man looked out the window, and, seeing the Confederates coming, he handed the prisoner his gun and said, "Now, Webb, I want you to take me and take care of me; you know I have treated you kindly."

Then to Danville Gano and his men moved out on the Harrodsburg Road over in the direction of Perryville to participate in the Perryville Battle. At a two-story residence several miles from the said pike they came upon a pretty heavy force of Federal Cavalry, and gave chase, for they made no fight. The Federals retreated in the direction of Perryville, until they came upon a heavier force of their Cavalry, where they formed a line of battle and withstood Morgan and his men. Gano, with his brigade, formed across the main road leading up toward Perryville. Colonel Chenault with his regiment on the right of the road. Colonel Cluke on the left. They had some pretty brisk fighting, Gano losing quite a number of his men, and his horse was killed also, which reared and fell back, Gano jumping off unhurt, but his saddle was broken all to pieces. A horse in the Federal lines which had had his rider shot off came galloping down the road toward the Southern lines, which Gano mounted and rode through the rest of the fight. The horse's ears were cropped off and the saddle was not at all suited to Gano's notion, but still they pressed on, driving the Federal Cavalry back up to their infantry.

The fight was ended for the day and Morgan, with his command, withdrew over to the Harrodsburg Pike. Gano with his brigade formed along the side of the pike, expecting to fight again within an hour or two.

Colonel Gano rode over to a house about a half mile distant, belonging to a man by the name of McLain, a well-to-do farmer who was known to have furnished some horses to a Federal Cavalry to go against Morgan on one occasion. Gano called him out and asked him if he could furnish him a horse to ride that evening. (72) That he would either buy his horse or ride him during the fight in the evening and return him to him the next day, as he had another horse back in the wagon train that would be up by that time. McClain said, "I have no horse." Gano told a negro man to get over the fence and see if there was a horse in the barn. Gano said, "Get over in the yard and look in that carriage house." The negro did so and said, "Yes sir, there is a fine grey horse." Gano ordered him to bring him out and put his saddle on him. Which he did. McLain said, "That is my wife's horse; you can't take him." Gano said, "Mr. McLain, I will ride your horse this evening and, if he is not killed, I will return him to you tomorrow, or, if you prefer, I will pay you for him now. If he should get shot, I will pay you for him tomorrow." McLain said, "You can't take that horse." Gano said, "I have already got him and I am going to do just as I told you." Major Dunlap, a grandson of McLain, and a Southern soldier in Gano's command rode up at this moment and said, "Grandfather, this is General Gano, and whenever he tells you he will do a certain thin, he will do it." McLain said, "Get out of my sight, I disinherit you forever!" Dunlap said, "Grandfather, I was only here to do you a favor and let you know that you could depend upon every word General Gano tells you. I am not here asking any interest in your estate and I don't care for any." Gano rode the horse up to his command. McLain went up to Morgan's headquarters and said, "General Morgan, one of your soldiers has taken my horse and insulted me." Morgan said, "Who was it?" McLain said it was General Gano. Morgan replied, "Now I know you have told me a lie. General Gano is a Christian gentleman and never abuses anybody, and never would ride a horse that was pressed; he always purchases his horses." McLain said, "Well, he had got my horse." Morgan said, "Well, go get your horse." McLain said, "I can't get my horse; I am not armed and Gano is." Morgan said, "Here, I will load you a pistol." McLain replied, "I don't want your pistol; I don't want to fight, but I want my horse." Morgan said, "Well, don't pester me any more (73) you have already told me a falsehood." McLain came down to where Gano was on his horse, walked up to the horse's head, and took hold of the bridle bits and said, "Morgan said for me to come and get my horse." General Gano said, "Have you a written order from General Morgan for this horse?" He said, "No sir, I haven's, but he told me to come and get my horse."

Gano said, "Well, you can't get his without a written order, so go back and get one." But McLain held to the horse's bits. Gano said, "You let go those bits and leave here." McLain still held to the bits. Gano said, "Cal (Cal Crozier from Dallas, Texas), take this old man a prisoner and take him up up there in the woods in the shade of the trees and keep him until he gets in his right mind. You will know when he comes to himself by the fact that he will want to go home, then turn him loose and let him go home." Cal rode forward, took the old man by the breast of his coat and said, "Come with me." McLain said, "You let me alone, I will go home right now." Gano couldn't return the next day to the neighborhood of McLain's but offered to turn the horse over to a nephew of McLain's who was a strong Union Man. But he wouldn't receive the horse, for he said if the Union men found that it had been left there by a Confederate they would take him away from him. Gano then turned the horse over to McLain's grandson, who was in his brigade, and told him if he got an opportunity to turn the horse over to his grandfather, and if he didn't get an opportunity he reckoned his grandson had just as well ride him as anyone else.

Morgan with his men rode over to Lancaster and joined Bragg's Army, which was moving in the direction of Crab Orchard, followed by Buell's Army. Morgan's men were formed on the southeast side of Lexington running along the brow of the hill, with Gano's command in the front of the center of Buell's Army and extending down to the Baptist Church on the right. Bragg sent word to this Cavalry command to hold their position at all hazards till night fell. Gano had a brother, Frank Gano, who had just joined (74) his command a few days before with a young friend Turpin from near Covington. They believed that in order to hold their position most of the cavalry would get killed. Frank Gano, thinking that he would certainly be killed, said to Turpin, "I shall not live through this fight, but when you see father and mother, you tell them that I loved them till the last, and that I loved my country and was willing to die for it." Turpin said "Frank, don't leave your message with me, I am going to be killed, but if you live through this battle tell my father and mother everything that you have been telling me." An Old Confederate soldier lying on the grass holding his old gray mare by the bridle and disposed to make fun of the boys, said, "Boys, if I get killed, just kill my old gray mare and lay my head on her side and leave me there." The boys got mad at the old man's sport and discussed the subject of death no longer. Gano with his surgeon and son rode down to the old Baptist church to take a view of his army from that position. Buell's army, seeing them there, fired a piece of artillery at them. It struck a plank fence around the church near where they were sitting on their horses, scattering splinters about in all directions. The doctor's horse wheeling around, came very near throwing him off, as he was sitting sideways, and he said hurriedly, "General Gano, we are doing no fighting here, suppose we ride back just over the brow of the hill." Buell's army, seeing this long line of men on foot, which was the cavalry dismounted and of course all over the hill, supposed that Bragg's Army was there and they didn't advance upon them that night. Next morning, as Bragg's Army had gone on to Crab Orchard, ten miles away, Morgan had a permit to return to Lexington with his soldiers.

As General Morgan and General Gano were standing around a fire, parching some corn in the ashes, the Federals fire a piece of artillery at them, which sent a ball in the fire between them, scattering ashes and coals about.

Gano and Morgan, losing their appetite for parched corn, mounted their horses and rode off in (75) in the direction of Lexington, Morgan telling Gano to remain behind his rear guard with about 100 men and then follow on down the Lexington pike. Gano stationed his hundred men in a cornfield near the pike, the corn was high enough to hide the men when dismounted, and he sent a true man named George Witton from Tarrant County, Texas, back in Lancaster with instructions to see what the enemy were doing, and if they should give pursuit for him to proceed down this pike close to this cornfield so as to bring them within range of Gano's guns. Some of the Federal Cavalry, seeing Witton up in the edge of the town, pursued him. They were about eight abreast when he came galloping down the pike. He would wheel into a fence corner, fire into them and turn out into the road, galloping down a piece further and repeat this method of fighting. When he got down to the cavalry which was stationed in the corn field, the Federals seemed to suspect a trap, for they turned their horses and rode back into Lancaster. Gano asked Witton why he used that method of firing on the Federals when there were so many of them firing on one. He said, "I had the advantage of them; they had only one to shoot at, and when I fired up the road, there were so many, I was sure to hit somebody."

(76) Gano with his men followed from Lancaster in the rear of Morgan's command in the direction of Lexington, overtaking him on the road, Morgan telling Gano to take his men down one turn-pike in Lexington and he would take his men down another. The Federal Cavalry had camped on the Fair Grounds, just in the city of Lexington. Morgan got there first and when Gano and his men reached Lexington, coming in from the opposite side, Morgan and the Federals were fighting. Some of the Federals fired upon Gano; he returned the fire, killing and wounding some of the Federals. Several of his men were wounded also. The Federals had surrendered to General Morgan just about the time General Gano had fired upon them. There would have been no need of Gano's firing if they hadn't fired first. George Morgan from Tennessee was shot in this fight, the ball entering his mouth and passing out the back of the neck...he died from the effects of the wound. A large mulatto negro among the Yankees, riding a fine gray horse, concluded that he wouldn't surrender and dashed across the fair grounds to the turnpike road, and through the gate leading down to the city of Lexington. Some of Gano's men fired at him and he fell dead in the road off his horse. A man by the name of Columbus Estes in Gano's command, a brave soldier who lived in Collin County, Texas, was shot in the jaw bone, the ball passing out the back of his neck, not striking the spine. The command thought that

he was mortally wounded and wanted to leave him for treatment, but he wouldn't submit to that, but got a buggy and one horse and followed behind the command every day, driving his own horse, having his wound dressed every night by the surgeon, and when they reached Tennessee, they sent him back to his home in Collin County. He recovered, and when the war was over and Gano became a minister, General Gano baptised him and his sister at Brackenridge in Collin, County, Texas.

General's Gano's father and grandfather were living at their home together in Bourbon County, Kentucky. They owned a yellow negro named Ike, who (77) ran away and joined the Federal Army, taking two good mules belonging to William Conn, Grandfather of General Gano, which he turned over to the Yankee Army. The negro left his wife at William Conn's residence and ventured through there one day to visit her, armed with a six shooter. Mr. Conn, hearing that he was at the cabin, went down there to drive him off the place. On entering the cabin, he said, "What do you mean by coming back to this place, sir?" "I came back to see my wife," he said. "Well, you had better get off this place as quickly as you can and never put your foot on it again, and if you can get Colonel Metcalfe to haul your wife into town, you can have her," Mr. Conn replied. The negro said, "I will come to see my wife as often as I want to." Mr. Conn, being unarmed, picked up a fire poker near the fireplace, and the negro, fearing to draw his six-shooter, jumped out the back window into the orchard. Mr. John Allen Gano, fearing some trouble might arise at the cabin, took a double barrelled shot gun and walked down there, reaching the cabin at about the time the negro jumped out the window and fled across the orchard. Colonel Metcalfe, a Federal officer, was in command of Paris. The negro went to Paris and reported to Colonel Metcalfe that Mr. Conn had struck him with an iron poker, for no other reason than that he belonged to the Union Army. Mr. Conn didn't strike the negro with an iron poker, but struck at him as he went out the window, the poker hitting the window facing.

Colonel Metcalfe, the Federal commander in Paris, sent a Dutch Captain with a company of cavalry out to Mr. Conn's residence to arrest him and bring him to Paris. Mr. Conn and John Allen Gano and his wife, who was formerly Miss Conn, were sitting in their room at the residence, when the house was surrounded by the cavalry. The Dutch Captain went to the door of the room where they were sitting and asked if Mr. William Conn was present. Mr. Conn replied, "That is my name, sir." The Dutchman said, "I am sent out here to arrest you and bring you back to Paris." Mr. Conn said, "Who sent you to arrest me?" "Colonel Metcalfe." Mr. Conn said, "You tell

Colonel that if he (78) has any business with me he can come out here and see me, I am not going in there to see him." The captain replied, "I have orders to take you to him dead or alive, and I am here to take you so there is no use in your resisting." Mr. Conn replied, "I suppose you have enough men to kill me, but you haven't men enough to take me alive. I am not going to surrender." Mr. Conn was a very determined man though about 80 years of age. Mr. Gano took his father-in-law, Mr. Conn, into an adjoining room and said, "Mr. Conn, I don't blame you for not surrendering to that old Dutchman, but we can avoid that without your forcing them to shoot. I will just give these fellows plenty of bacon and cabbage…give them a good dinner…and then hitch up my buggy and horse and take you with me into Paris. We will go to Metcalfe's office, but you will not be taken a prisoner. The Dutchman can follow along behind, if they want to."

Mr. Gano then proposed to the captain to give them their dinner, and he and Mr. Conn would go into town with them. They ate very heartily of the bacon and cabbage, and Mr. Gano took his horse and buggy, and he and Mr. Conn started to town, the company following on behind. Mr. Gano said to Mr. Conn, "Now, I am going to have some fun; those Dutchmen are so full of bacon and cabbage that they can't stand very much trotting." Mr. Gano let his horse out at a tolerable brisk trot, the company trotting on behind, trying to keep up, until their faces turned red and the captain said, "Halt!" Gano reined up his horse and the captain said, "What makes you drive so fast? You will trot us to death." Gano said, "Oh! are we driving too fast for you? I will drive a little slower." They rode on in a very slow trot for some time, then he said to Mr. Conn, "Now, we will have some more fun." And he let his horse out a little faster and faster by degrees, until they all got jolted up again, and the captain yelled out again, "Halt!" and came up and said, "What in the devil makes you go so fast? You will trot us to death I tell you!" Gano said, "My horse moves briskly; I will drive slow again." He drove slow again, and then said, "Well, we will give them another jolt"; and they did so (79) and were called down again in the same manner. They then reached Paris and drove up to Metcalfe's office on the court house square. Metcalfe's regiment was camped just below the town across a stream called Stony, and the Southern men about Paris had heard that Metcalfe had sent out men to arrest Mr. Conn and Mr. Gano, so they organized over 200 men armed with shotguns and pistols who had gone into Paris on different roads, and some of them who were living there. They elected a man by the name of William Rogers as their Captain, and were stationed around in all the stores. When they saw a buggy come in with Mr. Gano and Mr. Conn escorted by the

Dutch Company, Rogers sent orders around to his men that whenever they saw any Federal Officer start with Gano and Conn to the jail, a company of six men located near Metcalfe's regiment would charge up the pike and the men from all the stores and houses would pour in their shot from their double barrel shot guns, and they would slay them all. Metcalfe and his men knew nothing of this arrangement. When Gano and his father-in-law walked into his office the negro who caused all this trouble was there to be used as witness. Metcalfe asked, "Is Mr. William Conn present?" Conn said, "That is my name, sir." "Well," said Metcalfe, "You are accused of striking one of our men with an iron poker; is it true?" Conn replied," I struck that negro there." Metcalfe replied, "Don't you know it is a very serious offence to strike a Federal soldier, sir?" Conn replied, "Wouldn't you do it if a negro was to insult you?" Metcalfe replied, "I will have to fine you $500.00." Mr. Conn replied, "I wouldn't pay you a dollar to save your life." Metcalfe said, "Mr. Conn, you will have to pay this $500.00 or go to Northern prisons." Mr. Conn replied, "I suppose you have force enough to take me to Northern Prisons, but you can't rob me like you have been robbing these other men around here; I won't pay you a dollar." Mr. Gano, who had baptised Metcalfe's wife and mother, supposed that he might reach him by some measure, so he took him in an adjoining room and said (80) "Colonel Metcalfe, my father-in-law is an old man, and has only only one child in the world, and that is my wife. If he were to be sent to prison, she would go also, and so would I." Metcalfe replied, "Well, he will have to go or pay that $500." Mr. Gano said, "If you will never let him know anything about it, I will pay you that $500., but he means just what he says and he wouldn't pay it to save his life." Metcalfe replied, "I will never let him know anything about it." Gano gave him a check for $500.00 Metcalfe went into the other room where Mr. Conn was sitting and said, "Mr. Conn, you are an old man and if you were to be sent to Northern Prisons it would kill you; I am going to turn you loose and let you go home." Mr. Conn replied, "I told you that you would never get a dollar of my money." When Gano and Conn got into their buggy and returned home there was no such slaughter in Paris that day as was expected.

Kirby Smith was then in Lexington, Kentucky commanding a division of the Southern Army that had whipped the Federals out at Richmond, Kentucky, in which fight Colonel Metcalfe's regiment participated, but, getting whipped, they fled out of Lexington down the Cynthiana Pike and an old man by the name of Sidemer, living near the pike road and between Lexington and Cynthiana, was standing in the toll gate and saw Metcalfe's

Cavalry fleeing, but seeing no one after them, he said, "The wicked fleeth when no man pursueth." General Smith asked General Gano if he couldn't proceed down to Maysville on the Ohio River and capture that town: there were more than 400 men there that wanted to join the Southern Army but could not get out on account of the Federals. Gano said he could, so he took his brigade and moved down to Maysville.

When he got to within then miles of Maysville, he passed through a little town called Mayslick, where the people told him that the soldiers in Maysville had all the advantage, that they were in possession of the entire town and would fire on him from the houses, but Gano moved on with his command, until within four miles of Maysville (81); Here he came onto the little town of Washington, where the Federal Pickets were stationed. He charged them and captured several, some escaping to Maysville, giving the alarm, and when in about two miles of Maysville, some friends informed him, who were Southern sympathizers, that the Federals were in there with pretty strong forces, had possession of the houses and would fire upon him from the windows and doors and asked him not to go into Maysville. Gano thanked them for their information, but informed them then that he had come to take Maysville and he was going to do it. He rode with his command down into Maysville and turned up main street, but he saw no armed men, so he inquired, "Where is an officer to surrender the city to me." A citizen replied, "When the pickets brought the news that you were coming to take the town the soldiers fled across the Ohio River into Aberdeen, a little town across the river." Gano and his men could see them planting their artillery in the little town of Aberdeen as if they were going to sheel Maysville. Gano said if they do fire any artillery into this town, we will go up the river here two miles to a ford, cross the river and take an Ohio Town…but they never fired a gun. Gano said to the citizens, "Somebody has to surrender this town to me; where is your mayor?" They showed him up to the mayor's office and he very nicely surrendered the city, asking protection for the citizens. Gano marched out of the town with about 400 recruits for the Southern Army and a few Federal Prisoners. They slept that night not far from Maysville, and the next day moved on through Mayslick and on to the Blue Lick neighborhood, gaining recruits from Mayslick and all along the road, and in the evening before sunset, they came to the residence of Colonel Metcalfe, a stone house with some outhouses, one a warehouse, and a farm of several hundred acres, belonging to the said Colonel Leondis Metcalfe. Gano said, "This is a good place to camp," remembering the Five Hundred dollars he had taken away from his father. Mrs. Metcalfe invited Gano and his staff to stay in the house that night. She prepared them a good supper, night's lodging and breakfast (82). But before night, a soldier came into the house and said, "General Gano, did you know there was a barrel of whiskey out here in the warehouse and the men have found it out, and if you are not careful there will be some drunken men in our company tonight." Gano went out to the warehouse, had the barrel of whiskey rolled out into the road, knocked the head of the barrel in and let the contents run down the wagon tracks by a number of horse tracks. An old Confederate soldier, standing by, remarked with a twinkle in his eye, "General Gano, would you have any objections to an old Confederate Soldiers filling his canteen out of these horse tracks?" That night Gano fed over 2500 head of horses out of the oats and corn belonging to Colonel Metcalfe, and in the morning, before they left, they took several of Metcalfe's best horses and left their old sore backs and lame ones in exchange. So you must rest assured that Gano got back more than his grandfather's fine. Gano returned safely from the captured city on the Ohio River without the loss of any of his men. Colonel Wadsworth, who was a Kentucky Congressman in company with Metcalfe, was in command of those forces in Maysville that fled across the Ohio River. General Gano marched on into Lexington and turned his prisoners over to General Smith.

George Morgan, a Federal Officer stationed at Cumberland Gap, in command of the Federal Forces, when he found that the Confederates were about to invade Kentucky with full forces, determined to evacuate Cumberland Gap and cross with his forces over the Ohio River, General Kirby Smith ordered General J.H. Morgan to proceed out to East Kentucky and in front of George Morgan and hinder and delay him all he could until General Humphrey Marshall could reach them and then they would have forces sufficient to whip his Army. Gano with his command took possession of one of the roads along which George Morgan's army was proceeding, while J.H. Morgan would get a nearby position and make as strong a stand as he could. The (83) Federals would come up into shooting distance and they would fire on them and continue firing until they brought up sufficient force to drive them away, then they would fall back to another position and fire on them again in the same way. Every one of the skirmishes would delay George Morgan's command which was the object of Gano's fighting. But they had a number of heavy bush fights with some losses to the Federals, but Gano's losses were light, because he would always get in a strong position and would have cover. They were formed to retreat one cay, and one of his men, being hungry, requested Gano to let him have permission to stop in at a little house on the roadside and have some bread cooked. Gano gave him permission but told him to keep his eye open and not stay too far behind. While the good woman was cooking him some bread, he saw some Federals coming up the road some distance from the house. He hurried the woman up all he could, and when she gave him the bread, the Federals had got within shooting distance. He pocketed his bread, mounted his horse and dashed down the road. The Federals sent some bullets after him, but neither he nor his horse was struck. He said he acted a fool to stay so long, but he was awful hungry.

Every day, while these skirmishes were going on for the purpose of delaying George Morgan, the Southern forces were necessarily awaiting the arrival of Marshall, but he never got there. Gano sent runners to him several times asking him to hurry up, but all the reply he got was, "Check the enemy all you can until I get there." His command didn't seem to move any faster than Morgan's and he never was able to get in front of him. J.H. Morgan's men got up a little song on the strength of that raid. The chorus to which was, "If you don't want to fight just jin the infantry." And the Infantry boys retaliated by changing the chorus, which was, "If you don't want to fight just jin the cavalry." But we had a very lively time playing in front of George Morgan's Command, and no doubt he concluded that we were doing the fighting for the fun of it, so we had to let George Morgan go to the Ohio River.

(84) While Kirby Smith invaded Kentucky he passed with his army on the way to Richmond, Kentucky, through a place known as the Big Hill. General Bull Nelson, commanding the Federals, was sent with his command into Richmond to meet Kirby Smith, and drive his cavalry back, not permitting them to enter Richmond. General Gano had a friend, and old schoolmate by the name of Wharton Moore, who lived with his sister-in-law, Mrs. Billy Moore, near Russell's Cave. Wharton was not in the army, not taking any part in the war, but was known as a determined Union Man. His sister-in-law and family, with whom he lived, were resolute Confederates. Wharton Moore was in the city of Lexington when the Federals passed by Mrs. Moore's residence, and they, knowing her to be a Southern woman, took her carriage horses, moving on in the direction of Richmond. When Wharton Moore came home and found that they had taken his sister-in-law's horses, he determined to recover them. He went to Lexington and got letters from Old Dr. Robert Brackenridge and Colonel Goodlow, men of high authority among the Federals, to General Nelson, asking him to return to Mr. Moore his sister-in-law's horses. Reaching General Nelson in the town of Richmond, he presented his letters, and got an order from General Nelson for the horses to be returned to him. The next day he had his sister-

in-law's horses down at General Nelson's headquarters, and was about to return home, but learning that General Kirby Smith was coming over the hiss and that General Nelson was going out to meet him and capture him and his army, he asked General Nelson to allow him to go as an aid on his staff, as he had never been in a battle and desired very much to witness one. Nelson gave him his permission.

There was an old preacher living the valley just below the Big Hill and some of Kirby Smith's advanced cavalry passed his house and became engaged in fighting the Federal Calvary just about a quarter of a mile below. The fighting was very brisk. Some more of Smith's Cavalry, passing by this old preacher's house asked him if he had any milk they could drink. He replied, "Yes, there is a churn full of butter milk just churned," and (85) while they with their cups were emptying the churn, the Old Preacher, who was a Southern Sympathizer, said, with tears in his eyes, "Boys, how can you stand drinking buttermilk and listening at the rattling of guns down the road, knowing that your men are being killed." Some of the boys laughed, "Ha! Ha!" and said, "That's just the cavalry, wait till the infantry gets there and you will hear some shooting." The old preacher told this story to General Gano himself, after the war was over, and he said, "Judging by the firing, I thought all the men on both sides were killed."

Smith's men moved on down the valley toward Richmond till all the forces were engaged, and Nelson's men, retreating, were driven from the field, leaving many dead upon the ground, whom the Federals buried. When Nelson's forces were driven from the field, Wharton Moore fled in terror, and in such haste that he never could get back to his sister-in-law's horses, neither could he flee down to the turnpike road leading to the Kentucky river, for the Southerners had them cut off from the pike, so Wharton left his own saddle horse and fled on foot down to the cliff by the brink of the river, and swimming across the river he climbed up the cliff on the other side of the river with all possible haste for home, with bullets striking the rocks around him. He reached the top of the cliff without being wounded, then turned across the woodland toward home, running until he would get out of breath, then he would lay down on the grass, and, still hearing the firing, he would strike up at a run again, until, out of breath again, he would sink down on the ground. He finally reached Lexington without any of his horses and all of his muscles so sore that he could scarcely walk. He informed Gano of all this himself, and told him that he never wanted to see another battle; and he never did.

After the battle of Richmond, while Gano was riding through the city of Lexington with his command, there being a great crowd from the

(86) city and country on the street rejoicing over the great Confederate victory, Mrs. Billy Moore of near Russell's Cave, was in the crowd with her daughter, Mary, and having known Gano from his childhood, being members of the same church, she said when she saw him riding at the head of his command, "Why, there is Brother Gano; if he was down here I would kiss him." Gano dismounted from his horse, handed his bridle reins to Lieutenant Wall, his aid, telling him to lead on, and he turned through the crowd to greet his many friends, kissing Mrs. Moore and her daughter Mary, and all the ladies in the crowd thought that they must treat him likewise, and it has never been known horn many women he kissed, but Gano took a pain in the back of his neck from so much stooping, and when he returned to his command Lieutenant Wall said to him, "You had too big a job on hand, you ought to have commissioned me to have helped you out." Gano replied, "For the first time in my life I got tired of kissing and took a pain in the back of my Neck."

This remark was repeated to Miss Mary Moore, as General Gano had moved his command out on her farm and camped near her residence. The next morning she said to General Gano, "Never mind sir, I heard what you said." Gano said, "What could it have been Miss Mary? I certainly said nothing to hurt you." She said, "You said you got tired kissing the ladies and I was one of them." But just then General Gano's father, mother, sister and many cousins and friends in the neighborhood came up to see him. Gano and his command was drilling on the ground which the crowd was viewing when a messenger on horseback from Lexington came with an order from General Smith to General Gano, telling him to move with his command out to Eastern Kentucky to intercept George Morgan, who was coming through from Cumberland Gap. General Gano ordered his command to break up camp and get ready to move with his command out to Eastern Kentucky to intercept George Morgan. General Gano ordered his command to break up camp and get ready to move in 30 minutes. The friends and relatives who were visiting the command inquired "What does this mean?" Gano replied, "I am going out to meet George Morgan from Cumberland Gap." Then the ladies began to cry, for they could not realize how a man could go out to battle without the probability that (87) he would be killed. They all kissed General Gano goodbye, Mary Moore one of the number, although, She had just said two hours before, "I won't trouble you with another one of my kisses," but the impulses of their warm Southern hearts moves them on occasions like this. Oh, it was touching indeed when General Gano bid adieu to his parents, sister, and loving friends.

Russell's Cave, near Mrs. Moore's residence was quite a noted place, and barbecues, public speeches, and political discussions were frequently held there. It was at this place that Casis M. Clay and Sam Brown, two noted men of Kentucky had their fight and Clay cut Brown so badly with his Bowie knife. (88) Gano, with Morgan's entire command, was camped near a church in Tennessee on a hill not many miles from Snow's Hill. Gano was writing in his tent when one of his soldiers came to the tent and remarked, "General, come out here; here is a man from Grigby's regiment who has beat Holsell jumping, and we don't want him to go back and brag that he has beat our regiment." Gano replied, "I am busy now." Holsell said, "Please come and make just one jump." Gano laid down his pen and went out and made one jump, jumping about three inches over Grigby's man, "He jumped and jumped, but never could get up to Gano's jump." One of Gano's men remarked to Grigby's man, "You need not jump yourself to death; if you were to jump over Gano's jump, he would just come out here and beat you again." The man inquired, "Hos far can Gano jump?" They replied, "We don't know, but he can jump about two or three inches over any other man."

Morgan went out to meet a heavy force of Federal Cavalry in Tennessee not far from Snow's Hill. The Federal Cavalry dismounted and formed along a line of Worm Fences. Morgan ordered Gano with his men to attack the Federals' right on our left, who were lying behind a stake and rider fence. Gano charged upon the hill toward the fence, bullets firing in the thicket in their front while Morgan was moving upon the side of the hill to attack the Federals on their left. As Gano's men moved up the hill, a little rabbit jumped up out of the grass and ran into a thicket. One of Gano's officers remarked, "Run cottontail, if I hadn't any more reputation at stake than you have, I would run too." Before they reached the fence a bullet passed through the head of Stephen Gano, a cousin of General Gano, who was visited by General Gano after the thing was over, but was stiff and cold in death. Gano drove the Federals from the stake and rider fence, and his men were clamoring over the fence to capture them when a tremendous yell arose from the Federals. Reinforcements from the woods about a quarter of a mile back, composed of infantry, cavalry, and artillery, had arrived. Just then an order came up the line (89) from General Morgan to General Gano to fall back immediately, which they did, having won the fight as far as it went, but had lost several men. The Federals' loss was heavier than the Confederates, notwithstanding the protection they had from the fence most of the time. It was a terrific though brief fight.

While Morgan and Duke were both absent from the command, Gano was in command of the entire cavalry. They were camped on the south part of Snow's Hill. The Federals sent their cavalry up to drive the Confederates from the hill, which they failed to do, for Gano, after a brisk fight, drove them back. The Federal Cavalry, reinforced with artillery, came up again on the hill to drive the Confederates off. They stationed their artillery on three elevated positions and shelled the Confederates while the cavalry was fighting. One battery aimed its artillery at position where Gano was standing and succeeded in throwing dirt on him. Gano had only two small pieces of artillery and it looked for a while as if the Federals would be successful in driving them off, but they drove them from the hill again. The Federals reinforced and once more charged them with infantry, artillery, and cavalry. They placed their artillery on some hills, confronted Gano's line of cavalry with infantry and endeavored to flank his command on both sides of his cavalry. Gano saw that he wouldn't hold his position long, but hated to fall back, having whipped them twice, but he fought a little longer than he should have done, and when he ordered his men to fall back, the Federal Cavalry had flanked them enough to give them an infilading fire, which got Gano's command into a stampede. Gano's brother, Frank, was cut off in the charge and, when dashing across the field, one of Gano's soldiers, running on foot, named Billy Right, said, "Frank, for God's sake take me up behind you." Frank did so and away they went double, the Federal Cavalry pressing them pretty closely. When he came to a low fence; Frank jumped down and took off two or three rails and Billy Right (90) jumped the horse over the fence, thinking by this time there was no chance for Frank Gano, left him and dashed off on his horse. Frank offered to surrender to the Federals, but they wouldn't take his surrender, but shot at him. He ran a few steps to the head of a gully, jumped into it and ran down it. The Cavalry pursuing him lost sight of him. He continued to run down this steep gully until he came in sight of a regiment dressed in blue. They demanded his surrender. He replied, "Yes, I am willing to surrender, but I offered to surrender back here, but your soldiers wouldn't acknowledge my surrender, now, if you intend to kill me, say so, and we will fight it out to the best of our ability." They said, "What command do you belong to?" He said, "Gano's Brigade." They said, "Come up and surrender; we will treat you as a prisoner of war." Gano moved forward, looking down to the ground, not knowing what minute they would shoot him down. When he got up pretty close to the head of the cavalry, they laughed, "Ha! Ha!" On looking up he saw it was a regiment of Duke's men. They were dressed in blue overcoats captured from the Yankees. Frank Gano said, "I am a good mind to shoot you every one." But Frank got out safely, got another horse and joined his command the next day, after his friends had been hunting him all day over the battleground, thinking he was dead.

The Federal cavalry pursued Gano's command along Snow's Hill, passing Beckwith's Tavern, and Gano seeing they had gotten away from their artillery and infantry, knew he could whip the cavalry back if he could just rally his men. He sent two different orders to the front to form and protect the rear, but Colonel Brackenridge, who was in command of the front, said, "No such order ever reached the front; the only order I had was 'Double quick and go faster.'" Gano determined to rally his men, so ran his horse through a gap at the lower end, cutting off a number of his cavalrymen, whom he appealed to as Kentuckians to rally and make a stand. (91) A soldier in the battle who was a Kentuckian said to a man by the name of Clark Farris, who was also a Kentuckian, and was running by his side, "General Gano appeals to us as Kentuckians to rally and fight." Clark Farris, seeing nothing but destruction if they turned around, replied, as he whipped up his little horse, "I am a Tennessean." Gano succeeded in rallying 25 men. There were fences on either side of the road, and the woods on either side were densely overgrown with underbrush. Gano formed his men across the road from one side to the other in a line. When the regiment of Federal cavalry, 640 in number, were coming rapidly down the road, he ordered him men not to fire a gun until he told them, and they said they wouldn't. The Federals reached the 25 men formed in the road and lined up not more than 75 yards distant. There were eight men abreast and the eight men in front fired into Gano's men, but Gano's men sat as cool as a May morning, and never returned the fire. This frightened the Federals who thought that they must have all of Morgan's men there in the woods. The leader ordered a halt and the men, being frightened, got terribly tangled up in the road. Gano, seeing that this was his time, stood up in his stirrups and yelled across the woods to the right, "Forward charge!" Then, turning to the left, he repeated the command. The Federal regiment then ordered a retreat, and Gano ordered his 25 men to charge them. Gano's men continued to pursue them and shoot at them until they passed Beckwith's Tavern, and in the road above Beckwith's Tavern was a terrible mudhole. Gano and his men ran the Federals into this mudhole, and, some of the horses falling, they captured 42 prisoners out of that mudhole, so Gano, with 25 men, chased a whole regiment of 640 men off the field.

That night Gano went up to Beckwith's tavern, and while he was there Mrs. Morgan came into the hotel parlor and sat on the sofa beside him. She said to him, "General Gano, I saw the most wonderful sight I ever witnessed in my life. I went upon the house top where I could see good, and I saw 20 Confederates run a thousand Yankees (93) up the road into that mudhole and they captured about 100 prisoners." Just then Dr. Eilain, Morgan's horse Doctor, came into the parlor and said, "Mrs. Morgan, why are you telling General Gano? He commanded that little squad of men that whipped that regiment." She turned to General Gano and asked, "Were you there?" He replied, "I was." She drew back her fist and said, "I am a great mind to hit you." What did you let me tell you for?" He replied, "Because I was in it and couldn't see it very well and wanted to hear a description of it from a lady who was on the house top; you give a very good description of it. You say 20 men whipped a thousand, and we had 25 men and they whipped 640, and you said they captured 100 prisoners and they captured 42, so you have given a pretty good description for a woman upon a housetop."

Colonel W.C.P. Brackenridge wrote out a description of Gano's charge on Snow's Hill after the war. He said: "Gano, with a little squad of 25 men, charged an entire regiment. Riding this thoroughbred blue-grass horse, his hat in his hand, his hair and whiskers flowing back in the breeze, charging about thirty times his number, he drove them clear off the hill, and if I should live to be a hundred years old I would never forget that brilliant charge of General Gano on Snow's Hill."

Gano with his command was ordered down to McMinnville, and there engaged the enemy several miles out of McMinnville in the woods. It was a very hot battle, fighting behind trees and protecting themselves as well as they could. This fight was so close that in several instances they grabbed each others' guns, and in one case a Federal got a Confederate's gun and the Confederate got the Federal's gun. (94) One of Gano's soldiers, Lieutenant Wilson, was wounded in that fight. General Gano, learning that he was dangerously wounded, went down to the college, which was used as a hospital, to see him. Lieutenant Wilson had never made a profession of religion, but his father and mother were both Christians. Wilson knew that he was speedily dying. His face was pale, almost as white as his pillow. His hair curled gently back from his forehead. He was indeed a handsome young man. He said, "Tell father and mother when you see them that I loved them till the last. I send my love to them by you. Tell them that I loved my country and gave my life for it. But don't tell them one word about my future." When Gano met them after the war and delivered Wilson's message to them, the weeping mother said, "General Gano, what did he say about the future?" Gano couldn't tell her one word. He was not willing to tell her about what he had said about the future. Wilson did say that he regretted that he hadn't done his duty, but that would have been too sad to have told her.

Just before Gano left McMinnville, a gentleman came to him and asked him to buy his saddle mare. Gano said, "I haven't any use for her; I have all the horses I need on hand." "General," he said, "The Federals will take her away from me when they come in here, and I will lose her; Please, get on her and rider her just 100 yards." Gano did so, and can truthfully say that he never sat on a better saddle animal. He purchased her at $150.00. Later he was offered $500 for her, after that, $1000, after that $2000 and then $2,500, then $3000, after that $4000 and finally he was offered $5000 for her; he could have purchased with it a nice little farm in Texas. This, of course, was in declining Confederate money. He rode that little mare in many battles, and she was completely deafened by the artillery. She died in a Blue-grass pasture in Kentucky after the close of the war; the General's children having learned to ride upon her, Old Bird.

When the Confederates were about to evacuate Lexington, one of Gano's soldiers was sick with typhoid fever in the hospital; being too sick to move him, they had to leave him in the hospital where he would be taken care of. When he saw the city was deserted, he inquired, "What has become of all the soldiers?" They replied, "They have left the city to go south." He said, "I am not going to fall into the hands of the Federals." They said, "You can't leave here; you are too sick; you will be taken care of by friends." He got up and dressed himself and said, "I am not going to fall into the hands of the Federals. He left the hospital walking in the direction of Harrodsburg, toward the South. When he had gotten out about three miles, he could not walk any longer. He stopped at a house by the roadside and asked if he could stop over there till he died, that he was not going to get well. They good man of the house said, "I can't take you in here; if I were to do so the Federals would abuse me and mistreat me," so the poor man journeyed a little further on down the road, coming to a beautiful residence with beautiful maple trees in the front lot before the yard. He thought to himself, "I will go in here and lay in the shade of one of those trees and die there; these people will bury me." The man of the house, Dr. Barkly and his family were in at dinner; when they came out from dinner to the front porch, Dr. Barkly saw this man lying in the shade of the tree in the front yard. He said, "Let's go down there and see who it is, I reckon it is some drunken fellow." They went down and talked to the sick man, and he told his story, "I came in here to lie down in the shade of these trees to die and let you people bury me." Dr. Barkly said,

"My friend, we will take you to the house and put you in a good bed and take care of you and nurse you back to health if we can do so; but if you should (95) die, we will give you a decent burial." So they took him into the house and put him in bed, and Dr. Barkly, who had quit practicing medicine, said, "Wife, I will go after the doctor; and while I am gone, you can give him a good hot boot bath," which she did.

While she was bathing his feet she asked, "Are you a professor of religion?" He said, "Yes, my wife and I are both members of the Christian Church; they call us Campbellites sometimes down in our country, but we both are trying to serve the Lord and go home to Heaven." "Why!" she said, "You belong to the same church we do." "Well," he said, "Thank God! I have been put in the hands of good people." He said, "I am sick and wounded and can never reach home again, but I have fallen in the hands of Good Christian people; member of the same church we are…I want you to write this to my wife. Tell her, 'They are doing everything in their power to save me, but I am going to die. Train up our little ones in the nature and admonition of the Lord, and let us try to meet in that bright home above.'" He died and they buried him, and the old gentleman who had turned him away from his door for fear he would be persecuted by the Yankees attended the funeral. Seeing the sad funeral he said with tears in his eyes, "If God will forgive me, I will never turn another sick man away from my door, for the Bible says, 'Sometimes we turn away angels unawares.'"

Just after Billy Brackenridge's command was moved out in Eastern Kentucky, They met a large force of Federal Cavalry and engaged in a battle down in a valley between two big hills. Before the fight had begun, some soldier handed Gano some pawpaws, which he put in his overcoat pocket, not being very fond of them, but thinking in some hungry moment he might eat them. While engaged in a very warm fight, Brackenridge's regiment, not being accustomed to it, never having been in a battle before, were in danger of giving away. Gano rode out in front of Brackenridge's regiment, crossed his legs over his mare's neck, saying, "Give it to them, boys, they can't stand it long. These bullets won't hurt much." Some man (96) was heard to remark, who had seen men falling on his right and left…"No, they don't hurt, they go through and through." Gano went to eating his pawpaws and the men, all thinking that Gano saw victory just ahead, stood their ground, and the Confederates won the fight, capturing some of the Federals and driving the rest back. Some soldiers asked Gano how he could stand to eat pawpaws under such heavy firing; he replied, "I did it just to keep those men in line so we could win the victory."

Brackenridge in that fight was struck in the abdomen by a spent ball. The ball didn't enter his body, but made a large blue place. Brackenridge asked Gano what he thought about it. He, being a physician of eight years practice, replied, "It is not likely to injure you seriously, but be careful, make some applications to remove the soreness, for sometimes a ball that doesn't enter the body will kill a man by the inflammation brought about by the bruise." Presently Brackenridge, lying on the grass, remarked, "I wish you hadn't told me that, for I feel like my wound is mortal now."

Jerome Kirby of Dallas, Texas, one of Gano's boys, was cut off from the army, and, to avoid being captured, he taught school, putting on some citizens clothing. He had some pretty well grown boys in his school; some very fine students. Kirby said, "I never had to study so hard in my life as I did to keep ahead of those boys."

Note: At the bottom of the page, Trans-Mississippi fighting comes in here. Copied in book. Gano made brigadier general in this fighting.

Balance missing

"Recollections of a Kansas Pioneer"

Dr. George A. Moore

LEAVENWORTH TIMES, MARCH 8, 1914

ON THE FIRST SCHOOL BOARD

When under the law of 1864 the Leavenworth Board of Education was organized, I was a member, and was elected as its first president; David J. Brewer was chosen as superintendent and that board deserves the credit of having laid the foundation of the excellent public school system for which Leavenworth became noted.

It was during this year, a formative one for the Kansas State University, that I was appointed one of its regents.

Not long after that adjournment of the Legislature, I was commissioned to carry the soldiers' poll lists to the military headquarters in St. Louis and deliver the same to the commanding general, Thomas Ewing, Jr., whose home was in Leavenworth, and who personally was well-known to me. One evening while conversing with the General, knowing that he himself had aspirations toward the United States Senate, I asked him if he had not encouraged Governor Carney to bring on the premature senatorial election with a view to his political "killing off." Ewing laughingly denied having done so, and calling in his chief of staff told him of my question. They both laughed, treating the matter as a good joke, and I joined in their hilarity; but all the same my suspicion was not removed.

General Ewing was a man of unusual ability, and exceptionally well qualified to represent his state in the Upper House of our National Legislature. He was, before the war, a member of the law firm of Sherman, Ewing & McCook, all the members of which became conspicuous in military affairs, the senior member of the firm being the distinguished General William T. Sherman and the junior member dying a Brigadier General.

Returning from St. Louis I traveled over the North Missouri railroad, now I believe a part of the Wabash System; to its junction with the Hannibal and St. Joseph Railroad; thence over the latter road to St. Joseph, and thence by river steamer to Leavenworth. Only a few days before the train had been held up at Centralia, Missouri, by Bill Anderson and his band of guerrillas and some two hundred federal recruits taken off, lined up and shot. Every man on my train was armed, and all the way I sat with a loaded musket between my knees and a revolver by my side; but we met with no enemy or misadventure en route. I well remember the bright winter weather and the beauty of the country, which was covered with a mantle of pure snow, and the many charming forms of hoar frost crystals that adorned the forest trees and shrubbery along our way.

At Centralia our train was boarded by a body of soldiers, part of a cavalry force, that pursued, overtook and exterminated Anderson and his band. One of the soldiers showed me a small confederate flag and a booklet taken by him from the dead body of one of the guerrillas. The booklet was a manual of a secret order composed of guerrillas, their friends and sympathizers and contained a ritual including passwords and signals.

The soldier, referring to Anderson and his death, said that when he was shot he was riding his horse at full gallop, the bridle rein thrown over the horn of his saddle, a revolver in each hand and a bowie knife between his teeth; bravely facing his foes and firing as he charged upon them. Though a cut-throat, Anderson was fearless, and but for the demoralizing influences of war he might have been a valuable citizen; as fearless in the performance of civic duties as he was in leading his guerrillas.

TO FORT SMITH

During the summer of 1864 General Thayer, the commandant of the Union forces at Fort Smith, Arkansas, sent me word that he and other officers at his headquarters required the professional services of a dentist, and that if I would come to Fort Smith for a few weeks he would guarantee me receipts of $2,000. I considered this a good offer and, after talking the matter over with my partner, Dr. DuBoise, it was decided that I should go. I traveled by stage to Fort Scott, from which place I was to go on with a government wagon train. I was obliged to wait in Fort Scott for several days while the train was being assembled and loaded and during this waiting I was several times warned that the train was doomed to capture and that it would be wise for me to delay my departure. The confederate General Sterling Price, with a considerable force was slowly wending his way northward, and was supposed to be somewhere not far from the line of travel we were to follow. But I considered the reports in circulation as idle rumors and having made all my arrangements for the trip, and having come so far I decided to keep on in accordance with my plan.

In the train there were one hundred and twenty-five six mule government wagons laden with valuable stores of clothing, provisions and ammunitions, and in addition to these there were twenty settlers' wagons loaded with all manner of settlers' supplies. The train was escorted by an armed military guard numbering five hundred under command of Major Hopkins and was also accompanied by about six hundred unarmed recruits on their way to the front. The brigade-wagon master was named Anthony, a competent man, and a right good fellow. My trunk containing my clothing, instruments, etc., was on one of the government wagons; I was provided with a good saddle horse and armed with a volcanic repeating rifle, purchased of my friend I.S. Kalloch, a revolver and bowie knife. Our train traveled about fifteen miles each day. When we camped in the late afternoon at designated places, we did so in regulation order; the encampment having its tents disposed in military array and all ate and slept in tents. I enjoyed the novel experience and got on very comfortably.

Nothing of particular interest or to occasion alarm occurred for several days, or until we were well within the Indian Territory. Then one night scouts brought intelligence of an approaching enemy. The camp was quietly awakened, the teams were quickly attached to the wagons and at 3 o'clock in the morning, with wagons forming a double line, and in the advance, rear and side guards, we silently and cautiously moved forward over the prairies intent upon reaching Cabin Creek as soon as possible, where was a stockade and a detachment of infantry that for some weeks had been engaged in putting up hay. The creek had considerable forest growth upon each side, which thinned off to scattering scrub oaks as it approached the prairies. The stockade, with a building in its center, was amid scrub oak on the south side of the creek. After our train in the order mentioned had traveled about twenty miles, we arrived at and crossed Cabin Creek and about noon our wagons were deployed for a mile or more along the edge of the prairie, but no tents were erected.

THE ENEMY AT HAND

The scouts reported that the Confederate General Standwaite, with a brigade of General Price's Army and two batteries of howitzers, was approaching determined upon the capture of our train. On the other hand it was reported that a body of Union troops, cavalry and artillery were hastening to our aid.

In few of these reports the loose disposition of the train wagons certainly indicated a lack of prudence upon the part of somebody. It was a September Sunday, a warm and delightful day, our dinner and supper were cooked and eaten in the open air, and notwithstanding the possibility, not to say probability of impending disaster, no one seemed worried or troubled. When bedtime came, without disrobing, I rolled up in a blanket, stretched out in the wagon which contained my trunk and was soon in sound slumber. About one o'clock in the morning I heard the sonorous voice of Anthony calling out to the teamsters. "Tumble out quick and hitch up!" I sprang to the ground, the moon was shining brightly and I observed that the whole camp was in motion; teamsters were hurriedly harnessing their teams, and attaching them to the wagons, and the order given directed that the wagons should be driven nearer the stockade and a close corral formed in which the animals, women and non-combatants should be placed; a disposition of the train which should have been made when it arrived upon the ground.

Officers and soldiers were running toward the prairie and I followed, soon coming to a double line of battle formed upon the open prairie. In the dim distance I could see the dark line of the Confederates, and hear their shouts, but the distance was too great for words to be distinguished. After speaking to some of the officers with whom I was acquainted, I started on my return to the wagons containing my trunk, but had not reached it when our soldiers, mistaking the sound of hoofs of a runaway band of mules, for those of a charging body of Confederate cavalry, discharged a volley of musketry, and the scene of confusion that immediately followed is indescribable. The teams stampeded, and entirely beyond control were running in various directions, and I was in the midst of the tumult. The wild grass was so high that I could not see the teams until they were almost upon me and no sooner did I spring from before one team than I would find myself directly in front of another, and for a few minutes I am sure that I performed such dexterous feats of leaping backward, forward and sideways, as would excite the admiration and envy of an Australian kangaroo. It seemed almost miraculous that I escaped injury.

Of our train of government wagons but ten, including the one containing my trunk, reached the stockade; the rest, many of them in a more or less wrecked condition, were scattered through the small timber. A number of wagons were precipitated into a deep gulch, their animals and I think some of teamsters killed, and their loads spilled. I saw several wagon bodies with loads intact but minus their running gear and others to which were still attached but one, two or three, of the original complement of six animals. Most of the teamsters, mounting their respective saddle mules, had fled northwardly. As to the sutler's wagons, I do not know what became of them, but presumably most of them were captured.

BATTLE OF CABIN CREEK

Major Hopkins placed me in command of a small company of Cherokee Indian soldiers, and informed me that he would immediately make an attempt to meet and hasten the coming of re-enforcements, said to be but a few miles distant.

Order having been restored, a systematic mode of defense was agreed upon in the hope that we could maintain our position until reinforcements arrived. We had all told a force of almost six hundred fighting men, all infantry, except the Cherokee Indians, who belonged to a cavalry regiment. We had no cannon. The enemy numbering about 2,500 consisted of infantry and cavalry and two howitzer batteries. Evidently he did not know how weak we were, and feared to come to close quarters. Until morning the attack was confined to shelling, but he did not get our range, and the shells flew above us. We could see the burning fuses and their horrible howling caused an involuntary ducking of heads, but no one was hurt.

With the coming of daylight the battery fire became more accurate and caused us some loss. At times solid shot were used and we could see an approaching ball, and after it had passed, its ricocheting appearing much the same as is often seen by spectators at a baseball game.

A little later the battery commenced peppering us with grape shot and it was this that caused most of our loss. While the batteries were firing we lay flat upon the ground but when it ceased firing and the confederate infantry advanced we sprang to our feet, opened fire and forced them back. And thus the battle waged. Near where I was stationed, flat upon his back, with extended limbs, was the body of an Indian soldier; stretching at full length upon it, with nose under the dead man's chin, lay his faithful dog guarding his master's body, and growling when any one approached. In this position he remained during the continuance of the fighting, and when I left the field he was still there.

At 9 o'clock in the morning, all hope of re-enforcements was abandoned, and it became evident that it was a question of minutes only as to when we should be compelled to surrender. Already the confederates had driven back our right wing, and were running off our captured wagons, and setting fire to such as could not be moved. Very soon they would be in our rear and escape would be impossible. I hesitated as to my best course. I was extremely desirous of getting to Fort Smith and at first thought I would surrender and take the chances of being released and able to resume my onward journey; but on second thought, remembering that Stand Waite's force was largely Indians, and reflecting that I could hardly claim to be a non-combatant, and yet was not an officer or enlisted soldier, I felt so doubtful as to what, if captured, my fate would be that I decided that I would go with the retreating party and share its fate.

THE RETREAT

I then ran to the wagon containing my trunk with the intent of securing the most valuable of my portables, and was in the act of assembling them, when a charge of grape shot came hurtling through the top of a scrub oak within three feet of the wagon. I leaped to the ground and lay upon it until the firing ceased, and then, grabbing a blanket, I caught and mounted a raw-boned mule and attempted to ride over the ridge to the road beyond. The ungainly beast balked and I was obliged to dismount and, with a club, stimulate the onward progress of the inconsiderate brute. While thus surmounting the ridge four charges of grape shot hissed by me, one shot cut off the foot of a nearby mule, and another cut through the backbone of another and dropped him in a heap just as a young soldier of the 16th Kansas Regiment, a boy not more than seventeen years of age, was about to mount him. The expression on the boy's face was curious. He was not frightened, but he had an injured and disappointed look which seemed to say: "What did you let them do that for, and leave me to walk clear back to Fort Scott?"

I admit that I was badly scared and very likely the hair upon my head stood on end, and I had little hope of living to get over the ridge and out of the line of fire. But kind Providence favored me and I reached the northern side of the ridge unhurt, sat down by the roadside to gain my breath and give thanks to God.

My friend, William Martin of Leavenworth, who had been captured a few days previous by Stand Waite's force, always insisted that through a field glass he saw and recognized me, as I urged my gothic mule over the ridge, and he used to relate the story with much humor.

By this time I had passed through the strip of forest bordering the creek and reached the prairie beyond. I found myself one of a party of sixty, including three ladies, two of whom rode in an ambulance, our only vehicle, and one mounted upon a mule. As we moved out upon the prairie, we saw upon distant bluffs to the west a small detachment of Confederate cavalry, evidently sent out to intercept federal fugitives, but they made no attempt to cut off our retreat, thinking no doubt that we were too strong for them.

We had traveled some two miles over the prairie when, looking back, we saw emerging from the wood six of our soldiers; and at the same time they were also seen by the watching confederates who immediately started to intercept them. Our soldiers at the same moment discovered the enemies and divined their purpose. Then commenced a race the like of which neither before nor since have my eyes seen; a race for life, Captain Clark of our party believing the soldiers were of his own regiment, not-withstanding his fine horse was already wounded in the neck, bravely rode back to share his comrades' fate and he joined them a few moments before the clash came. The whole scene was in plain view and we watched the result with breathless interest, but for want of horses, were unable to render assistance. Both parties were riding at utmost speed, and when they met and exchanged shots two confederates and one federal soldier dropped, and others on either side wavered in the saddle, showing they were hit. But our remaining men came on and when they reached us but one of them was found to be seriously wounded. He, poor fellow, was shot in the back, the large musket ball passing clear through his body and lodging under the skin of the abdomen whence I extracted it. The injured man realized that his would was a mortal one, and his great desire was that he might live to reach Fort Scott and once more see his wife and children, whose home was there. We placed him as carefully and comfortably as possible in the ambulance, the women were very kind to him, and he lived not only to reach Fort Scott but for several days thereafter, and died with his family about him.

During our retreat we saw no more confederates though we were once fired upon from a clump of bushes, but no one was hurt. Soon after the tragic incident related we met a large party of mounted Osage Indians hastening forward to join other Union forces with a view to intercept Standwaite. We regretted they had not come to our assistance in time to save our train.

As evening approached we arrived at an abandoned camp where we had expected to find a small detail of soldiers and food. As we had eaten nothing since the previous day our crowd was hungry as well as tired. We killed a heifer near the camp and divided the flesh and soon everyone was occupied roasting meat upon the end of a stick held over some of the several fires that had been kindled for that purpose. I was fortunate enough to find an empty salt pork barrel, from the inside of which I scraped enough salt to season and make palatable my own and several other roasts.

RELIEF COMES

After eating, and resting for an hour or more, we resumed our weary way, camping by the roadside as darkness gathered. Early next morning we broke camp and moved forward; in the afternoon we met a relief party and from it obtained some hardtack and brown sugar and at night we camped by the nearly dry bed stream wherein some pools of water were. The night was chilly but several large fires illuminated the forest and gave a cheerful aspect to the camp, though everyone seemed to be in a rather gloomy state of mind.

Following the example of others, I rolled up in my blanket and slept. At four o'clock in the morning a relief wagon arrived with a supply of hardtack, brown sugar, roasted coffee in the berry, and three pounds of bacon. As we had no coffee mill the question was "how can we grind the coffee?" After several unsuccessful attempts had been made, I suggested that the soldiers use their tin cups as mortars and the muzzles of their carbines as pestles; this plan worked well and soon we had half a dozen kettles of fragrant, steaming hot coffee, abundance for all. I failed to secure any of the bacon, but a soldier kindly loaned me a small piece with which to smear my hardtack and give it a flavor, and so I fared quite well. The food and coffee, especially the latter, infused new life and vigor into all and from this and other experiences I have had I am convinced that, when one is cold, hungry, tired and depressed nothing so quickly invigorates, warms and cheers as does a cup of good, hot coffee.

In dreams during the first two nights after the Cabin Creek affair, all its experiences were lived over again, thus indicating the profound mental effect of those exciting hours. On the third day of our retreat we arrived at the Osage Indian Catholic Mission, the good monks gave us a kindly reception and well provided for our hungry stomachs. That night, wrapped in my blanket, I slept a sound, dreamless sleep upon the hay at the foot of a large hay stack and after our early breakfast, upon the invitation of Colonel Hoyt, I rode with him and several companions to Fort Scott, from which point I took stage for home, arriving there in good physical condition though somewhat out of pocket. I never saw any published report of the Cabin Creek fight but I was informed that the killed upon the Union side did not exceed thirty. The property loss to the government and to sutlers was very heavy; in the aggregate it must have amounted to several hundreds of thousands of dollars.

Battle Map

September 19, 1864

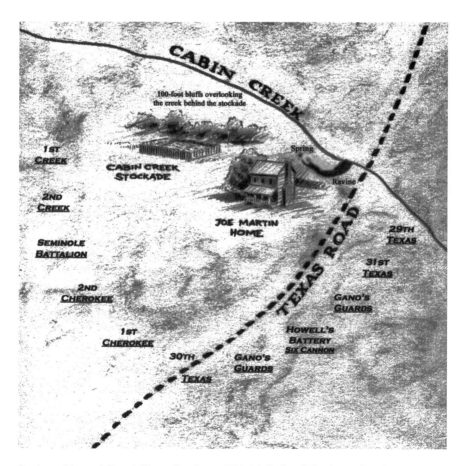

Battle positions of Gano's Texas Cavalry and Watie's Indian Brigade as of 1:00 a.m., September 19, 1864. *Courtesy Warren Entertainment.*

APPENDIX IV

The Moon During the Second
Battle of Cabin Creek

DONALD W. OLSON, DEPARTMENT OF PHYSICS
SOUTHWEST TEXAS STATE UNIVERSITY
SAN MARCOS, TEXAS

Author's note: The following information was sent to me by Dr. Olson in August 1998 after I had inquired about his work on the position of the moon during the wounding of Stonewall Jackson by his own men during the Battle of Chancellorsville in May 1863. I asked him about the moon's position and the moonlight intensity as reported by Confederate soldiers during the Second Battle of Cabin Creek, Indian Territory, on the night of September 18–19, 1864. Dr. Olson's entire e-mail follows.

I have had a little more time to do careful calculations of the Moon as it appeared at the second battle of Cabin Creek

Two things worth special mention.

First, one of your sources may have mentioned an artillery bombardment lasting until the Moon went down and then resuming at sunrise. In fact, the Moon did not go down during the battle that night. The Moon rose on the previous evening [September 18, 1864, at 7:56 p.m., LMT], was above the horizon during the night action, and was still high in the sky (48 degrees above the western horizon) when the Sun rose at 5:46 a.m. LMT on Sept. 19, 1864. If the moonlight went away during the night, it may have been because of clouds, but it was not because the Moon set.

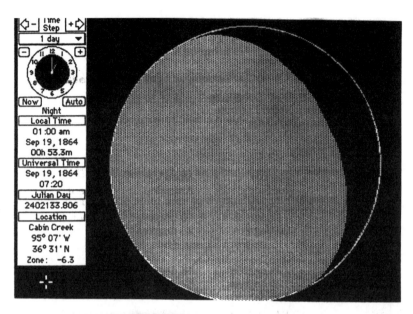

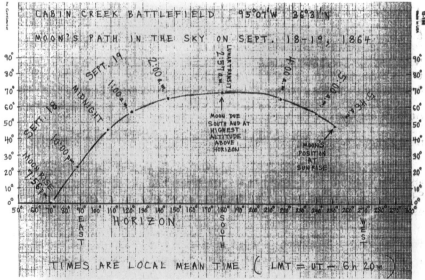

A chart showing the moon's path over the Cabin Creek Battlefield on September 19, 1864. *Courtesy Dr. Donald W. Olson.*

Second, the times listed below are in Local Mean Time for the site, which is 6 hours and 20 minutes west of Greenwich, England.

(Local Mean Time)   (UT)—(6 hours 20 minutes)

The abbreviation UT stands for Universal Time, which is sometimes referred to as Greenwich Mean Time. Local Mean Time is the time system that was used during the Civil War, since modern time zones were not adopted in the U.S. until 1883. Oklahoma now uses Central Standard Time, which is exactly 6 hours earlier than Greenwich, and Central Daylight Time, which is 5 hours earlier than Greenwich mean time. If someone else tries to check my calculations and gets slightly different results, it may be because their computer program is using modern time zones.

Full Moon: Sept 15, 1864
Last Quarter: Sept. 22, 1864

Cabin Creek Battlefield 95 degrees 07 minutes West   Longitude
                        36 degrees 31 minutes North   Latitude
                        LMT = UT—6 hours 20 minutes

MOON'S PATH IN THE SKY

LMT	Moon's Azimuth	Moon's Altitude	Event
Sept. 18, 1864			
7:56 p.m.	71 degrees	0 degrees	Moonrise
10:00 p.m.	88 degrees	23 degrees	
Sept. 19, 1864			
Midnight	108 degrees	46 degrees	
1:00 a.m.	123 degrees	57 degrees	
2:00 a.m.	146 degrees	56 degrees	
2:57 a.m.	180 degrees	69 degrees	Lunar Transit
4:00 a.m.	218 degrees	65 degrees	

LMT	Moon's Azimuth	Moon's Altitude	Event
5:00 a.m.	240 degrees	56 degrees	
5:46 a.m.	252 degrees	48 degrees	Sunrise

Note:
LMT = Local Mean Time
UT=Universal Mean Time
GMT=Greenwich Mean Time
Azimuth = compass direction (0 degrees = North, 90 degrees = East, 180 degrees = South, 270 degrees = West)
Altitude = angle above the horizon
Lunar Transit = Moon is then due south and near its highest altitude in the sky for the night.

The Moon was in the waning gibbous phase (that is, between Full Moon and Last Quarter). At 1:00 am LMT, the Moon had an illuminated fraction of 84% (that is, 84% lit and 16% dark) and stood high in the sky (57 degrees above the southeastern horizon).

APPENDIX V

Historical Mileage

It is interesting to note the actual mileage of some of these historic sites using a Global Positioning System, or GPS unit. The following are some mileage figures provided by researcher Joe Poplin. He used his GPS unit to mark the old sites of the Texas-Military Road. It should be noted the GPS is a straight-line system.

- The distance from the Horse Creek camp to the Cabin Creek ford is 17.8 or 18 miles. Major Hopkins wrote in his report that the distance from Horse Creek to Cabin Creek was 15 miles.
- From their camp on Wolf Creek, Gano and Watie's forces had to travel 11 miles in order to reach the Cabin Creek stockade.
- After the Battle of Flat Rock, the Confederates were only 32 miles from the Cabin Creek stockade. R.M. Peck wrote in 1904 that he believed the distance to be 35 miles.
- Major John Foreman's relief column of six Indian companies had to travel 63.6 or 64 miles to reach the Cabin Creek stockade from Fort Gibson on the branch of the Texas Road, which is located on the east side of the Grand River.
- After the capturing the wagon train, the Confederates traveled south on the Texas Road for about 16 miles before encountering Colonel J.M. Williams's Second Brigade near Pryor's Creek.

- Colonel Williams's black soldiers had to march at the double-quick roughly 40 miles from Fort Gibson to a point where they first encountered the Confederate advance guard protecting the wagon train. From this point, they were pushed back by the Southerners about 3.5 miles, where they formed their battle line at Pryor's Creek.

List of Officers with Escort to Supply Train

OFFICERS WITH ESCORT TO SUPPLY TRAIN EN ROUTE TO FORT GIBSON, CHEROKEE NATION AS LISTED IN THE RECORDS OF FORT SCOTT, KANSAS, FOR SEPTEMBER 1864

Name	Rank	Regiment	Company
H.P. Ledger	Captain	Sixth Kansas Cavalry	L
J.W. Duff	Captain	Sixth Kansas Cavalry	M
Thomas Stevenson	Captain	Fourteenth Kansas Cavalry	H
M.O. Leeple	Captain	Fourteenth Kansas Cavalry	I
Pat Cosgrove	Captain	Second Kansas Cavalry	L
James Brooks	First Lieutenant	Sixth Kansas Cavalry	M
J.C. Anderson	Second Lieutenant	Sixth Kansas Cavalry	M
N.B. Lucas	Second Lieutenant	Sixth Kansas Cavalry	G
W.H. Shattuck	Second Lieutenant	Sixth Kansas Cavalry	G

Name	Rank	Regiment	Company
L.F. Stewart	Second Lieutenant	Sixth Kansas Cavalry	I
J. Graham	Second Lieutenant	Sixth Kansas Cavalry	L
L.L. Jennings	First Lieutenant	Fourteenth Kansas Cavalry	D
J.A. Heuff	First Lieutenant	Fourteenth Kansas Cavalry	F
William C. Smith	First Lieutenant	Fourteenth Kansas Cavalry	C
E.C. Lowe	Captain	First Indian Home Guards	F
A.F. Broking	First Lieutenant	First Indian Home Guards	A
James McVay	First Lieutenant	First Indian Home Guards	B
Johnth	Captain	First Indian Home Guards	K
Lots.ca.ha.jo	Second Lieutenant	First Indian Home Guards	D
B.F. Whitlow	First Lieutenant	Third Indian Home Guards	K
Moses Price	Captain	Second Indian Home Guards	B|
A.J. Waterhouse	First Lieutenant	Second Indian Home Guards	H|
Alick Hawk	Second Lieutenant	Second Indian Home Guards	B

Information courtesy of Arnold W. Schofield, historian at Fort Scott National Historic Site, Fort Scott, Kansas.

POWs Captured at Flat Rock and Cabin Creek, Indian Territory

C amp Ford was located about four miles northeast of Tyler, Texas. It was made a prison by the Confederate Trans-Mississippi Department in July 1863. The Union prisoners captured at Flat Rock and Cabin Creek were forced to march roughly four hundred miles to Camp Ford. All of the Kansas prisoners were released from the prison on May, 22, 1865.

Name	Rank	Regiment	Company	Place Captured	Date
Ainsworth, W.F.	corp	2nd KS Cav	G	Nr Ft. Gibson, CN	9/16/1864
Bates, W.J.	pvt	2nd KS Cav	C	Nr Ft. Gibson, CN	9/16/1864
Biegert, David	pvt	2nd KS Cav	C	Nr Ft. Gibson, CN	9/16/1864
Carson, Jas.	pvt	2nd KS Cav	H	Cabin Creek, CN	9/19/1864
Clark, Enoch	corp	2nd KS Cav	G	Nr Ft. Gibson, CN	9/16/1864

Name	Rank	Regiment	Company	Place Captured	Date
Crookham, A.J.	sgt	13th KS Cav	D	Flat Rock, CN	9/16/1864
Davis, A.W.	corp	2nd KS Cav	C	Nr Ft. Gibson, CN	9/16/1864
Dean, M.D.	pvt	2nd KS Cav	G	Nr Ft. Gibson, CN	9/16/1864
Farmer, John Q.	sgt	2nd KS Cav	C	Nr Ft. Gibson, CN	9/16/1864
Foldmann, Levi	pvt	2nd KS Cav	C	Nr Ft. Gibson, CN	9/16/1864
Frohm, A.	sgt	13th KS Cav	D	Cabin Creek, CN	9/19/1864
Fuller, Jay	pvt	2nd KS Cav	G	Nr Ft. Gibson, CN	9/16/1864
Goodwin, Elijah	corp	2nd KS Cav	G	Nr Ft. Gibson, CN	9/16/1864
Gugles, G.T.	sgt QM	2nd KS Cav	C	Nr Ft. Gibson, CN	9/16/1864
Hanna, A.J.	sgt	2nd KS Cav	G	Nr Ft. Gibson, CN	9/16/1864
Harman, John	pvt	2nd KS Cav	G	Nr Ft. Gibson, CN	9/16/1864
Holland, James N.	pvt	2nd KS Cav	C	Nr Ft. Gibson, CN	9/16/1864
Kirkley, Thos	pvt	2nd KS Cav	C	Nr Ft. Gibson, CN	9/16/1864

Name	Rank	Regiment	Company	Place Captured	Date
Londogin, John	pvt	12th KS Cav	L	Cabin Creek, CN	9/19/1864
Mahoney, Jas.	pvt	2nd KS Cav	G	Nr Ft. Gibson, CN	9/16/1864
McMathen, Geo. W	corp	2nd KS Cav	C	Nr Ft. Gibson, CN	9/16/1864
Milliman, Robt	pvt	2nd KS Cav	C	Nr Ft. Gibson, CN	9/16/1864
Nance, John M.	sgt	2nd KS Cav	C	Nr Ft. Gibson, CN	9/16/1864
O'Conner, T.S.	1Lt	2nd IT Cav	C	Cabin Creek, CN	9/19/1864
Parker, J.R.	pvt	2nd KS Cav	G	Nr Ft. Gibson, CN	9/16/1864
Peterson, Chas.	pvt	2nd KS Cav	E	Cabin Creek, CN	9/19/1864
Shaunnessey, Ed	pvt	2nd KS Cav	C	Nr Ft. Gibson, CN	9/16/1864
Smith, Pete	pvt	2nd KS Cav	C	Nr Ft. Gibson, CN	9/16/1864
Stone, P.W.	2nd Lt	2nd KS Cav	C	Nr Ft. Gibson, CN	9/16/1864
Stubblefield, Wm	pvt	2nd KS Cav	C	Nr Ft. Gibson, CN	9/16/1864
Sutherland, D.M.	1st Lt	1st KS Inf (C)	K	Flat Rock, CN	9/16/1864

Name	Rank	Regiment	Company	Place Captured	Date
Taylor, Amos	pvt	2nd KS Cav	C	Nr Ft. Gibson, CN	9/16/1864
Test, E.B.	pvt	2nd KS Cav	G	Nr Ft. Gibson, CN	9/16/1864
Thornhill, A.	pvt	2nd KS Cav	D	Nr Ft. Gibson, CN	9/16/1864
VanHorn, John	pvt	2nd KS Cav	C	Nr Ft. Gibson, CN	9/16/1864
White, Frank	corp	2nd KS Cav	G	Nr Ft. Gibson, CN	9/16/1864
Whitely, Henry. D	pvt	2nd KS Cav	D	Nr Ft. Gibson, CN	9/16/1864
Wortham, A.K.	pvt	2nd KS Cav	C	Nr Ft. Gibson, CN	9/16/1864
Yalkin, Ryan	pvt	2nd KS Cav	C	Nr Ft. Gibson, CN	9/16/1864

CIVILIAN TEAMSTERS CAPTURED WITH WAGON TRAIN AT CABIN CREEK

Brookover, W.H.
Irwin, R.
Lanes, Theodore
McDonough, Wm.
McKay, Alfred
Moore, W.F.

Pall, D.
Starks, W.H.
St. Glisaro, C.S.
Thornton, A.
Tucker, A.
Young, C.W.

Civilians Listed as Captured at Cabin Creek

Babbit, Wm
Finney, Thomas
Leaky, Peter
Railery, Wm
Wright, James

All of the captured civilians and teamsters were also sent to Camp Ford, Texas and were paroled at the same time as the Kansas soldiers.

APPENDIX VIII

In Memoriam

Captain Benjamin W. Welch, the commanding officer of Company K of the First Kansas Colored Volunteer Infantry, was not present at the Battle of Flat Rock. He was recovering from a thigh wound he received at the Battle of Poison Springs, Arkansas, on April 14, 1865, and was on detached service. Captain Welch was later killed on November 19, 1864, in a skirmish at Timbered Hills, Indian Territory.

The following list was compiled by Curtis Payne of Tulsa, Oklahoma, from service records located at the National Archives in Washington, D.C.

CASUALTIES OF COMPANY K, FIRST KANSAS COLORED INFANTRY, AT THE BATTLE OF FLAT ROCK, INDIAN TERRITORY, ON SEPTEMBER 16, 1864

First Lieutenant D.M. Sutherland	captured
Sergeant James Brown	reported killed, returned October 24, 1865
Sergeant Isom Wood	captured
Corporal John Hays	killed
Corporal James Lee	killed
Private Jacob Miller	killed
Private George Nelson	killed

Private Jacob Perkins	killed
Private James Polk	killed
Private Stephen Pinket, Bugler	killed
Private Colman Richardson	killed
Private Charles Straws	killed
Private George Tibb	killed
Private Austin Terrill	killed
Private Jessee Vaughn	killed
Private Perry Clarkson	captured
Private John Gains Reported	killed
Corporal Brown Wood	captured
Private Gordan Thompson	captured
Sergeant Samuel Wilson	killed
Private Henry Adams	killed
Private Scott Boler	killed
Private Horace Butler	killed
Private Amos Curnel	killed
Private Hugh Curry	killed
Private Gariel Clark	killed
Private Alfred Collins	killed
Private Washington Irving	killed
Private Lewis Edwards	killed
Private Gilford Spercer	killed
Private James Graham	killed
Private Thomas Homilton	killed
Private Martin Irvin	killed
Private Richard Johnson	killed
Private Newton Johnson	killed
Private Frank Lindsey	killed

In Memorium

Private Newton Johnson	killed
Private Frank Lindsey	killed
Private Ellis Myers	killed

The First Kansas Colored Infantry designation was officially changed to the Seventy-ninth U.S. Colored Volunteers on December 13, 1864.

CASUALTY LIST FOR COMPANY C, SECOND KANSAS CAVALRY, AT THE BATTLE OF FLAT ROCK

Captain Edger A. Barker	escaped
James M. Carlton	captured/escaped
Corporal Robert Hampton	killed
Private James H. Davis	killed
Private James Ledgewood	killed
Private Bailey Duval	killed
Private Marion Thompson	killed

CASUALTY LIST FOR COMPANY G, SECOND KANSAS CAVALRY, AT THE BATTLE OF FLAT ROCK

Sergeant John McDougal	killed
Private John W. Smith	killed

APPENDIX IX

Stand Watie Surrender Document

STAND WATIE SURRENDERED BY THE FOLLOWING ARTICLES ON JUNE 23, 1865, FROM AN ORIGINAL COPY OF THE WATIE SURRENDER DOCUMENT IN THE LIBRARY OF THE THOMAS GILCREASE MUSEUM, TULSA, OKLAHOMA

Treaty stipulations made and entered into this 23rd day of June 1865 near Doaksville Choctaw Nation between Sent. Colonel A.C. Mathews and W.H. Vance U.S. Vol. commissioners appointed by Major General Herron U.S.A. on part of the military authorities of the United States and Brig. General Stand Watie Governor and Principal Chief of that part of the Cherokee Nation lately allied with Confederate States in acts of hostilities against the Government of the United States as follows to wit:

ARTICLE I. All acts of hostilities on the part of both armies having ceased by virtue of a convention entered into on the 26th day of May 1865 between Major General E.R.S. Gantry U.S.A. comdg. Mil. Division West Miss, and General E. Kirby Smith C.S.A., Comdg. Trans. Miss Department. The Indians of the Cherokee Nation here represented lately allied with the Confederate States in acts of hostilities against the Government of the United States.

Do agree at once to return to their respective homes and there remain at peace with United States, and offer no indignities whatever against the whites or Indians of the various tribes who have been friendly to or engaged in the service of the United States during the war.

ARTICLE II. It is stipulated by the undersigned commissioners on part of the United States, that so-long as the Indians aforesaid observe the provisions of article first of this agreement, they shall be protected by the United States authorities in their person and property, not only from encroachment on the part of the whites, but also from the Indians who have been engaged in the service of the United States.

ARTICLE III. The above articles of agreement to remain and be in force and effect until the meeting of the Grand Council to meet at Armstrong Academy, Choctaw Nation on the 1ˢᵗ day of September A.D. 1865 and until such time as the proceedings of said Grand Council shall be ratified by the proper authorities both of the Cherokee Nation and the United States.

In testimony whereof the said Lieut. Col. A.C. Mathews and adjutant W.H. Vance commissioners on part of the United States and Brig. General Stand Watie Governor and Principal Chief of the Cherokee Nation have hereunto set their hands and seals.

Signed.
A.C. Mathews, Sent. Col.
W.H. Vance, Adjr. Commissioners.
Stand Watie Brig. Gen., Governor and Principal Chief Cherokee Nation

Notes

CHAPTER 1

1. Whit Edwards, "Civil War Operations in Indian Territory," a speech made before the Tulsa Civil War Round Table, July 2000. Edwards presented a list of Civil War battles that were fought in Indian Territory and gave it to roundtable members.
2. *St. Louis Dispatch*, "A Terrible Quintette." A copy of the article is in Walter B. Stevens's Scrap Book No. 278, State Historical Society of Missouri.
3. Rod Martin, personal interview at Sand Springs, Oklahoma, 1991. Martin is the great-great-grandson of Greenbrier Joe Martin, whose Pensacola Ranch encompassed the area around the Cabin Creek ford. He is also the great-grandson of Richard Martin.
4. Burch, *True Story of Charles W. Quantrell*, 224.
5. Ibid., 264.
6. *Oklahoma's National Register Handbook*, Oklahoma State Historic Preservation Office, July 2000, 63. The caretaker is Herman Stinnett, who owns the property south of the battlefield park. The park is open from daylight to dusk, seven days a week, 365 days a year. In 2011, the Civil War Trust, in cooperation with the Friends of Cabin Creek and the Oklahoma Historical Society, purchased a total of eighty-eight acres of the battlefield that included the Stinnett property.

7. Program of the *Cabin Creek Monument Dedication*, Flavius J. Barrett Chapter 1829 of the United Daughters of the Confederacy, Vinita, Oklahoma, June 2, 1961. The Vinita UDC chapter purchased the ten-acre tract, which is now the battlefield park, for $800. Members raised the money in sixty days via bake sales, home talent shows, rummage sales and private donations. The largest contribution, of $100, came from the Oklahoma Historical Society. The land was deeded to the Vinita UDC chapter in February 1952.

8. The Friends of Cabin Creek Inc. will remedy this situation by building an outdoor kiosk to better explain to visitors the engagements fought around the Cabin Creek ford.

9. Although the portion of Mayes County where the battlefield lies is rural, the Cabin Creek Battlefield is still threatened by residential development. As of August 24, 2012, the battlefield is on the U.S. government's list of secondary battlefields to save. It is listed as Preservation Priority: III.3 (Class C) Battlefield in need of additional protection by the American Battlefield Protection Program. An update to the Civil War Sites Advisory Commission Report on the Nation's Civil War Battlefields done in May 2010 by the National Park Service identified 2,161 acres of land encompassing the historic extent of the battle as it rolled across the landscape. The report also listed 575 acres that represent the core area, representing the direct areas of engagement on the battlefield.

10. Rod Martin interview. Martin explained that he walked the creek many times as a child and as a college student. He remembered the creek as always being rather wide in his lifetime. However, at the ford, Martin noted that the water was always relatively low, perhaps always relatively low or ankle deep. He recalled that sometimes the water was very low and described it as "just like wet gravel on a driveway."

11. Foreman, *Down the Texas Road*, 8. For an eyewitness account of traveling down the old Texas Road, see Works Progress Administration's Indian-Pioneer Papers, Project S-149, Western History Collections, University of Oklahoma Libraries (hereafter cited as I-PP), Emma Herrington interview, January 24, 1938, 436–39; a description from memory as to the layout of the road can be found in I-PP, W.A. Patilla interview, March 14, 1938, 63–68.

12. Foreman, *Down the Texas Road*, 7.

13. Letter from Paul Venamon to the author dated October 18, 1999. Also included were other materials, including copies of Irving's original

journal and a chapter from McDermott's book, *Journal II*, pages 89–123. Venamon mentioned McDermott's footnote 42 at the bottom of page 103 that notes, "The last entry for October 5th is almost completely undecipherable. It seems to refer to their camping place on the (west?) branch of Cabin de Planch (Plank Cabin) Creek, and is followed by another of Irving's Osage transcriptions." Venamon wrote that he read it as "East bank of Cabin de Planch." This would place the campsite just east of the Cabin Creek military ford, across the creek from the present-day Civil War monuments. Venamon also noted at this point that McDermott seems to be out of step with the Irving's original journal. According to the original journal, "Entry made with the Journal reversed" is not the story of the dialogue between Brother Vail and the Indian but rather about the "Indian that had 200 head of cattle." The story of Brother Vail and the Indian appears in the later October 6 entry. It is Venamon's belief that the Vail/Indian dialogue occurred while they were camped at Cabin Creek on the morning of October 6, 1832. Brother Vail had joined the party on October 1 at Harmony Mission. The mission was located near the present-day small town of Metz, Missouri. Venamon also pointed out McDermott's footnote 3 at the bottom of page 107 notes that "Hopefield Mission was below Cabin Creek." This is incorrect, according to Venamon. Hopefield was on the Grand River just east of the mouth of Cabin Creek. It was upstream above Cabin Creek, not below.

14. Davis, *Jefferson Davis*, 53. The chimney of the cabin where Lieutenant Davis was quartered is marked by the Oklahoma Historical Society at the Fort Gibson Military Park.

CHAPTER 2

15. Mayes County Historical Society, *Historical Highlights of Mayes County*, 185.
16. Ibid.
17. Ibid.
18. Ibid.
19. D.E. "Bill" Martin, personal interview with the author, Sand Springs, Oklahoma, 1991. Martin was the great-grandson of "Greenbrier"

Joe Martin and the grandson of Richard Martin. He explained that
the Pensacola Ranch ran along the west side of the Grand River and
extended in length from present-day Ketchum, Oklahoma, to the area
of present-day Salina, Oklahoma. In width, it stretched across the
rolling prairie about twelve miles. Since he was of Cherokee blood, Joe
Martin leased the acreage from the Cherokee tribe at the rate of half
a cent to one cent per acre. Tribal members had the right to own the
property where their improvements (including their house, barn and
other outbuildings) were located. Bill and his wife, Jennie, saw a lot of
Oklahoma history themselves. An attorney by trade, he served as an
early district attorney for Muskogee County. Martin later became an
agent for the Federal Bureau of Investigation and served on the White
House detail to guard President Harry Truman. One of Rod Martin's
most prize possessions is a piece of White House stationery with the
inscription, "To Rod, Harry Truman." Jennie Martin also had a few
tales to tell about her brush with history. While a student at Oklahoma
A&M College (which would later become Oklahoma State University),
she would often watch barnstormers in their early planes display daring
feats above crowds of students and local townsfolk. After learning
that the pilots sold rides for five dollars each, she was determined to
try out this new form of transportation. So the next time one of the
barnstormers visited the campus, she rode in an airplane. This is how
she met and flew with Wiley Post. Jennie's reputation as a dancer was
also well known in her college social circles. She could really "cut a rug."
At one of her sorority dances, a tall, handsome gentleman asked her
for a dance. He told her that he had heard through the local grapevine
about her dancing abilities. She accepted and danced with the stranger,
who never told her his name. It wasn't until several days later that she
finally discovered the identity of the handsome stranger. His name was
John Dillinger.

20. Interview with Sam Vann, ex-slave, I-PP, 98.
21. Mayes County Historical Society, *Historical Highlights of Mayes County*, 185.
22. Rod Martin interview. Also based on aerial photographs taken by Rick Harding of Sun-Up Productions/Warren Entertainment during the production of the television documentary *Last Raid at Cabin Creek*. The photos show the old Martin house site sitting beside a short branch of the Texas Road. The branch ran east to west from the main road to the house site.

23. D.E. "Bill" Martin and Rod Martin interviews. Also see Mayes County Historical Society, *Historical Highlights of Mayes County*, 185.

24. D.E. "Bill" Martin and Rod Martin interviews.

25. Ibid.

26. Ibid.; see also I-PP, Vann interview, 100.

27. Ibid.; see also I-PP, Vann interview, 100.

28. Rod Martin interview.

29. D.E. "Bill" Martin and Rod Martin interviews; see also I-PP, Cunnie Martin interview, 383–84.

30. D.E. "Bill" Martin and Rod Martin interviews.

31. Ibid.

32. Ibid.

33. Ibid.

34. Ibid.

35. Military service record of Major Joseph L. Martin, compiled from the service records of the Second Cherokee Mounted Volunteers, Confederate States Army, National Archives publications, microcopy rolls 79, 80 and 90.

36. "D.E. "Bill" Martin and Rod Martin interviews.

37. Circular, General Orders No. 11, United States Army, By Order of Major General Blunt, Fort Scott, August 23, 1863. A copy of this order is located in the library of the Thomas Gilcrease Museum, Tulsa, Oklahoma.

38 Ibid.; see also Boeger's "Stand Watie and the Battles of First and Second Cabin Creek," 53.

CHAPTER 3

39. For death totals among the Indian nations, see Gibson, *American Indian*, 239; Wardell, *Political History of the Cherokee Nation*, 175; Wright, *Guide to Indian Tribes of Oklahoma*, 250–51; Debo, *Road to Disappearance*, 163, 178–79.

40. *American Scene* 8, no. 3, Diary of Hanna Hicks, 22.

41. Ibid.

42. Foreman, *Five Civilized Tribes*, 24; Boydson, "Fort Gibson Barracks," 289.

43. United States War Department, *Official Records of the Union and Confederate Armies*, Davis to Congress, December 12, 1861, series IV, vol. 1, 785 (hereafter after cited as *OR*).

44. Franks, *Stand Watie*, 114.

45. Maxey to Marilda Maxey, July 11, 1862, Lightfoot Family Papers.

46. Smith, *War with Mexico*, 17, 25; *Returns of the Regular Army*, Seventh Infantry, February 1847, 391.

47. Johnston, *Narrative of Military Operations*, 176–78; see also *OR*, vol. 24, pt. 3, John Adams to John Pemberton, May 13, 1863, 871.

48. S.S. Anderson to Maxey, December 11, 1863, Maxey Papers.

49. Maxey to Anderson, January 12, 1864, Maxey Papers.

50. *Time*, "Washington's Baptism," September 5, 1932.

51. *Memorial and Biographical History of Dallas County*, 999.

52. *Biographical Souvenir of the State of Texas*, 315.

53. Ibid., 316.

54. Speer, *Encyclopedia of the New West*, 176.

55. Ibid., 177.

56. Letter from Claire Witham to the author, July 2, 1991. Witham was one of General Gano's great-granddaughters.

57. See the "War Record of Brigadier General Richard Montgomery Gano."

58. Letter from Claire Witham to author, July 2, 1991.

59. Duke, *History of Morgan's Cavalry*, 197–98.

60. Branda, *Handbook of Texas*, 325.

61. Bower and Thurman, *Annals of Elder Horn*, 54.

62. Grady and Felmly, *Suffering to Silence*, 131–38.

63. Maxey to Marilda Maxey, February 25, 1864, Maxey Papers; see also Maxey to H.E. McCullough, March 21, 1864, Letter Book A, Maxey Papers.

64. Franks, *Stand Watie*, 158; see also Horton, *Samuel Bell Maxey*, 35.

65. Examples of these different caliber Indian weapons are on display at the Council House Museum, Okmulgee, Oklahoma.

66. *OR*, vol. 34, pt. 3, Captain J.J. Duboise to Maxey, February 25, 1864, 998.

67. Madeus, "Use of the Percussion Shotgun," 165–66.

68. Ibid.

69. Circular, Headquarters District Indian Territory, Confederate States Army, Brigadier General Samuel Maxey, Fort Towson, Choctaw Nation, May 14, 1864, Gilcrease Museum.

Chapter 4

70. *OR*, vol. 34, pt. 2, 945–46.

71. *OR*, vol. 41, pt. 2, 1,082.

72. *Journal of the Provisional Congress*, vol. 4, 26. On May 6, 1864, Confederate president Jefferson Davis placed Watie's name into nomination, and on May 10, the Confederate Senate confirmed Watie's appointment to brigadier general.

73. "A Short History of Stand Watie"; Wright, "Name of General Stand Watie," 252–53.

74. Genealogy of Ridge-Watie-Boudinot in Dale and Litton, *Cherokee Cavaliers*, 302 and following.

75. Franks, *Stand Watie*, 111.

76. DeMoss, "J.R. Williams Recovery Committee," vol. 41, pt. 3, 300. In November 1998, Robert DeMoss of Cleveland, Oklahoma, led a diving expedition to look for the remains of the *J.R. Williams* in the old Arkansas River channel now inundated by the Robert S. Kerr Reservoir near Tamaha, Oklahoma. Although visibility was poor, divers were able to find a long man-made structure on the bottom of the lake. Scanning of the object revealed its measurements to be 155 feet long and 45 feet wide. Artifacts were brought to the surface and included what appeared to be a section of a steamboat wheel and hand-hewn wood from the side of an old boat. DeMoss was led to the spot by Larry Peck, a local resident, who claimed that his father showed him the wreck of the *J.R. Williams* lying in the Arkansas River in about 1946. From local stories collected by DeMoss, apparently many local residents saw the remains of the vessel during dry years when the water level of the river was low. One story indicates that the boat may have not burned completely to the water line as first thought. During the 1930s, one man boarded the wreckage, took window frames still on the boat and placed them on his house. Reports indicate that the *Williams*'s smokestack could still be seen rising from a sandbar in the river until the late 1940s. One family even had a reunion photograph taken at an angle showing a portion of the river with the wreck of the *J.R. Williams* behind them. In September 2000, the U.S. Army Corps of Engineers attempted an underwater scanning survey close to the site where DeMoss found the submerged vessel and the artifacts. Results from the survey were inconclusive. The Army Corps of Engineers may attempt another study of the site if the funding is available to determine if the wreck is indeed the remains of the *J.R. Williams*.

77. Gano to Maxey, August 29, 1864, Maxey Papers; *OR*, vol. 22, pt. 1, Cooper to Steele, 457–61.
78. *OR*, vol. 41, pt. 1, Maxey to Anderson, September 3, 1864, 279; *OR*, vol. 41, pt. 2, Maxey to Kirby Smith, August 18, 1864, and Boggs to Maxey, August 25, 1864, 1,072 and 1,078.
79. *OR*, vol. 41, pt. 1, Cooper to Scott, September 14, 1864, 781; Bearss and Gibson, *Fort Smith*, 287.
80. *OR*, vol. 41, pt. 1, Watie to Heiston, 786.
81. *OR*, vol. 41, pt. 2, 1,082; *OR*, vol. 41, pt. 1, 780–82, 785. Camp Pike was located near present-day Whitefield, Oklahoma, by the Canadian River.
82. Maxey File, Letter Book A, 85, Texas State Archives, Austin, Texas; see also Payne, *Thundering Cannons*, 52.
83. *OR*, vol. 41, pt. 2, Maxey to Boggs, October 7, 1864, 780; *OR*, vol. 41, pt. 1, Gano to Cooper, 789; *OR*, vol. 41, pt. 1, Watie to Heiston, 785. Maxey wrote that Watie agreed to serve under Gano. However, historian Anne Bailey claimed that Gano had agreed to serve under Watie. It was decided that each man would retain individual command over each of their regiments, with Gano serving as the overall commander, *Confederate General*, vol. 2, 155. Historian Robert Kerby also wrote that Gano "played an important part in allowing Watie, the only nonwhite (general) officer in either Civil War army, to prove he had the capacity to conduct 'one of the most brilliant and skillfully managed cavalry raids of the war.'"
84. *OR*, vol. 41, pt. 1, Gano to Cooper, 789–91.
85. Ibid.

Chapter 5

86. *OR*, vol. 41, pt. 1, Watie to Heiston, 785.
87. Ibid., Gano to Cooper, September 29, 1864, 788.
88. Ibid., Watie to Heiston, 785.
89. Ibid., Gano to Cooper, September 29, 1864, 788.
90. Ibid. Watie to Heiston, p. 785.
91. Payne, *Thundering Cannons*, 56.
92. *OR*, vol. 41, pt. 1, Watie to Heiston, 785.
93. Ibid., Gano to Cooper, 788.
94. See "Notes on the Nigger Creek Fight."

95. *OR*, vol. 41, pt. 1, Gano to Cooper, 788.

96. Ibid., September 29, 1864, 788.

97. Ibid., Gano to Cooper, 788.

98. *OR*, vol. 41, pt. 1, Barker to Adjutant General, September 20, 1864, 772.

99. Military service record of Captain Edgar A. Barker, Junction City, Kansas, National Archives.

100. *OR*, vol. 41, pt. 1, Barker to Adjutant General, 772.

101. Ibid.

102. Ibid.

103. Ibid.; see also Britton, *Civil War on the Border*, vol. 2, 245; Payne, *Thundering Cannons*, 57.

104. *OR*, vol. 41, pt. 1, Barker to Adjutant General, 772.

105. *OR*, vol. 41, pt. 1, Gano to Cooper, 788.

106. Payne, *Thundering Cannons*, 58; see also Burke, *Official Military History of Kansas Regiments*, 420.

107. Britton, *Civil War on the Border*, vol. 2, 246.

108. Baird, *Creek Warrior for the Confederacy*, 95.

109. *OR*, vol. 41, pt. 1, Barker to Adjutant General, 772.

110. Baird, *Creek Warrior for the Confederacy*, 96.

111. Yeary, *Reminiscences of the Boys in Gray*, 46.

112. Battle Creek is a stream, 3.5 km (2.2 mi) long, heads at 36Â° 00' 11" N, 95Â° 22' 29" W, flows southeast to North Bay in Fort Gibson Lake, 3.2 km (2 mi) northeast of Wagoner. The stream is the site of the Civil War battle of Flat Rock (September 16, 1864) in which black Union soldiers were killed, Wagoner County, Oklahoma, sec. 1, T.17N. R.18E. Indian Mer., 35Â° 59' 03" N, 95Â° 20' 56" W; USGS map—*Wagoner East* 1:24,000; "Not Nigger Creek," BGN Decision List 1990, 22; see also *Wagoner Record Democrat*, "Battlefield Search May Be Easy for Society President."

113. *OR*, vol. 34, pt. 2, Maxey to Kirby Smith, February 26, 1864, 994.

114. Baird, *Creek Warrior for the Confederacy*, 96.

115. Sarah C. Watie to Stand Watie, June 8, 1863, in Dale and Litton, *Cherokee Cavaliers*, 128.

116. Peck, "Wagon Boss and Mule Mechanic," 8. The *National Tribune* was a weekly paper printed by the Grand Army of the Republic from 1879 to the late 1930s. It was the forerunner of the *Stars-N-Stripes*.

117. *Muskogee Phoenix*, "Nigger Creek."

118. Yeary, *Reminiscences of the Boys in Gray*, 733. Stroud remembered the brothers' surname was "Holden." Howard captured his brother John. However, while doing research for his book, Curtis Payne discovered the

brothers' family name was actually "Holland." *Report of the Adjutant General of the State of Kansas*, vol. 1, *1861–1865* lists John Holland as a private in Company C of the Second Kansas Cavalry. He enlisted at Humbolt, Kansas, on December 6, 1861. Howard Holland appears on the muster roll of Howell's Texas Battery compiled in Payne's *Thundering Cannons*, 92.

119. Yeary, *Reminiscences of the Boys in Gray*, 684.

120. *OR*, vol. 41, pt. 1, Gano to Cooper, 788; *OR*, vol. 41, pt. 1, Watie to Heiston, 785.

121. *OR*, vol. 41, pt. 1, Gano to Cooper, 788.

122. Ibid., Barker to Adjutant General, 772.

123. Britton, *Civil War on the Border*, vol. 2, 246–47.

124. *OR*, vol. 41, pt. 1, Gano to Cooper, 788.

CHAPTER 6

125. *OR*, vol. 41, pt. 1, Hopkins to Thomas, September 22, 1864, 766.

126. Military service record of Major Henry Hopkins, Second Kansas Cavalry, National Archives.

127. Hopkins, "Henry M. Hopkins," 276.

128. Burke, *Official Military History of Kansas Regiments*, 449; see also *OR*, vol. 32, pt. 1, Captain Henry Hopkins's report to Colonel William A. Phillips, July 21, 1863, 456–57.

129. *OR*, vol. 41, pt. 1, 767; Dr. George A. Moore, "Recollections of a Kansas Pioneer," *Leavenworth Herald*, March 8, 1914. A copy of the article is on file in the library of the Kansas State Historical Society, Topeka, Kansas. Moore remembered that the train was guarded by an armed military guard of five hundred men under the command of Major Hopkins. He also wrote that about six hundred unarmed recruits accompanied the train on the way to the front; see also Peck, "Wagon Boss and Mule Mechanic."

130. Ibid.

131. Ibid.

132. Ibid.

133. Ibid.; see also Britton, *Union Indian Brigade in the Civil War*, vol. 2, 441.

134. Peck, "Wagon Boss and Mule Mechanic." In his article, Peck also wondered why Gano allowed Whitlow and Palmer to reinforce Hopkins.

Peck suggested that Gano was confident that his forces would capture the wagon train.

135. Ibid.

136. Ibid.

137. *OR*, vol. 41, pt. 1, Cooper to Scott, September 14, 1864, 781.

138. *OR*, vol. 34, pt. 4, 609.

139. *OR*, vol. 22, pt. 1, 379–31.

140. Epple, *Civil War Battle of Cabin Creek*, 26.

141. *OR*, vol. 41, pt. 1, Gano to Cooper, September 29, 1864, 789.

142. Ibid.

143. D.E. "Bill" Martin and Rod Martin interviews; Richard Martin, undated letter typewritten at Pensacola, Indian Territory.

144. Peck, "Wagon Boss and Mule Mechanic," 8; Moore, "Recollections of a Kansas Pioneer"; D.E. "Bill" Martin and Rod Martin interviews.

145. *OR*, vol. 41, pt. 1, Gano to Cooper, 789; D.E. "Bill" Martin and Rod Martin interviews. The author visited the site of the camp where Gano and his cavalry troopers waited for Watie and the rest of the Confederate force. The area is well sheltered and cannot be seen from a distance. There is no doubt that Gano's placement of his cavalry force in the small ravine helped to confuse Hopkins as to the actual size of the Confederate force.

146. *OR*, vol. 45, pt. 1, Jennison to Hampton, 773.

147. *OR*, vol. 41, pt. 1, Hopkins to Thomas, 769.

148. Peck, "Wagon Boss and Mule Mechanic," 8.

149. Ibid.

150. Moore, "Recollections of a Kansas Pioneer."

151. I-PP, Mrs. Vernon Purlee interview, May 5, 1938, 11. Mrs. Purlee was the daughter of Greenbrier Joe Martin and Lucy Martin Rogers.

152. *OR*, vol. 41, pt. 1, Watie to Heiston, September 23, 1864, 786; *OR*, vol. 41, pt. 1, Gano to Cooper, September 29, 1864, 789.

153. D.E. "Bill" Martin interview. Among the stories his grandfather (Richard Martin) told him when he was a child, Martin remembered that Richard told him how he led Gano and his four hundred troopers to an area southeast of the Cabin Creek stockade using another ford to cross Cabin Creek. According to Martin, this ford was located southeast of the military ford.

CHAPTER 7

154. *OR*, vol. 41, pt. 1, Gano to Cooper, September 29, 1864, 789; *OR*, vol. 41, pt. 1, Hopkins to Thomas, September 25, 1864, 770; Moore, "Recollections of a Kansas Pioneer"; see also Peck, Wagon Boss and Mule Mechanic," 8.
155. *OR*, vol. 41, pt. 1, Watie to Heiston, 786. A bright moon is also reported in Dr. Moore's account of the battle.
156. Ibid., Gano to Cooper, 490.
157. Grady and Felmly, *Suffering to Silence*, 160. The authors wrote that General Gano ordered his men to dismount and then fired a shot in the air with his revolver to get the attention of the Union pickets.
158. Hermon, "Early Sheriff Faced Wild Times."
159. *OR*, vol. 45, pt. 1, Jennison to Hampton, September 22, 1864, 773.
160. In his autobiography, Grayson wrote that the man who approached the Confederate lines was drunk. He also remembered the man as being Mexican and guessed that he was probably one of the teamsters with the wagon train. See Baird, *Creek Warrior for the Confederacy*, 100.
161. *OR*, vol. 45, pt. 1, Johnson to Morris, September 20, 1864, 775.
162. *OR*, vol. 41, pt. 1, Gano to Cooper, September 29, 1864, 789.
163. *OR*, vol. 45, pt. 1, Jennison to Hampton, September 22, 1864, 773.
164. *OR*, vol. 41, pt. 1, Hopkins to Thomas, September 25, 1864, 768.
165. I-PP, James R. Carselowey interview, July 15, 1937, 156. Carselowey was a field worker gathering material for the Indian-Pioneer Papers project. He was acquainted with Nick Thomas, a Cherokee Indian, who as a Confederate soldier fought at the Second Battle of Cabin Creek and drove one of the captured wagons. See also Britton, *Civil War on the Border*, vol. 2, 251.
166. *OR*, vol. 45, pt. 1, Gano to Cooper, September 29, 1864, 789; *OR*, vol. 41, pt. 1, Hopkins to Thomas, September 25, 1864, 770; Moore, "Recollections of a Kansas Pioneer"; see also Peck, "Wagon Boss and Mule Mechanic," 8.
167. Peck, "Wagon Boss and Mule Mechanic," 8.
168. *Northern Standard*, "Letters of a Private"; *Northern Standard*, letter to the editor from Colonel DeMorse (private) dated September 29, 1864, at Camp Bragg.
169. Moore, "Recollections of a Kansas Pioneer."
170. Peck, "Wagon Boss and Mule Mechanic," 8.
171. Letter of George W. Trout, age eighty-three, dated September 30, 1930; *OR*, vol. 41, pt. 1, Watie to Heiston, September 23, 1864, 786.

172. Over the years, historians have assumed that the moon set before the battle was over. In 1998, Dr. Donald W. Olson of Southwest Texas State University did a study of the phases of the moon during the Second Battle of Cabin Creek. Dr. Olson concluded in his study that the moon was indeed bright, just past full and high in the sky in the early morning hours and may have played a significant role in lighting up the battlefield. However, Olson's research also found that the moon did not set during the battle and was still high in the sky (48 degrees above the western horizon) when the sun rose at 5:46 a.m. LMT on September 19, 1864. He theorized that if the moonlight went away during the night, it may have been due to clouds, but it was not because the moon set, *OR*, vol. 41, pt. 1, Gano to Cooper, September 29, 1864, 790; *OR*, vol. 41, pt. 1, Watie to Heiston, 787.

173. *OR*, vol. 41, pt. 1, Gano to Cooper, September 29, 1864, 790.

174. Grady and Felmly, *Suffering to Silence*, 161.

175. *OR*, vol. 41, pt. 1, Gano to Cooper, 790.

176. *OR*, vol. 41, pt. 1, Watie to Heiston, 787.

177. Baird, *Creek Warrior for the Confederacy*, 102; Cunningham, *General Stand Watie's Confederate Indians*, 155.

178. *OR*, vol. 41, pt. 1, Gano to Cooper, 790.

179. Ibid., Watie to Heiston, 787.

180. Ibid., Gano to Cooper, 790.

181. Crane, "Excerpts from a Diary"; see also *Field Manual for the Use of Officers*, 23. According to the *Field Manual*, canister was a tin cylinder with iron heads filled with cast-iron balls packed in sawdust. Grapeshot was composed of nine small cast-iron balls of a size approximate to the caliber, disposed in three layers of three balls each. A stand of grape was held together by two rings and a plate at each end of the stand, connected by a rod or bolt. Spherical case shot was developed by Colonel Schrapnell of the British army and hence was often called "shrapnel." The projectile consisted of a thin cast-iron round shell filled with lead musket balls. Each of the twelve-pound spherical case shot projectiles fired by Howell's Texas Battery at the Second Battle of Cabin Creek contained ninety lead balls and one ounce of black powder.

182. *OR*, vol. 45, pt. 1, Johnson to Morris, September 20, 1864, 774.

183. Britton, *Civil War on the Border*, vol. 2, 250.

184. *OR*, vol. 41, pt. 1, Gano to Cooper, 790.

185. Ibid.; Crane, "Excerpts from a Diary."

186. *OR*, vol. 41, pt. 1, Gano to Cooper, 790.

NOTES TO PAGES 75–82

187. The author, along with researcher Steven B. McCartney, found Alfred
    Collins's account and Dr. George A. Moore's article in the archives of the
    Kansas Historical Society in Topeka.
188. Peck, "Wagon Boss and Mule Mechanic," 8.

CHAPTER 8

189. Yeary, *Reminiscences of the Boys in Gray*, 353.
190. *OR*, vol. 41, pt. 1, Hopkins to Thomas, 771; *OR*, vol. 41, pt. 1, Gano to
    Cooper, 791; *OR*, vol. 41, pt. 1, Watie to Heiston, 784.
191. Letter of T.S. Bell, Company E, Thirtieth Texas Cavalry, September
    30, 1864, Archives Division, Oklahoma Historical Society.
192. *OR*, vol. 41, pt. 1, Watie to Heiston, 787.
193. Ibid., Gano to Cooper, 788.
194. *OR*, vol. 41, pt. 3, Curtis to Rosecrans, September 20, 1864, 278. For
    this book, I wanted to find a formula to see what the value of the goods in
    the captured wagon train would be worth today. According to historian/
    author Alfred Nofi, there really isn't any valid way of comparing the
    relative value of money over so great a period. There are several "official"
    conversion figures, including one by the Bureau of Labor Statistics, but
    these are not based on serious historical research—basically they try to
    compare the price of a handful of basic items. Nofi gave one example.
    Consider that as a fairly successful lawyer, Abraham Lincoln was only
    making $1,500 per year on the eve of the war. This would only be about
    $30,000 based on the BLS conversion rate—hardly enough today to
    be considered doing well with a family of four. Instead, Nofi multiplied
    the 1860s dollar by about 350. Today, this would give Abe a $525,000,
    income, a not impossible figure for an attorney of his stature. Nofi noted
    that there is really no valid way to compare the value of money over the
    past 150 years given the enormous changes in the quality and availability
    of goods, not to mention the tremendous increase in the nature of what
    we buy.
195. *OR*, vol. 41, pt. 1, Gano to Cooper, 788.
196. Ibid., Gano to Cooper, 788.
197. D.E. "Bill" Martin interviews.
198. Yeary, *Reminiscences of the Boys in Gray*, 830.

199. *OR*, vol. 41, pt. 1, Hopkins to Thomas, September 28, 1864, 769.

200. Moore, "Recollections of a Kansas Pioneer."

201. Peck, "Wagon Boss and Mule Mechanic," 8.

202. *OR*, vol. 45, pt. 1, Jennison to Hampton, September 22, 1864, 772.

203. Maxey Files, Texas State Archives, quoted by Payne in *Thundering Cannons*, 71.

204. *OR*, vol. 41, pt. 1, Foreman to Blair, September 20, 1864, 766; *OR*, vol. 45, pt. 1, Johnson to Morris, September 20, 1864, 774; see also Kerby, *Kirby Smith's Confederacy*, 355.

205. *OR*, vol. 41, pt. 3, Forman to Wattles, September 22, 1864, 301.

206. Yeary, *Reminiscences of the Boys in Gray*, 251.

207. Maxey Papers, Gilcrease Museum, quoted by Payne in *Thundering Cannons*, 72.

Chapter 9

208. *OR*, vol. 41, pt. 1, Williams to Blair, September 20, 1864, 765. See also Hancock, "Second Battle of Cabin Creek," 422. The author's father, Leon Warren, lived on a farm near Vinita, Oklahoma, in the 1930s when many rural families still relied on horses, mules and wagons for transportation. According to conversations with Warren, a good four-mule team could pull a wagon about three to four miles per hour. Joe Poplin of Pryor, Oklahoma, whose father also lived on a farm during the Great Depression, confirmed this fact. Considering that many of the Union supply wagons were pulled by six-mule teams, and if Gano and Watie had the remaining wagons rolling south immediately after the Union garrison surrendered at about 9:00 a.m., it is feasible that the Union skirmishers encountered the first captured wagons driven by Confederates north of Pryor's Creek at about 11:00 a.m. on the morning of September 19.

209. Yeary, *Reminiscences of the Boys in Gray*, 643.

210. *OR*, vol. 41, pt. 1, Gano to Cooper, September 29, 1864, 788; Peck, "Wagon Boss and Mule Mechanic."

211. Rampp, "Negro Troop Activity in Indian Territory," in *Kepis & Turkey Calls*, 211.

212. *OR*, vol. 41, pt. 1, Williams to Blair, September 20, 1864, 765.

213. The author examined artifacts from the Pryor's Creek Battlefield that clearly show that Williams's gunners fired Parrott projectiles, as well as Hotchkiss projectiles made for Parrott rifled guns.
214. Wilson, *Black Phalanx*, 240; Payne, *Thundering Cannons*, 73.
215. *OR*, vol. 41, pt. 1, Gano to Cooper, September 29, 1864, 788; see also Britton, *Union Indian Brigade in the Civil War*, 445.
216. *OR*, vol. 41, pt. 1, Watie to Heiston, October 3, 1864, 784.
217. Anderson, *Life of General Stand Watie*, 25.
218. *OR*, vol. 41, pt. 1, Williams to Blair, 765.
219. Ibid.
220. Graton correspondence, MS 918.02, Microfilm division, Kansas Historical Society.
221. Payne, *Thundering Cannons*, 74.
222. *OR*, vol. 41, pt. 1, Foreman to Blair, September 20, 1864, 766.
223. Ibid.
224. Peck, "Wagon Boss and Mule Mechanic."
225. Ibid.
226. Letter of Christian Isley to Eliza, October 19, 1864, Isley Family Papers.
227. Ibid.

CHAPTER 10

228. *OR*, vol. 41, pt. 1, Gano to Cooper, 791.
229. Chase, *Index to the First Cherokee Mounted Volunteers*, Holt's Squadron and the Second Cherokee Mounted Volunteers, rolls 79, 80 and 90. Clem Rogers served as a lieutenant in Company G of Stand Watie's First Cherokee Mounted Volunteers. He finished the war with the rank of captain.
230. Anderson, *Life of General Stand Watie*, 25–26.
231. Ibid. Mayes may have been romanticizing his story just a little bit. The author grew up near the Verdigris River, and its waters have always been muddy, never clear.
232. Debo, *Tulsa*, 34; see also Hancock, "Second Battle of Cabin Creek," 422; Yeary, *Reminiscences of the Boys in Gray*, 643.
233. I-PP, James R. Carselowey interview, 156.
234. *OR*, vol. 41, pt. 1, Johnson to Morris, September 25, 1864, 776.

235. Pocket diary of Master Sergeant Septimus Stevenson (1839–1918). Stevenson's diary contains entries from January 1, 1864, to November 17, 1864. Stevenson survived the war and lived in Sturgeon Bay, Wisconsin. His diary is in the private collection of Chuck Larson.

236. Letter of Richard Martin, Pensacola, Indian Territory, not dated.

237. Yeary, *Reminiscences of the Boys in Gray*, 46.

238. *OR*, vol. 41, pt. 1, Gano to Cooper, 791.

239. *New York Times*, September 27, 1864.

240. *New York Times*, September 28, 1864.

241. Dale and Litton, *Cherokee Cavaliers*, 190.

242. Miller, *Photographic History of the Civil War*, vol. 8, 47.

243. Sherman, *Memoirs of William T. Sherman*, vol. 2, part 4.

244. Ballard, *Staff Ride Guide*, 65.

245. Wesley Walk Bradly to Nancy Bradly, *Bradly Civil War Letters*.

246. James Rumsey to George Rumsey, November 20, 1864, written at Camp zano. Courtesy of Howard Coleman Jr., San Angelo, Texas. Coleman is the great-great-grandson of Lieutenant James Rumsey.

247. I-PP, Judge J.T. Parks interview, 64.

248. Portlock to Inspector-General Bonham, October 13, 1864, AGO, *Confederate Archives*, chapter 2, no. 59, no. 81, 64.

249. DeMorse as "private," *Northern Standard*, October 10, 1864.

250. Gano to Maxey, October 4, 1864, and Maxey to Marilda Maxey, October 12, 1864, Maxey Papers.

251. Fields, "Texas Heroes of the Confederacy."

252. Ibid.

253. Wilmeth, "Thoughts and Things as They Occurred." With Gano out of action, Colonel Charles DeMorse assumed command of the Texas brigade at the Battle of Poison Springs, Arkansas; see also *OR*, vol. 34, pt. 3, 766; Evans, *Confederate Military History*, vol. 11, 407, mentions that Gano was severely wounded in the left arm while serving in Arkansas.

254. *OR*, vol. 34, pt. 3, 766; Evans, *Confederate Military History*, vol. 11, 407, mentions that General Gano "was severely wounded in the left arm while serving in Arkansas."

255. *OR*, vol. 41, pt. 1, 792–94; see also Harwell, *Confederate Reader*, 310–15.

256. Congratulatory General Order 81 of Major General Edmund Kirby Smith, October 12, 1864. A copy of this order is in the library of the Thomas Gilcrease Museum; see *OR*, vol. 41, pt. 1, 794.

257. *Journal of the Congress of the Confederate States of America*, Senate Document 234, vol. 7, 495.

258. Britton, *Union Indian Brigade in the Civil War*, 460–62; *OR*, vol. 41, part 4, Thayer to Wattles, 74–75.
259. *OR*, vol. 48, pt. 1, Grant to Halleck, 391.
260. Peck, "Wagon Boss and Mule Mechanic."

CHAPTER 11

261. L.P. Chouteau to James M. Bell, January 21, 1865, in Dale and Litton, *Cherokee Cavaliers*, 200–210.
262. A copy of the actual surrender document and treaty signed by Watie and Matthews is in the library of the Gilcrease Museum, Tulsa, Oklahoma.
263. See surrender document.
264. DeMorse, *Northern Standard*, June 14, 1865.
265. H.E. McKee to Stand Watie, Fort Smith, Arkansas, 1867, in Dale and Litton *Cherokee Cavaliers*, 258–59. The sutler firm of McDonald & Fuller also claimed a $60,000 loss from goods lost in the Cabin Creek raid; see Monaghan, *Civil War on the Western Border*, 310.
266. R. Armstrong to Stand Watie, August 30, 1867, Cherokee Nation Collection.
267. Dale and Litton, *Cherokee Cavaliers*, 266.
268. Fields, "Texas Heroes of the Confederacy."
269. Ibid.; Yeary, *Reminiscences of the Boys in Gray*, 251. Gano counted more than 6,800 persons whom he alone had baptized. However, he did not count those who responded to his preaching when visiting other churches. It is the opinion of the author that he simply lost count. Many writers of Christian Church/Church of Christ history agree that the number of people he baptized was more than 16,000; see also Eckstein, *History of the Churches of Christ*.
270. See *Memorial and Biographical History of Dallas County*.
271. The ad also ran in the issues of December 6 and December 20, 1873. Gano advertisement from the collection of Claire Witham; *Biographical Souvenir of the State of Texas*, 316.
272. Casey, *Soldiers, Ranchers and Miners*, 150–51; see also *Map of Southern Part of Presidio County* by John T. Gano in Texas State Land Office, Austin, Texas.
273. Casey, *Soldiers, Ranchers and Miners*, 150–51.

274. *Handbook of Texas Online*, located on the Internet at www.tsha.utexas. edu/handbook/online; *Men of Affairs of Houston and Environs*, 132–33. Howard Hughes's grandfather, Howard Robard Hughes, graduated from Harvard University in 1897. He patented a rock drill bearing the Hughes name and organized the Sharp-Hughes Tool Company. In 1905, he married Gano's daughter, Alene.

275. *Dallas Morning News*, "Gen. Richard M. Gano Claimed by Death."

276. *Handbook of Texas Online*; see also Scarbrough, *Land of Good Water.* The town of Gano was on Farm Road 486, six miles south of Thorndale in southeastern Williamson County on the Milam County line.

277. Military service record of Major Henry Hopkins, Second Kansas Cavalry.

278. *Daily Capital*, "Maj. Henry Hopkins."

279. Hopkins, "Henry M. Hopkins," vol. 6, 280.

280. Gable, "Kansas Penitentiary," vol. 14, 395.

281. Ibid.; Hopkins, "Henry M. Hopkins," 280.

282. *Kansas Herald*, "Death of Commissioner Hopkins."

283. Gable, "Kansas Penitentiary," vol. 14, 428.

284. Peck, "Wagon Boss and Mule Mechanic."

285. Statement of Allen Ross located in the Special Collections Department of the McFarlin Library, University of Tulsa; see also Chase, *Indian Home Guards*, 144.

286. D.E. "Bill" Martin and Rod Martin interviews; I-PP, Granville A. Cunnie Martin interview, 387; I-PP, Mrs. Vernon Purlee interview, 4.

287. I-PP, Lula Poole Kelley interview, April 6, 1937, 65–68.

288. D.E. "Bill" Martin interview; I-PP, Stella Evelyn Carselowey Crouch interview, January 20–21, 1938, 418–19. In her interview, Mrs. Crouch described the tornado as "the worst storm in the history of Indian Territory. It traveled up the Grand River at 12 o'clock noon and almost took the country clean."

289. D.E. "Bill" Martin and Rod Martin interviews.

290. Several of Martin's letters and articles printed in Indian Territory newspapers can be viewed on microfilm, including Vinita's the *Indian Chieftain*, the *Cherokee Advocate* and the *Cherokee News*; see also I-PP, Mrs. Vernon Purlee interview, 4.

291. Mayes County Historical Society, *Historical Highlights of Mayes County*, 185.

292. *Cherokee News*, "Greenbrier Joe Martin"; *Cherokee Advocate*, "Joseph L. Martin."

293. Mayes County Historical Society, *Historical Highlights of Mayes County*, 185; D.E. "Bill" Martin and Rod Martin interviews.

294. Mayes County Historical Society, *Historical Highlights of Mayes County*, 185; D.E. "Bill" Martin and Rod Martin interviews.

295. D.E. "Bill" Martin and Rod Martin interviews. Richard Martin's house at Rock Creek is still a private residence and stands southwest of the bridge where State Highway 28 crosses Big Cabin Creek.

296. Kappler & Merillat to Richard Martin, May 28, 1907, Collection of Paul and June Venamon, Pryor, Oklahoma.

297. *Adair Weekly Ledger*, August 17, 1911.

298. Ibid.; D.E. "Bill" Martin and Rod Martin interviews.

299. *Leavenworth Times*, "Reunion"; James M. Williams's military service record highlights, located at the American Civil War Research Database, http://www.civilwardata.com; biography of James M. Williams, typewritten manuscript in the library of the Kansas Historical Society, Topeka.

300. Ulysses S. Grant to Andrew Johnson, January 1866, Adjutant General's Office Records, NA RG 94. Henry Stanberry, U.S. attorney general, wrote on the back of Maxey's brochure of letters, "I recommend a pardon in this case." It is dated July 20, 1867.

301. Maxey to Dora Maxey, February 2, 1874, Maxey Papers; see also Horton, *Samuel Bell Maxey*, 54.

302. Horton, *Samuel Bell Maxey*, 193.

303. *Handbook of Texas Online*.

304. Military service record of Edgar A. Barker, Second Kansas Cavalry.

305. Burgess, "Eighteenth Kansas Volunteer Cavalry," vol. 13, 534–38. The Eighteenth Kansas Cavalry was raised for duty in 1867. Barker is listed as captain of Company B of the Eighteenth Kansas Cavalry on a muster roll dated July 15, 1867, that is found in Crawford, *Kansas in the Sixties*, 404; see also Jenness, "Battle on Beaver Creek," vol. 9, 1906, 443–52.

306. Military service record of Edgar A. Barker, Second Kansas Cavalry.

307. Sutherland family papers and records, courtesy of Mrs. Pat Sutherland Mittelsteadt, a direct descendant of David M. Sutherland.

308. Payne, *Thundering Cannons*, 72

309. Hermon, "Early Sheriff Faced Wild Times."

310. Patrick Cosgrove obituary, *Olathe Register*, July 13, 1916.

311. Griffin, *University of Kansas*, 693.

312. *Men of the Pacific Coast*, 395.

313. Chapman, "Founding of El Reno," 79–108.

CHAPTER 12

314. War of 1861, Declaration for Invalid Army Pension of Richard M. Roark, Polk County, Missouri, dated April 2, 1882, courtesy of Jack and Norma Jean Mullen, Pryor, Oklahoma.

315. Ibid.

316. Letter of George W. Trout, age eighty-three, dated September 30, 1930. Copy located in the Oklahoma Historical Society Library.

317. Henry Trout memoirs, typed manuscript in private collection of Kelly Kirkpatrick, Big Cabin, Oklahoma.

318. Ibid.

319. *Tulsa World*, "Veteran Recalls Oklahoma Battle," September 29, 1929, Sect. 4, 7.

320. *Oklahoma*, 268–69.

321. Ibid.

322. United Confederate Veteran Camps in Oklahoma, http://www.usgennet.org/usa/ok/county/woodward/military/vetcamp.html.

323. General Order No. 5, Headquarters United Confederate Veterans, New Orleans, Louisiana, March 29, 1924.

324. Commander of the Trans-Mississippi Department, UCV, *Confederate Veteran*, May 1924.

325. Yeary, *Reminiscences of the Boys in Gray*, 407.

326. Application for Charter, Grand Army of the Republic, dated Stafford, Kansas, January 26, 1884, Kansas Historical Society Archives.

327. R.M. Blair, Post Commander of Henry Hopkins Post No. 301, to H.T. Devendorf on post stationery, dated February 11, 1884, Kansas Historical Society Archives.

328. Reports of Adjutant and Quartermaster, Henry Hopkins Post No. 301, for the year ending December 31, 1934, Kansas Historical Society Archives.

329. Grand Army of the Republic (GAR) Posts in Oklahoma, http://suvcw.org/garposts/ok.pdf.

330. If you have any information about the Military Cemetery located near Pensacola, Oklahoma, contact the Craig County Genealogical Society via e-mail at ccgs484@hotmail.com or write to the society at P.O. Box 484, Vinita, Oklahoma, 74301.

CHAPTER 13

331. On different occasions, the author had the opportunity to speak privately with each of the listed historians about the story of the cannon in Cabin Creek.

332. Interview with Lee Good, March 1990. At the time of the interview, Mr. Good was the director of the J.M. Davis Gun Museum in Claremore, Oklahoma.

333. I-PP, Stella Evelyn Carselowey Crouch interview, 415.

334. Jennie Martin interview, Sand Springs, Oklahoma, November 1990.

335. *Tulsa Tribune*, "Hunt for Civil War Cannon Is Fruitless."

336. *Tulsa World*, "Civil War Musket Found," January 23, 1964.

337. Interview with Jack Mullen, Pryor, Oklahoma, April 1990.

338. Telephone interview with Steve Cox, Van Buren, Arkansas, May 2001.

339. I-PP, Mrs. Josephine Spence interview, July 29, 1937, 337.

340. Roster and record of Iowa Soldiers in the War of the Rebellion, American Civil War Research Database, www.civilwardata.com.

CHAPTER 14

341. The Vinita chapter of the United Daughters of the Confederacy always that believed the ten-acre plot included the Confederate graves from the second battle, though no evidence of graves within the present-day battlefield park has ever been found. George Trout wrote that the Confederate dead from the second engagement were "buried west of the creek up on the flat. Was buried up the creek from the ford about one half-mile west on the south bluff on the banks of Cabin Creek," Letter of George Washington Trout, September 30, 1930, Oklahoma Historical Society Library.

342. Yeary, *Reminiscences of the Boys in Gray*, 118.

343. "Record Book of Burials," Fort Gibson, 42–43. The Flat Rock dead are marked 1433 through 1444 (11 total). The Cabin Creek dead are numbered 1405 through 1419 (14 total).

344. Anderson, *Life of General Stand Watie*, 48.

345. Ibid., 50.

346. *Dallas Daily Herald*, August 7, 1885, reporting remarks made by Gano at a Confederate Veterans reunion in Fort Worth, Texas.

Bibliography

Books, Booklets and Pamphlets

Abel, Annie Heloise. *The American Indian as a Slave Holder and a Secessionist.* Cleveland, OH: Arthur H. Clark Company, 1915.
————. *The American Indian as Participant in the Civil War, 1861–1865.* Cleveland, OH: Arthur H. Clark Company, 1919.
————. *The American Indian Under Reconstruction.* Cleveland, OH: Arthur Clark Company, 1925.

Abbott, Wayne E. *History of Southeastern Wagoner County, Oklahoma.* N.p.: privately printed, n.d.

Albaugh, William A., III. *Tyler, Texas: The Story of the Confederate States Ordinance Works at Tyler, Texas 1861—1865.* Wilmington, NC: Broadfoot Publishing Company, 1993.

American Scene 13, no. 3 (1979). Diary of Hanna Hicks. Thomas Gilcrease Institute of American History and Art, Tulsa, Oklahoma.

Anderson, Mabel Washburn. *Life of General Stand Watie.* Pryor, OK: Mayes County Republican, 1931

Bailey, Anne. *The Confederate General.* 6 vols. Harrisburg, Pennsylvania, 1991.

Baker, T. Lindsay, and Julie P. Baker. *The WPA Oklahoma Slave Narratives.* Norman: University of Oklahoma Press, 1996.

Ballard, Ted. *Staff Ride Guide: Battle of Ball's Bluff.* Washington, D.C.: Center of Military History, U.S. Army, 2001.

Bearss, Edwin C. *Steele's Retreat from Camden and the Battle of Jenkin's Ferry*. Little Rock, AK: Democrat Printing & Litho Company, 1995.

Bearss, Edwin C., and A.M. Gibson. *Fort Smith: Little Gibraltar on the Arkansas*. Norman: University of Oklahoma Press, 1969.

Biographical Souvenir of the State of Texas. Chicago, IL: F.A. Battery & Company, 1889.

Bower, John Wilson, and Claude Harrison Thurman. *The Annals of Elder Horn*. New York: Richard Smith Inc., 1930.

Branda, Eldon Stephen, ed. *The Handbook of Texas*: A Supplement. Vol. 3. Austin: Texas State Historical Association, 1975.

Britton, Wiley. *The Civil War on the Border*. 2 vols. New York: G.P. Putnam's Sons, 1899.

———. *Memoirs of the Rebellion on the Border—1863*. Chicago, IL: Cushing, Thomas & Company, 1882.

———. *The Union Indian Brigade in the Civil War*. Kansas City, KS: Franklin Hudson Publishing Company, 1922.

Burch, J.P. *A True Story of Charles W. Quantrell and His Guerilla Band*. Vega, Texas, 1923.

Burke, W.S. *Official Military History of Kansas Regiments During the War for the Suppression of the Great Rebellion*. Ottawa: Kansas Heritage Press, n.d.

Cabin Creek Monument Dedication. Program. Flavius J. Barrett Chapter 1829 of the United Daughters of the Confederacy, June 2, 1961.

Calhoun, William G., comp. *Fort Scott: A Pictorial History*. Fort Scott, KS: Sekan Printing Company, 1991.

Campbell, O.B. *Vinita, I.T.: The Story of a Frontier Town in the Cherokee Nation 1871–1907*. Oklahoma City, OK: Metro Press, 1972.

Cantrell, Marc Lea, and Mac Harris, eds. *Kepis & Turkey Calls: An Anthology of the War Between the States in Indian Territory*. Oklahoma City, OK: Western Heritage Books, 1982.

Casey, Clifford B. *Soldiers, Ranchers and Miners in the Big Bend*. Washington, D.C.: National Technical Information Service, 1969.

Castel, Albert. *A Frontier State at War: Kansas, 1861–1865*. Ithaca, NY: Cornell University Press, 1958.

Cavalry Tactics: Single Rank Formations and Skirmish Drill for Mounted Rifles, For the instruction of the forces of the Confederate States, in the Department of Indian Territory. Boggy Depot, Cherokee Nation, May 1863. Reprint, Tulsa, OK: Gilcrease Museum, 1965.

Chase, Marybelle W., ed. *Index to the First Cherokee Mounted Volunteers, Holt's Squadron, and the Second Cherokee Mounted Volunteers*. Compiled from the service records of these organizations that are National Archives publications on microcopy, 258 rolls. Rolls 79, 80 and 90. Tulsa, OK: privately printed, n.d.

————. *Index to the Second Cherokee Mounted Volunteers, Confederate States Army.* National Archives publications, microcopy, 258 rolls. Rolls 79, 80 and 90. Tulsa, OK: privately printed, n.d.

————. *Indian Home Guards Civil War Service Records.* Tulsa, OK: privately printed, 1993.

Cornish, Dudley Taylor. *Kansas Negro Regiments in the Civil War.* State of Kansas Commission on Civil Rights, 1969.

————. *The Sable Arm: Negro Troops in the Union Army, 1861–1865.* New York: Longmans, Green and Company, 1958.

Crawford, Samuel J. *Kansas in the Sixties.* Chicago, IL: A.C. McClurg & Company, 1911.

Cunningham, Frank. *General Stand Watie's Confederate Indians.* San Antonio, TX: Naylor Company, 1959.

Dale, Edward Everitt, and Gaston Litton. *Cherokee Cavaliers.* Norman: University of Oklahoma Press, 1969.

Davis, William C. *Jefferson Davis: The Man and His Hour.* New York: HarperCollins Publishers, 1991.

Debo, Angie. *The Road to Disappearance: A History of the Creek Indians.* Norman: University of Oklahoma Press, 1941.

————. *Tulsa: From Creek Town to Oil Capital.* Norman: University Of Oklahoma Press, 1943.

DeMorse, Charles. *An Editor's View of Early Texas.* Ed. Lorna Geer Sheppard. Austin, TX: Eakin Press, 1998.

DeMoss, Robert W. "J.R. Williams Recovery Committee Information Packet." Cleveland, Oklahoma, 1999.

Duke, Basil W. *A History of Morgan's Cavalry.* Cincinnati, OH: Miami Printing & Publishing Company, 1867.

Dyer, Frederick A. *A Compendium of the War of the Rebellion.* 3 vols. New York: Thomas Yoseloff, 1959.

Eckstein, Stephen Daniel. *History of the Churches of Christ in Texas, 1824–1950.* Austin, TX: Firm Foundation Publishing House, 1963.

Epple, Jess C. *Civil War Battle of Cabin Creek.* Muskogee, OK: Hoffman Printing, 1964.

Evans, Clement A., ed. *Confederate Military History.* 12 vols. Atlanta, GA: Confederate Publishing Company, 1899.

Faulk, Odie B., Kenny A. Franks and Paul F. Lambert, eds. *Early Forts and Military Posts in Oklahoma.* Oklahoma City: Oklahoma Historical Society, 1978.

The Field Manual for the Use of Officers on Ordnance Duty. Richmond, VA: Ritchie & Dunnavant, 1862. Reprinted as *The Confederate Field Manual with Photographic Supplement* by Dean S. Thomas, Gettysburg, Pennsylvania, 1984.

Fischer, Leroy H., ed. *The Civil War in Indian Territory*. Los Angeles, CA: Lorrin L. Morrison, 1974.

Fleck-O'Keefe, Marlynn Ann. *Fort Towson, Indian Territory: A Link to the West*. Wolfe City, TX: Hennington Publishing Company, 1997.

Foreman, Grant. *Down the Texas Road: Historic Places Along Highway 69 through Oklahoma*. Norman: University of Oklahoma Press, 1954.

———. *The Five Civilized Tribes*. Norman: University of Oklahoma Press, 1934.

———. *Fort Gibson*. Norman: University of Oklahoma Press, 1936.

———. *A History of Oklahoma*. Norman: University of Oklahoma Press, 1945.

Fox, William F. *Regimental Losses in the American Civil War, 1861–1865*. Albany, NY: Albany Publishing Company, 1889.

Franks, Kenny A. *Stand Watie and the Agony of the Cherokee Nation*. Memphis, TN: Memphis State University Press, 1979.

Gibson, Arrell Morgan. *The American Indian: Prehistory to the Present*. Norman: University of Oklahoma Press, 1971.

Grady, John C., and Bradford K. Felmly. *Suffering to Silence: 29th Texas Cavalry Regimental History*. Quanah, TX: Nortex Press, 1975.

Grayson, George W. *A Creek Warrior for the Confederacy: The Autobiography of Chief G.W. Grayson*. Ed. W. David Baird. Norman: University of Oklahoma Press, 1988.

Griffin, Clifford S. *The University of Kansas*. Lawrence: University Press of Kansas, 1974.

Harwell, Richard B., ed. *The Confederate Reader*. New York: Longmans, Green and Company, 1957.

Hauptman, Lawrence M. *Between Two Fires: American Indians and the Civil War*. New York: Free Press, 1995.

Horton, Louise. *Samuel Bell Maxey*. Austin: University of Texas Press, 1974.

Johnston, Joseph E., ed. *Narrative of Military Operations Directed During the Late War Between the States*. Ed. Frank Vandiver. Bloomington: Indiana University Press, 1959.

Journal of the Provisional Congress of the Confederate States of America, 1861–1865. 7 vols. Included in the United States Senate Documents No. 234, 58th Congress, 2nd Session. Washington, D.C.: Government Printing Office, 1904.

Kerby, Robert L. *Kirby Smith's Confederacy: The Trans-Mississippi South*. New York: Columbia University Press, 1972.

Knight, Wilfred. *Red Fox: Stand Watie's Civil War Years in Indian Territory*. Glendale, CA: Arthur H. Clark Company, 1988.

Lord, Francis A. *Civil War Sutlers and Their Wares*. New York: Thomas Yoseloff, 1969.

Mayes County Historical Society. *Historical Highlights of Mayes County*. Pryor, OK: privately printed, 1977.

McKee, W. Reid, and M.E. Mason Jr. *Civil War Projectiles II: Small Arms & Field Artillery with Supplement*. Mechanicsville, VA: Rapidan Press, 1980.

Melton, Jack W., and Lawrence E. Paul. *Introduction to Field Artillery Ordnance 1861–1865*. Kennesaw, GA: Kennesaw Mountain Press, 1994.

The Memorial and Biographical History of Dallas County, Texas. Chicago, IL: Lewis Publishing Company, 1892.

Men of Affairs of Houston and Environs: A Newspaper Reference Work. Houston, TX: Houston Press Club, 1981.

Men of the Pacific Coast. Containing portraits and biographies of professional, financial and businessmen from California, Oregon and Washington, 1902–3. San Francisco, CA: Pacific Arts Company, n.d.

Miller, Francis T. *The Photographic History of the Civil War*. 10 vols. New York: Review of Reviews, 1911.

Monaghan, Jay. *Civil War on the Western Border, 1854–1865*. Boston: Little, Brown and Company, 1955.

Morris, John W., and Edwin C. McReynolds. *Historical Atlas of Oklahoma*. Norman: University of Oklahoma Press, 1965.

Morris, Lerona Rosamond, ed. *Oklahoma: Yesterday, Today and Tomorrow*. Gutherie, OK: Cooperative Publishing Company, 1930.

Oates, Stephen B. *Confederate Cavalry West of the River*. Austin: University of Texas Press, 1961.

Oklahoma Genealogical Society. *An Index to the 1890 United States Census of Union Veterans and Their Widows in Oklahoma and Indian Territories (Including Old Greer County) and Soldiers Stationed at Military Installations in the Territories*. Oklahoma City: Oklahoma Genealogical Society, 1970.

Oklahoma State Historic Preservation Office. *Oklahoma's National Register Handbook*. Oklahoma City, OK: self-published, 2001.

Payne, Curtis. *Thundering Cannons: Howell's Texas Battery in the Indian Nations*. Privately printed on CD, 1995.

Phisterer, Frederick. *Statistical Record of the Armies of the United States*. New York: Charles Scribner's Sons, 1881–83. Reprint by the Archive Society, 1992.

Rammp, Lary C. "Negro Troop Activity in Indian Territory." In *Kepis & Turkey Calls: An Anthology of the War Between the States In Indian Territory*. Ed. Marc Cantrell and Mac Harris. Oklahoma City, OK: Western Heritage Books, 1982.

Rampp, Lary C., and Donald L. *The Civil War in Indian Territory*. Austin, TX: Presidial Press, 1975.

Report of the Adjutant General of the State of Kansas. Vol. 1. *1861–1865*. Leavenworth, KS: Bulletin Co-operative Printing Company, 1867.

Returns of the Regular Army. Seventh Infantry, February 1847. National Archives, Record Group 94, Washington, D.C.

Richards, Ralph. *Headquarters House and the Forts of Fort Scott.* Fort Scott, OK: Fort Scott Tribune, 1954.

Scarbrough, Clara Sterns. *Land of Good Water: A Williamson County History.* Georgetown, TX: Williamson County Sun Publishers, 1973.

Sherman, William T. *Memoirs of William T. Sherman.* 2 vols. New York: D. Appleton & Company, 1889.

Smith, Justin H. *The War with Mexico.* Vol. 2. New York: McMillian Company, 1919.

Speer, William S., ed. *The Encyclopedia of the New West.* Marshall, TX: U.S. Biographical Publishing Company, 1881.

Starr, Emmett. *The History of the Cherokee Indian.* Oklahoma City, Oklahoma, 1922.

Thoburn, Joseph P., and Muriel H. Wright. *Oklahoma: A History of the State and its People.* 4 vols. New York: Lewis Historical Publishing Company, 1929.

Tyler, Ronnie C. *The Big Bend: A History of the Last Texas Frontier.* Washington, D.C.: National Park Service, 1975.

United States War Department. *Atlas to Accompany the Official Records of the Union and Confederate Armies.* Washington, D.C.: U.S. Government Printing Office, 1891–95.

————. *The War of the Rebellion: A Compilation of the Official Records of the Union and Confederate Armies.* 128 vols. Washington, D.C.: U.S. Government Printing Office, 1880–1901.

Wallace, Ernest. *Charles DeMorse: Pioneer Editor and Statesman.* Lubbock: Texas Tech Press, 1943.

Wardell, Morris L. *A Political History of the Cherokee Nation, 1838–1907.* Norman: University of Oklahoma Press, 1938.

Webb, Walter P. *The Handbook of Texas.* 2 vols. Austin: Texas State Historical Association, 1952.

Williams, J.M., Brevet Brigadier General. "Historical Sketch of the First Kansas Colored Infantry, Lately Known as the 79th U.S. Colored Volunteers." Undated typewritten history presented to the adjutant general of Kansas. Kansas Historical Society, Topeka, Kansas.

Wilson, Joseph T. *The Black Phalanx: A History of the Negro Soldiers of the United States in the Wars of 1775–1812, 1861–1865.* Hartford, CT: American Publishing Company, 1888.

Witham, Claire. *Coyle-Gano & Witham-Foust Ancestors.* Houston, TX: privately printed, 1990.

Wright, Marcus J., ed. *Texas in the War 1861–1865.* Ed. Harold Simpson. Hillsboro, TX: Hillsboro Junior College Press, 1965.

Wright, Muriel. *A Guide to Indian Tribes of Oklahoma.* Norman: University of Oklahoma Press, 1951.

Yeary, Mamie. *Reminiscences of the Boys in Gray, 1861–1865.* Reprint, Dayton, OH: Morningside House, 1986.

ARTICLES

Adair Weekly Ledger. "Murder and Suicide: Richard L. Martin Shoots Wife and then Takes Own Life with Same Gun." August 17, 1911.

Barry, Louis. "The Fort Leavenworth—Fort Gibson Military Road and the Founding of Fort Scott." *Kansas Historical Quarterly* 11 (May 1942): 115–29.

Blunt, James G. "General Blunt's Account of His Civil War Experiences." *Kansas Historical Quarterly* 1 (May 1932): 211–65.

Boeger, Palmer. "Stand Watie and the Battles of First and Second Cabin Creek." *Journal of the Indian Wars* 1 (Autumn 2000): 45–68.

Boydson, Q.B. "Fort Gibson Barracks, Powder Magazine and Bake Oven." *Chronicles of Oklahoma* 50 (Autumn 1972).

Brown, D. Alexander. "The Million Dollar Wagon Train Raid." *Civil War Times Illustrated* 7 (October 1968): 12–20.

Burgess, Henderson L. "The Eighteenth Kansas Volunteer Cavalry, and Some Incidents Connected with Its Service on the Plains." *Kansas Historical Collections* 13 (1915): 534–38.

Chapman, Bernard. "The Founding of El Reno." *Chronicles of Oklahoma* 34 (Spring 1956): 79–108.

Cherokee Advocate. "Joseph L. Martin." November 23, 1891. Tahlequah, Indian Territory.

Comtois, Pierre. "Frontier Battle of Honey Springs." *America's Civil War* 10 (November 1997): 54–60.

Crane, D.O. "Excerpts from a Diary." *Osage City Press*, December 14, 1882.

Cubage, Annie Rosser. "Engagement at Cabin Creek, Indian Territory." *Chronicles of Oklahoma* 10 (March 1932): 44–51.

Daily Capital. "Maj. Henry Hopkins." December 23, 1883.

Dallas Morning News. "Gen. Richard M. Gano Claimed by Death." March 27, 1913.

Debo, Angie. "Southern Refugees of the Cherokee Nation." *Southwestern Historical Quarterly* 35 (April 1932): 255–66.

Fields, Mrs. S.M. "Texas Heroes of the Confederacy." *Dallas Times Herald*, May 10, 1925.

Fischer, LeRoy H. "The Impact of the Civil War in Oklahoma: Death and Destruction." *Oklahoma State Alumni Magazine* 5 (September 1964): 10–12.

Foreman, Grant. "The Centennial of Fort Gibson." *Chronicles of Oklahoma* 2 (June 1924): 119–28.

Franzmann, Tom. "The Final Campaign: The Confederate Offensive of 1864." *Chronicles of Oklahoma* 63 (Fall 1985): 266–79.

Gable, Frank M. "The Kansas Penitentiary." *Collections of the Kansas State Historical Society* 14 (1918): 379–433.

Good, Mary Elizabeth. "Just Before the Battle." *Tulsa World*, September 13, 1964.

Hancock, Marvin J. "The Second Battle of Cabin Creek." *Chronicles of Oklahoma* 39 (Winter 1961–62): 414–26.

Hazel, Michael. "Riding with Morgan's Raiders: Richard Gano and His Cavalry, 1862–63." *Legacies* 4 (Spring 1992): 11–19.

Hermon, Gregory. "Early Sheriff Faced Wild Times." *Olathe (KS) Daily News*, September 5, 1984.

Holabird, S.B, Brevet Brigadier General. "Ordnance Notes—No. 189: Army Wagon Transportation." *Journal of the Military Service Institution of the United States* (April 15, 1882) Washington, D.C.

Hood, Fred. "Twilight of the Confederacy in Indian Territory." *Chronicles of Oklahoma* 41 (Winter 1963–64): 425–41.

Hopkins, Florence M. "Henry M. Hopkins." *Collections of the Kansas State Historical Society* 6 (n.d.): 276–84.

Horton, L.W. "General Sam Bell Maxey: His Defense of North Texas and the Indian Territory." *Southwestern Historical Quarterly* 74 (1971): 507–24.

Jenness, George B. "The Battle on Beaver Creek." *Kansas Historical Collections* 9 (1906): 443–52.

Johnston, Carolyn Ross. "The Panther's Scream Is Often Heard: Cherokee Women in Indian Territory During the Civil War." *Chronicles of Oklahoma* 78 (Spring 2000): 84–107.

Kansas Herald. "Death of Commissioner Hopkins." December 19, 1883.

Leavenworth Times. "A Reunion: A Perfect Love Feast Held at G.A.R. Hall." October 18, 1890.

Madeus, Howard Michael. "The Use of the Percussion Shotgun in Texas Prior to and During the American Civil War, 1861–1865." *Armax: The Journal of the Cody Firearms Museum* 5 (1995): 165–66.

Morrison, W.B. "Fort Towson." *Chronicles of Oklahoma* 8 (June 1930): 226–32.

Morton, Ohland. "Confederate Relations with the Five Civilized Tribes, Part II." *Chronicles of Oklahoma* 31, (Autumn 1953): 299–322.

Muskogee Daily Phoenix. "Ebbing Confederacy Fortunes Bolstered by Cabin Creek Win." June 23, 1961.

Muskogee Phoenix. "Nigger Creek: How a Little Stream in the Cherokee Nation Got Its Name." December 17, 1891.

Northern Standard. "Letters of a Private." September 29, 1864; October 1, 1864; and October 15, 1864. Clarksville, Texas.

Oates, Stephen B. "Recruiting Confederate Cavalry in Texas." *Southwestern Historical Quarterly* 66 (April 1961): 463–77.

Patrick Cosgrove obituary. *Olathe Register,* July 13, 1916.

Peck, R.M. "Wagon-Boss and Mule Mechanic: Incidents of My Experience and Observation in the Late Civil War." *National Tribune,* November 3, November 10 and November 17, 1904.

Rain, Gene Wharton. "History of the R.M. Gano House." Five typewritten pages, undated, from the collection of Claire Witham.

St. Louis Dispatch. "A Terrible Quintette." November 22, 1873.

Time. "Washington's Baptism." September 5, 1932.

Tulsa Tribune. "Hunt for Civil War Cannon Is Fruitless." No date. Oklahoma History Files—Civil War, Tulsa City-County Library, Tulsa, Oklahoma.

Tulsa World. "Civil War Musket Found." January 23, 1964.

———. "Veteran Recalls Oklahoma Battle." September 29, 1929.

Vinita Daily Journal. "Two Battles Fought Near Cabin Creek." June 10, 1961.

Wagoner Record Democrat 98, no. 19. "Battlefield Search May Be Easy for Society President" (September 19, 1990).

Warde, Mary Jane. "Now the Wolf Has Come: The Civilian Civil War in the Indian Territory." *Chronicles of Oklahoma* 71 (Spring 1993): 64–87.

Watts, Mr. Charles R. "Nigger Creek Skirmish and the Maneuvers of the Confederacy after the Fight." Two typewritten pages. Oklahoma Historical Society Library, Oklahoma City, Oklahoma.

Windham, William T. "The Problem of Supply in the Trans-Mississippi Confederacy." *Journal of Southern History* 27 (May 1961): 149–68.

Wright, Muriel H. "The Name of General Stand Watie of the Cherokee Nation." *Chronicles of Oklahoma* 34 (Autumn 1956).

Wright, Muriel H., and LeRoy Fischer. "Civil War Sites in Oklahoma." *Chronicles of Oklahoma* 44 (Summer 1966): 158–215.

Zellar, Gary. "Occupying the Middle Ground: African-Creeks in the First Indian Home Guard, 1861–1865." *Chronicles of Oklahoma* 76 (Spring 1998): 48–71.

NEWSPAPERS

Adair Weekly Ledger
Cherokee Advocate
Cherokee News
Dallas Daily Herald
Dallas Morning News
Dallas Times Herald
Fort Worth Weekly Democrat
Frank Leslie's Illustrated
Indian Chieftain
Kansas Herald
Leavenworth Times
Muskogee Daily Phoenix
Muskogee Phoenix
National Tribune (Grand Army of the Republic)
New York Times
Northern Standard
Olathe (KS) Daily News
Olathe Register
Osage City Press
St. Louis Dispatch
Topeka (KS) Daily Capital
Tulsa Tribune
Tulsa World
Vinita Daily Journal
Wagoner Record Democrat

PERIODICALS

America's Civil War. Leesburg, Virginia, 1987–present.
Civil War Times Illustrated. Harrisburg, Pennsylvania, 1961–present.
Confederate Veteran. 40 vols. Nashville, Tennessee, 1893–1932.
North & South. Tollhouse, California, 1997–present.

MANUSCRIPTS

Anderson, Mabel Washbourne. "A Million-Dollar Hunch." WPA Transcripts. Vertical Records File, Oklahoma Historical Society Library, Oklahoma City, Oklahoma. Two typewritten pages.

Cherokee Nation Collection. Western History Collections, University of Oklahoma Library, Norman, Oklahoma.

Foreman, Grant. "Indian-Pioneer History." 113 vols. Indian Archives Division. Oklahoma Historical Society, Oklahoma City, Oklahoma.

Gano, Daniel W. "History of the Gano Family." Forty-six-page typewritten manuscript, Houston, Texas.

Graton correspondence. MS 918.02, Microfilm division. Kansas State Historical Society, Topeka, Kansas.

Isley Family Papers. Wichita State University, Wichita, Kansas.

Lightfoot Family Papers. Texas State Library, Austin, Texas.

Maxey, Samuel Bell. Maxey Papers. Gilcrease Museum, Tulsa, Oklahoma.

National Archives, Washington, D.C. Service records of Edgar A. Barker, Henry M. Hopkins, Richard M. Gano, Stand Watie and James M. Williams.

"Nigger Creek Skirmish and the Maneuvers of the Confederacy after the Fight." Undated. WPA Transcripts. Vertical Records File, Oklahoma Historical Society Library, Oklahoma City, Oklahoma.

"Notes on the Nigger Creek Fight." Oklahoma Historical Society Library, Oklahoma City, Oklahoma.

"Record Book of Burials at Fort Gibson, Indian Territory." Original book located in the office of Fort Gibson National Cemetery, Fort Gibson, Oklahoma.

Ross, Allen. Statement written in long hand. Special Collection Department, McFarlin Library, University of Tulsa, Tulsa, Oklahoma.

"A Short History of Stand Watie." Cherokee Nation Collection. Western History Collections, University of Oklahoma Library, Norman, Oklahoma.

Stephenson, Septimus. Unpublished diary. Private collection of Chuck Larson. Stephenson served as a sergeant in Company H, Third Wisconsin Cavalry.

Sutherland Family Records and Papers. Private collection of Pat Sutherland Mittelsteadt.

Trout, George Washington. Letter dated Big Cabin, Oklahoma, September 30, 1930. Two typewritten pages. Trout (1847–1933) wrote the letter at the age of eighty-three.

Trout, Henry. Interview with Henry Trout, Big Cabin. Three typewritten pages in Kelly Kirkpatrick Collection.

"War Record of Brigadier General Richard Montgomery Gano." Typed manuscript. Claire Witham Collection, Dallas Archaeological Society, Dallas, Texas.

Wilmeth, James R., Reverend. "Thoughts and Things as They Occurred in Camp A.D. 1864." Unpublished diary. Vertical File, Center for Restoration Studies, Abilene Christian University, Abilene, Texas.

Works Progress Administration. Indian Pioneer Papers. Western History Collections, University of Oklahoma Libraries, Norman, Oklahoma.

ONLINE SOURCES

American Civil War Research Database. http://www.civilwardata.com.

"Bradly Civil War Letters, Grayson County, Texas 1862–1865." Compiled by George Warren Blankenship Jr., Kathleen Blankenship Dophied and Sarah Blankenship Dye. http://truittb.home.texas.net/WWBradly.htm.

Civil War Soldiers & Sailors System. http://www.itd.nps.gov/cwss.

Grand Army of the Republic (GAR) Posts in Oklahoma. http://suvcw.org/garposts/ok.pdf.

The Handbook of Texas Online. http://www.tshaonline.org/handbook.

Kansas Adjutant General's Report, 1861–65. http://www.kshs.org/p/kansas-adjutant-general-s-report-1861-1865/11175.

United Confederate Veteran Camps in Oklahoma. http://www.usgennet.org/usa/ok/county/woodward/military/vetcamp.html.

TELEVISION DOCUMENTARY

Last Raid at Cabin Creek. Warren Entertainment, 1992.

Index

About the Author

Steven L. Warren is a native Oklahoman. A veteran writer-producer, he has national and regional credits in the areas of television broadcasting, national cable television and advertising. Among his numerous history projects, Steve wrote and produced the award-winning Civil War documentary *Last Raid at Cabin Creek*. In 2010, the United Daughters of the Confederacy bestowed the Jefferson Davis Historical Gold Medal on Warren for his work on the Battles of Cabin Creek. He continues to write articles on the American Civil War and is in demand as a speaker.

In his spare time, Steve enjoys metal detecting and searching for lost Civil War sites.

Warren received his MA in journalism and mass communication from the University of Oklahoma. He also holds a BA in communications from the University of Tulsa. Steve and his wife, Amy, have two daughters, Emma and Alli.

For more information on the Battles of Cabin Creek, be sure to visit the Brilliant Victory Facebook page, www.facebook.com/brilliantvictorybook.

Visit us at
www.historypress.net